True Tales from the Land of Digital Sand

To Jackie,

Enjoy!

Mike A. V...

True Tales from the Land of Digital Sand

relatable memoirs of a career tech support geek

Michael Anthony White

VOX GEEKUS LLC

All events and conversations in this book have been accurately chronicled to the best of the author's rather sound mind and exceptional memory. Names, genders, & titles have been changed to protect the privacy of individuals, businesses, and employers — innocents and reprobates alike.

First Printing, 2021

ISBN 978-1-7377921-0-9 (hardcover)
ISBN 978-1-7377921-2-3 (paperback)
ISBN 978-1-7377921-1-6 (ebook)
ISBN 978-1-7377921-3-0 (audiobook)

Published by Vox Geekus LLC

CONTENTS ▮

CONTENTS

CONTENTS

SIX

The Empire, Part I: Joining The Ranks

SEVEN

The Legendary Battle Of The Motherboard

CONTENTS

EIGHT

The Empire, Part II: Settling In

NINE

Timing Is Everything

CONTENTS

ELEVEN

Another World

CONTENTS

FOURTEEN

'Tis All Fun & Games

*For all who have suffered calling for support
and those who have sincerely assisted them*

Embracing a Lonely Word

"Okay, go pick an album!"

My Mom had decided it was time to show me how to use the record player.

I'd become a music lover pretty early in life, being captivated with piano music. When offered to select an album, there was one artist whose work I was already familiar with that instantly came to mind: The Piano Man himself, Billy Joel.

Flipping through the records on the shelf, I spied *52nd Street*, smiling as I snatched it quickly. I'd heard my parents playing it before, but that momentous occasion inspired me to focus as I listened to it in its entirety.

It was the first pop album that won my full undivided attention. I made certain to follow along to all the printed lyrics, having already developed a fifth grade reading level.

When it finished, I immediately played it again. I was drawn to it.

It didn't matter that I was five years old; kids know everything one needs to about appreciating music. It's in the soul, in one's heart, in their being.

Absorbing all the emotions I could from those songs, I acknowledged the intensity and realized the expertise in the brass player's tone. I appreciated the articulation and dynamics of each note from every instrument... although lacking said vocabulary at the time to describe the complexity of what I'd experienced.

You don't merely *listen* to your favorite music — you feel it and breathe it.

One song in particular left quite an impact. It reinforced many lessons my parents had taught me regarding a crucial moral facet to uphold.

Some times prove more difficult than others to retain this. When you don't find the strength to wield it, people are often hurt. You're usually hurt too. Many lack the fortitude to keep it despite its utmost importance:

"Honesty."

I don't pretend to have understood the full depth of every verse at that age, but that's what makes our favorite songs special. As we mature, so do our interpretations of their lyrics.

I've recently turned 40 years old, marking 22 years in my career as a technical support agent.

It's difficult work.

Trials have been far from exclusively mental; emotional challenges have thoroughly and often tested the extremities of my moral compass.

I know very well what it's like to be a customer, as well as the employee in the world of technical support; I've undergone the nastiest of experiences playing each of these roles.

Witnessing a growing number of *questionable* trends in the industry throughout my career, I've begun to frequently suspect if I really want to do this anymore.

I've come forward to share a bit of knowledge and my most memorable experiences to both entertain and enlighten. Numerous tales are humorous, and many are intense. Some painfully angering, others absurd enough to tease disbelief.

Nonetheless, you'll find no hackneyed internet myths here. The only modifications present henceforth are the random scramblings of names and genders to protect the guilty.

I hereby offer my stories, my experiences, and by the lessons instilled in me by my parents, teachers, and Billy Joel... complete honesty.

ONE

Twas All Fun & Games... Until My Eyeball Drifted

Scar Tissue & Household Chores

It was 1986 in Atascadero, California. Truth be told it was 1986 everywhere, but in my innocent young mind I was certain I'd never move away.

I was six years old and had recently made some new friends after starting the second grade at Santa Margarita Elementary School.

Life's priorities were simple yet adventurous, sprinkled with that expected smidgen of recklessness that kids seem to thrive on. Always thoroughly enjoying recess, math, and music, my favorite daily pastime was still yet to come after the final bell rang.

My friends and I would hop on the school bus only to be let out three miles away at the stop on Santa Clara Road. From there we could always be seen running home as quickly as possible to jettison our backpacks.

Minutes later, we'd meet back at the U-shaped dirt driveway in front of my house with our bikes at the ready.

If my older sister wasn't busy experimenting with a new hairdo or catching the latest videos on MTV, she would join the fun.

The cult classic film *Rad* had just been released on VHS. Having already seen it countless times, we'd become obsessed with assembling our own makeshift bike ramps out of any materials we could find outside.

Our hobby's bread and butter was a variety of corner-worn bricks, questionably stable two-by-fours, and oddly shaped plywood scraps. We couldn't *wait* to see what new styles of jumps and obstacles we could construct each day as we constantly tried to one-up our former masterpieces.

The education we gained from such a simple activity was both substantial and impressive. Although we didn't realize it at the time on an academic level, what began as trial & error very quickly developed into the craft of troubleshooting.

This hands-on experience provided us with an admirable number of lessons involving principles of motion and momentum, structural integrity and failure, leverage, speed and acceleration, and several other fundamentals of physics that we didn't even know the terms for yet.

We were just kids being kids.

As expected, we... also became rather adept in our first aid skills.

Pain is a harsh yet fair teacher. Being young children comfortable with life in the country, we were beyond the phase of whimpering upon first impact of injury.

Bragging rights entered our social scene as visible scabs, scars, and bandaging meant popularity and respect amongst friends and fellow students. If they *weren't* readily visible, we were more than willing to peel back a sleeve or roll up a pant leg to reveal the trophy wounds on elbows and shins, earning that ever-gratifying unison, "woah...!" from our responding classmates.

Playground reputations aside, we still knew and respected the risks of shirking a certain level of logic and safety. You can't ride bikes with friends every day when nursing a broken limb. We were well aware of the clear distinction between a kid with guts and a kid with little brains and no judgment, so we avoided major injuries.

For that we were proud.

Whenever darkness or rainy weather entered the skies to strike the driveway wipe-outs from my schedule, I had plenty of dry entertainment options indoors.

MTV and Nickelodeon, Nintendo, and the Speak & Math were way up there on the list. It was also a rare event for my sister and I to miss our favorite Saturday morning cartoons. Those thrilling memories have yet to dwindle.

Like most events or activities in life, entertainment and recreation are much more appreciated when unique and in short supply. *We* especially cherished every moment because after the cartoons ended, we were to begin our weekend chores.

Our parents rewarded us for our household duties with an allowance. The base pay was ten dollars per month, but we'd often get additional opportunities each week if we helped out or offered to pitch in with small projects. Cleaning up the yard, tidying the basement, and doing extra dishes were typical tasks.

Upon finishing our chores it was right back to playtime, and on weekend afternoons I was usually found in front of my most precious purchase: my first home computer.

Before we had moved from Huntington Beach the prior year, I had saved over $150 from allowance and birthday cards over a grueling fifteen months.

Accompanying my Mom during an otherwise routine shopping trip to Kmart in Costa Mesa had resulted in my first major financial transaction at age five.

Unbeknownst to me, that purchase was the defining moment that would set my career in motion.

To Catch One's Eye

As we strolled by the electronics section of Kmart, a bright red box on the lower shelf boasting a bold tagline caught my eye:

"ATARI 65XE Personal Computer. Power Without The Price."

The sticker reading "$99.99" also had my attention.

I didn't care about the noted "65,536 Bytes of Random Access Memory" because I had no idea what that meant at the time. I only knew I had about $150, and I **really** wanted a computer.

Seeing the amount of energy pumping through me when I pointed at the box, chanting, "Mom! A Computer! It says 'Power Without The Price!'," she realized calming me down would be a moot effort.

She asked my over-excited bouncing self *several* times to confirm, "Are you SURE you want this one? It's $100 before tax, so you'll only have maybe $40 dollars leftover from your savings if you buy it."

My parents had recognized my interest in video games, pinball machines, robots, math, and all manner of electronic devices for years, so the acquisition of a computer was inevitable. I mean, hey — all the cool kids in TV shows and movies were great at using computers, and it looked awesome.

Inspector Gadget's niece Penny had a "computer book" that she used in order to anonymously solve her bumbling Uncle's cases for him. Ferris Bueller used his personal computer to hack into the school system to change his attendance records.

Doogie Howser and Wesley Crusher would soon join that list of legends supporting the geek tenets which had forever affirmed the following: If you were a kid that was a whiz with computers, you would get to do some super cool stuff.

Pressing countless buttons, using massive screens, traveling in spaceships, finding lost treasure, rescuing civilians, foiling villains' plans and saving the day...

What kid *wouldn't* want a computer?

So, I bought it. My family had yet to own a home computer or any peripherals at the time, thus we had no monitor or hard drive. Fortunately, a nearby sales clerk guaranteed us that the 65XE could easily connect to any modern television.

Upon checking out and leaving the store, every moment felt surreal. I was floating through kid-dom with a stunned glare and an unshakable smile plastered on my face.

I was in a daze from the ride home to the official moment that night when my Dad helped to unbox the computer, connect it through the coaxial matching transformer to our 25" Magnavox TV, and fire up the power for the very first time.

I had done it. I had saved up my money and purchased my very first computer.

The 65XE manual included a simple yet generous primer on "Atari BASIC," an easy to learn programming language specifically modified for that Atari series.

It would become my first recreational textbook.

I'd been reading since age three, enjoying the wonderful variety of stories from Dr. Seuss, the series of Little Golden Books, Garfield comics, Shel Silverstein poems, Beverly Cleary novels and more.

I loved to read. I'd be completely content reading all day every day.

I often did.

This was all fine and dandy until my parents had noticed that I was at times, blinking excessively while staring at pages.

During long periods of reading, one of my eyes would slowly start to drift outward. My vision would blur for a split second, and I'd instinctively blink to restore clarity. I wasn't experiencing any pain, but an annoyance so mild that I myself hadn't consciously noticed it.

After a visit to the ophthalmologist, the condition was identified.

I was suffering from Exophoria.

In short, my young growing eye muscles were stressed from reading several straight hours a day and they'd begun to rebel.

My prescription was to follow some basic eye exercises and take more frequent breaks. Doing so, the symptoms gradually vanished over a few weeks, but my love of reading never waned.

Though the treatment was simple and timely, my family and I still shake our heads and laugh about the predicament:

My parents once had to make a point of convincing their young child to stop reading for hours on end, and go outside and play once in a while.

That's quite literally one for the books.

My Mother Had Me Tested

Just a few weeks into my first year of Kindergarten in Huntington Beach, I was exhibiting substantial signs of boredom.

Several consultations soon took place between my parents and a school psychologist at Eader Elementary, after which a series of tests were scheduled to be administered — including the Stanford-Binet Intelligence Examination.

Having scored in the 99th percentile, it concluded that I was, "highly gifted," and was admitted to first grade GATE, skipping Kindergarten.

Despite the intense process, I never once felt treated like a lab rat by my parents, the school psychologist, my teacher, or any other adults working with me during that time. In fact, I had a blast.

...*Loads* of fun! I'd always gotten a kick out of *Highlights* magazines when finding them in classrooms or waiting rooms — and the mazes, puzzles, math problems & brain teasers I was being tested with were reminiscent of their content.

I'd learned young to view books as a source of knowledge that once absorbed would prove to be a gateway to another dimension, each of them constantly inviting me into their realm with curious fascination.

I'd also learned that other kids in elementary school generally weren't the most civil or kindhearted humans around. After many made it quite clear to me that I was a freakish teacher's pet once they'd learned I was a couple years younger than them, that only further encouraged me to find companionship within a book or computer screen.

I was happy to oblige.

Throughout that entire year after purchasing my computer, I could be found reading and re-reading that manual to absorb as much as I could.

All the work and practice that I would perform, the example programs I'd transcribe and run, and all the exercises I'd complete as directed by the manual would all be lost every day upon powering off the computer.

Such was life with no hard drive.

As repetition proves a solid method of retention, the payoff was learning the introductory concepts of programming at a fairly admirable rate for a child.

By the time we'd moved to Atascadero in '86, I had a proper understanding of most of the commands and was able to start experimenting by writing my own simple programs.

My favorites were in essence, conversations; it was exciting to simulate texting back and forth with a much more advanced computer possessing artificial intelligence.

KITT from *Knight Rider* was an inspiration, as was the Master Control Program from *TRON*.

For example, one program started with a blank screen and asked the user for their name. Upon typing a response and pressing enter, the program would then address the user by that name and proceed with canned small-talk.

It might ask what month of the year it was, to then reply with a generic comment about the likely weather. This mechanic would be repeated for a short time before the program gave its farewell and ended.

Other programs were simple guessing games in which the user was asked to guess a number between 1 and 1000, and the program would respond by teasing with a variety of hints. Some of them berating, some encouraging, but all of them silly.

"IS THAT THE BEST YOU CAN DO? IT'S HIGHER, STUPID... TRY AGAIN!"

Time went on, and I eventually purchased the *Mario Brothers* game cartridge for Atari XE systems, which I still have today.

That Christmas, my parents bought my sister and me the Nintendo Entertainment System Deluxe Set, which was our first official game console.

Though some friends down the street had an Atari 5200, the NES completely blew it away.

By 1990, my younger sister had her first birthday, the Game Boy was selling like hotcakes, and my treasured computer was showing its age.

We moved to the Santa Ynez Valley that year, and I finished out the fifth grade at Solvang Elementary School where I was properly exposed to the Apple IIe.

Its release date of 1983 notwithstanding, the Apple IIe was a far more powerful machine compared to mine and because of this was still prevalent in many schools.

Though its power and potential was much greater, the experiences I had with it didn't impress me. The school could afford only limited software titles, and their spinach-green monochrome displays weren't very fun to look at, as I'd been enjoying a pleasant color palette and the freedom of creation on my computer and TV at home.

It seemed the era of my earliest infatuation with computers had started coming to an end.

I was developing a love of outdoor activities, especially riding my bike around Solvang.

It would be a few years until my mind would once again be blown by another computer experience.

Meanwhile, I would explore the town that was my new home, try new hobbies, and make new friends — but that first encounter in which I got my initial glance into the digital world would be the most memorable, and the knowledge I retained from embracing reading at a young age and grinding through that manual remains fresh in my brain.

As of a few years ago, I can very sadly no longer power up my Atari 65XE due to a hardware failure upon boot.

I've still kept it, and I even pull it out of the box now and then just to hold it. I can close my eyes, smell the familiar plastic aroma of that case, feel the power switch and the keys and the buttons, and instantly be transported back in time.

Whenever I do, a jolt of that exhilaration always returns.

TWO

Glancing Through Windows

Keep Calm And RTFM

I'll always remember walking into room E-2 freshman year. It was my very first class in high school: Keyboarding & Computer Applications I.

The air was, initially, *so* shockingly brisk.

With 30 personal computers in the same room, air conditioning was crucial. Apart from ensuring every heat sink was caressed with limitless doses of freely flowing frigid fresh air, the filtration system drastically decreased the denizens of dust particles that would otherwise have accumulated inside them.

If you're keeping a PC tower on the floor of a warm carpeted room, it's probably housing chunks of angry, rabid dust bunnies that could use a good vacuuming up.

As to increase mitigation of said fuzzballs' presence, every tower sat upon its own elevated platform beside each desk.

Keyboarding, or touch typing was the course's first order of business. With several years of piano lessons under my belt, one would have thought that I'd already have learned to type by touch at a younger age, but no. Something about it seemed heavily daunting.

It was a skill flaunted by talented administrative assistants in movies, or college interns in Manhattan. The people you see on episodes of *Ripley's Believe It Or Not* or *That's Incredible* performing jaw-dropping stunts at insane speeds... *those* were the kinds of people it took to type fast.

I had somehow been convinced of that.

This ludicrous misconception was thoroughly rectified in the following weeks as proven by our entire class successfully touch typing at an average rate of 30 words per minute.

All The Right Type training software had made learning simple, therapeutic, and fun. It's much easier than it looks, and there's something gratifying about the rhythmic clickety-clack of the keys as you crank along.

As excited as I was to have learned a new skill, the surface of what those computers were capable of had yet to be scratched. It *had* been eight years since I'd purchased the Atari, and things had changed drastically.

They were running on 486SX 25 megahertz processors, 4 megabytes of RAM and had Super VGA Monitors. This *shamed* my 65XE's 1.7 megahertz processor and 64 kilobytes of RAM being hooked up to a console TV from 1985.

No longer would I be suffering spinach-green monitors like those from elementary school. These were vibrant, high resolution displays capable of over 16 million colors. Every computer was equipped with a mouse, and both sides of the symmetrical lab were connected to their own laser printer begging to spit out your document in less than twenty seconds.

I had to know more.

All the PCs were installed with MS-DOS (Microsoft Disc Operating System) version 6.0 which was configured on startup to arrive at an uncluttered screen titled, "MS-DOS Shell."

This was a file manager that the teacher had set up to offer a nominal selection of program titles to click on. One of them was the aforementioned *All The Right Type*, and the other was *Windows*.

Launching Windows 3.1 for the first time was a beautiful sight. It had a crisp appearance, and featured several colorful icons to launch utilities, games, accessories, and more advanced training software such as *Mavis Beacon Teaches Typing*.

We learned how to change fonts, window sizes and button colors. We could create and organize custom labeled icons and program groups however we pleased.

We could even generate our own clunky amateur drawings in a program called *Microsoft Paintbrush*, then save and select them to be shown as the "Desktop Wallpaper" in the background after Windows launched.

Different styles of mouse arrows and hourglass designs could be selected for display when the computer was "thinking."

Instead of the default hourglass, I preferred the animated option; when Windows was busy, the mouse cursor would be displayed as a small hourglass with its pixels of sand actually falling from the top into the lower bulb, filling it one grain at a time.

After a few seconds, the hourglass would rotate 180 degrees, and repeat the cycle. This provided the illusion I was staring into a very real living land of sentient pixels thriving on the other side of the monitor.

Also installed in the lab was a productivity suite called *Microsoft Works*. With it we created our first resume, learned how to design and organize spreadsheets, and acquired basic skills in creating and editing databases.

It wasn't long before I realized that Windows 3.1 contained a generous amount of documentation within most programs. Help menus abound had their own table of contents making it easy to find answers to a variety of questions.

There were also "readme" documents available — text files that often contained basic details and introductory tips for first-time users.

This land of digital sand had me mesmerized.

Before long, I'd repeated my pattern and read every help file and in-product tutorial I could click on, but was still left with several questions:

How does one install MS-DOS and Windows on a new machine?

How do you fix a program if something goes wrong?

If you uninstall a program, does all the saved work disappear with it?

Still so much to learn.

Luck was granted one morning upon arriving to class, and one of the doors on the short wide cabinets lining the walls of the lab was cracked open a smidge. I snuck a peek inside to find a *hoard* of books.

In fact, in order to comply with the software license agreements, those cabinets were housing thirty packaged copies of 3.5" Floppy Disks alongside manuals for every piece of software used in the lab.

Every. Single. One.

I asked the teacher if I could possibly come in at lunchtime and take a look at them, and he said I was welcome to do so, provided I didn't remove them from the lab.

I'd hit another knowledge jackpot: more books. As with my 65XE, all I needed to do was RTFM: Read The Flippin' Manual.

I surely had the time.

I hadn't really gotten anywhere making friends on campus aside from a select few in band. The primary student body was just as abrasive as the children in elementary school. The difference was that now popularity and classism had established a firm presence within their dismissals.

Giving a nod or daring to speak a friendly "hello" upon passing a classmate in hallways would often result in a "shut up" from arrogant jocks, or a "go *awaaaay*" from young women who had still retained their acquired valley-girl accent from their pretentious youth.

I knew to expect it, as John Hughes films did a wonderful job preparing me.

Some of the snootiest upper class students noted my medium dark skin tone of both Yaqui & Iberian roots, and asked me directly, "Shouldn't you be hanging out with the Chicanos?"

I *could* speak fairly fluent Spanish thanks to classes in junior high, and that girl's comments had me wondering if the Latino cliques would let me hang out with them.

They did not.

Just minutes after saying hello to those classmates that I'd gotten along with *just fine* back in junior high, they were sure to announce to me in front of their newfound older friends that they didn't want me hanging out with them because I, "...wasn't Mexican enough."

I discovered very quickly who my friends were, and for that I'm thankful.

My MS-DOS and Windows proficiency was soon acquired with gusto, and thus began my modern PC education.

Though it was 1993 and Windows would see drastic changes over the next couple decades, the foundation of knowledge I acquired in that very lab still remains imperative today.

The Arrival Of The Internet

I continued spending a fair amount of time in the computer lab throughout my freshman year. During both recess and lunch, everybody knew where they'd find me. Fellow classmates and teachers alike knew me by name a few weeks into the school year.

At first they would jest, asking if I was in some sort of trouble, at a lunchtime detention or such.

They really didn't know me.

They'd appear shocked when I told them I was reading more and beefing up my knowledge about computers.

Eventually, that gave way to being asked questions by a **lot** of other students. I'd help them with word processing, typing techniques, operating system preferences, file and folder structures... anything they'd ask I was glad to help out with.

"Geeking Out" defined.

I realized quickly that helping others with *their* questions regarding computer knowledge was an efficient way to expand my own, approaching things from different angles and viewing them from multiple perspectives.

Upon completing my freshman year, I dove in and signed up for more classes that were available during summer school. As word got around and people learned that I was still the resident computer geek, my fascination soon turned into profit!

My reputation had gotten the attention of the high school's IT Manager. He would end up hiring me during my sophomore year to install network cards in every computer in the lab, and perform the configuration on every machine to allow them to access the internet.

How could I say no to that?

For $7.25/hour, I spent several evenings after winter break performing my first hands-on hardware upgrade, and all 30 computers were eventually ready to surf the internet with one of the earliest browsers: Netscape Navigator.

Our high school computer lab was now online, and I'd acquired my first professional techie reference to slap on a resume.

Progress

Weeks before starting my junior year, Microsoft had released Windows 95 while IBM had in turn released a new line of personal computers:

"Aptiva."

After spotting it in a "PC Connection" magazine to then see their paid program on a shopping channel discuss it in great detail, I convinced my parents that the IBM Aptiva A90 was a steal for the sale price of $1479.

At the time, it truly was.

Flaunting respectable hardware, it included a generous suite of business applications and a large variety of games on CD-ROM.

Between my younger sister and me, we still have them.

That was when I and most people got introduced to Weezer, as their music video for "Buddy Holly" was featured in MPEG format, included with Windows 95.

That Aptiva was a champ for years to come.

It was eventually upgraded to Windows 98 SE, had the RAM increased, and an improved video card installed.

With more and more computer games blowing up the market, I quickly gained experience putting together several custom PCs for friends, and I was able to set up my parents with a smokin' fast machine for a great deal.

The computer I'd built for them was well under $1,000 and that number only decreased for subsequent builds.

Nearly all the personal computers I've owned since after high school have been custom built myself for a substantially cheaper price than those on the market. It's actually something practiced by most geeks because it always yields better bang for buck, and like typing by touch, is *much* easier than it sounds.

When I think about the progress made throughout the years in hardware and software, I'm most impressed with the size of the leaps taken right around the start of the new millennium.

We used to pay over $100 for mere megabytes of RAM while we can buy a stick of several gigabytes today for under $20.

A hard drive bigger than a few hundred megabytes was considered pretty hefty in 1994. Today people are filling up terabytes in no time, and for a fractional price.

Friends and I once joked upon hearing rumors early in high school about future technology, scoffing at the news that Intel's processors would soon press forward into the world of three digits, accomplishing clock speeds of over one hundred megahertz.

We wondered why *anybody* would need a CPU that fast. That was complete overkill, right?!

Yet, here I am today using a 3.3 gigahertz processor at home, and its price was less than a fancy steak dinner.

Though some aspects of the technology race have changed focus, there's always fierce competition *somewhere,* be it household smart devices or video game consoles.

Nintendo continues to be my favorite, and the next current entry in the *Legend Of Zelda* series is being teased for an upcoming release.

I grin just thinking about it.

Smartphones and mobile devices have continued to flaunt advances, sometimes doubling in price every few years of late. I've yet to be impressed; I don't do much with phones outside of talk, text, and occasionally use a browser or GPS when traveling. My $130 budget model from 2018 still performs beautifully.

Dropping $700 every two years for the latest release isn't justifiable for me, I guess.

In recent years, virtual reality experiences, and 4K & Ultra-HD displays have been trying their best to become more mainstream, and they're succeeding.

That's right up my alley, and I can't wait to see what happens in the near future.

Eventually, they'll only become more affordable.

Brace Yourself

I was 16 years old during the first half of my senior year, and I had a schedule I'd never dreamed of:

Government/Economics, Library Assistant, two band classes, and two computer lab classes.

Basically, I had to study for one class, and got to play for the other five.

That was appreciated, as Government/Economics was draining enough on the psyche.

By adulthood, many have grown accustomed to groups and governments all over the world often using pandering and exploitation as their primary tools of the trade, but I learned of it well on a personal level that first semester.

Santa Ynez is home to a native tribe, and they had opened a small facility in the mid 1990s that would eventually consist mostly of slot machines, and some [allegedly rigged] promotional drawings held under a large tent.

En route to the bus stop after my final class one day, I was flagged down by a brown-eyed male with dark brown skin, who looked to be in his early twenties.

He had a clipboard with a small pad of paper, and was loitering on the edge of the school campus. A local supporter of the aforementioned facility, he was on the lookout for other brown-eyed dark-haired kids with any semblance of a moderate tan.

"Hey bro, you got a second?"

I gave him a short audience.

"You look like you got some of our tribal blood, you wanna sign the petition? We need some signatures to approve a real building instead of just a tent..."

I shook my head, "Oh, sorry, no... I'm not from that tribe."

As I walked away, he shrugged as he offered his arm to me with pen in hand, wearing an unctuous grin.

"Hey, that's OK, you got dark enough skin, you could pass, you could pass... there could be big money and commissions for you if you sign, bro."

I kept walking.

I'm no stranger to being racially profiled due to my mixed race skin tone in such a manner, but that one really turned my stomach.

As I hopped on the bus I met up with my good friend Blake and told him what happened. He commended me for holding my ground, but I'd imagine anybody with a conscience would have done the same.

Blake and I were both into video games, and we would always be excited to head home after school to rent one of the latest titles.

I soon pushed that curbside encounter out of my mind, and was eager to enjoy my final semesters at school.

As luck would have it, catching a ride with Blake to campus later that week would put a kink into my easy-breezy final year.

His first car was a 1970-something Toyota Corona, and as we headed to school one November morning, we were listening to The Beatles on the 8-track deck that somehow still worked.

Being intelligent boys who didn't like the idea of moving violations, we were going 50mph in a 55 zone uphill.

We were a half mile away from our destination when an 81 year old driver in a sedan was pulling out of a residential neighborhood off the right side of the highway.

We'd both had eyes on them, as they'd pulled the classic hesitant driver trick: Creep out and stop, creep out and stop, creep out and stop...

There was hardly fair time for Blake to hit the brake after what happened next: Catching a glance through the driver's side window, we saw them turn their head hard right, and without an indicator they immediately floored the gas to turn left.

We were 20 yards away.

T-boning them hood-to-fender with *great* fortuitousness, everybody was alive and conscious.

Be that as it may, we'd still suffered a high speed impact into another vehicle, and were rather shaken.

Our hearts pumping full of adrenaline, my friend ejected the 8-track Beatles tape and cursed as he threw it into the back seat in a fit of rage.

My sentiments exactly.

A police car arrived at the scene in what seemed like the blink of an eye.

Medics followed soon after, who deemed Blake and I OK, suffering no visible injuries, but advising we get checked out by a doctor at the local urgent care.

We had already checked on the other driver who had remained in their seat, mystified and embarrassed. They made a statement to the officers that they couldn't recall what caused the crash.

We were more than happy to enlighten them, as were several witnesses, but nobody's testament was really necessary.

The positions of our cars and strips of rubber on the road had already made it abundantly clear as to exactly what happened.

The other driver was quickly found at-fault, being cited for failure to yield right-of-way.

Our Vice Principal was en route to work, and had stopped by upon noticing the accident to see if they could be of any help. We both accepted his offer to hitch a ride down the road to the school office so we could call our parents, since Blake's car was clearly totaled.

Later that day, the urgent care staff also found nothing wrong with me, saying I'd probably be a little stiff for a week.

The next morning my back was tight as expected, so my parents brought me to a local chiropractor in Solvang.

The visit took only 10 minutes.

"You've probably got a little whiplash, but you'll be fine in a few weeks. Expect some tightness in your muscles, but you can take some ibuprofen to help the pain."

The next week, I could hardly get out of bed, as pain was shooting from my upper neck all the way to my tailbone.

Worst. Chiropractor. Ever. I just didn't know it yet.

He'd actually retired soon after that year, which was for the best.

My parents found another recommended chiropractor covered by their insurance, Dr. Lori Sender in Goleta, which was about 30 miles one-way.

She was worth every mile of that drive.

She cared enough about me to take more than 10 measly minutes.

Learning of my car accident and seeing as I had no X-Ray on record, Dr. Sender quickly had one taken, followed by a brief acupressure massage and the first chiropractic adjustment of my life.

Tightness remained, but I could breathe a little deeper without as much stiffness in my back. She explained that my spine had suffered substantial trauma, and I'd probably need a few months of frequent adjustments to coax it back to its natural shape.

Sure enough, returning to go over the X-Ray results the following week revealed more than a *mild* whiplash.

The sight of my spine was unnerving, pun intended.

Viewing an X-Ray of a healthy human body from the side, the neck and spine are *supposed* to have a nice natural S-curve.

A moderate whiplash would be indicated by losing some of said curves, with bones being more straightened with higher impact.

I was a little worse off than that.

My middle back was completely straight. My neck wasn't lacking contours but slightly curving the *opposite* direction.

Brutal.

"Do you remember bracing yourself before impact? It's a natural defense when seeing an eminent crash to put your feet on the floor and tense up your legs."

I recalled every detail.

"Absolutely, we saw it coming since the other driver had crept out and stopped so many times, so when they pulled out, I had my legs fully braced to the floor. I even put my hands on the dash above the glove box, bracing my arms as a reflex action at the last moment. I guess I did everything I could to avoid that image of my body flying through the windshield."

She closed her eyes and nodded, wincing.

"I completely understand, it's tough not to trust your seat belt when you see an accident coming... but by bracing yourself and tensing up like that, it *really* worsens the damage to your body on impact..."

I was prescribed three visits a week: Monday, Wednesday, and Friday for three months minimum, with appointments to wane off more sparsely after that depending on my progress.

Luckily, it's true: Younger bodies heal quickly.

After three months, I went to two adjustments a week, and after six months, once a week.

Little did I know that much like the use of a retainer is required after having braces to keep the alignment of one's teeth, ongoing chiropractic care would become crucial to maintaining the health of my weakened, battered spine.

Learning of my passions, Dr. Sender was also certain to advise me to always remember to get out of the desk chair, as sitting for long hours every day was no way for a human body to thrive.

Looking back, I wish I'd have taken better notes, but I digress...

My parents were granted less than $5,000 compensation from the accident, and the first few months of corrective adjustments alone including transportation to an office 30 miles away exceeded that easily.

I remember pondering briefly, wondering if I should have signed that tribal petition — and quickly dismissed the idea upon feeling a nauseating lump in my gut even entertaining the thought.

Of course, there *were* other chiropractors located close-by in the Santa Ynez Valley, but they weren't within our current health insurance company's network at the time.

Gotta love the system.

Regardless, another X-Ray was taken about nine months after my treatment had begun, and my spine had been nearly restored to its natural shape. I was able to go about my day without any pain.

Despite that first terrible experience I'd had in Solvang, my appreciation of chiropractics, backed by not only how I felt but by visible X-Ray proof, was firmly established.

She was worth every mile of that drive.

THREE

It Annoys Me Just As Much As It Annoys You

The Big Six

No matter how many books I've read, no matter how much experience I've acquired, I will still on occasion find calling for technical support unavoidable.

Usually this occurs when documentation is either absent or poorly assembled. I might not have the time to spare in certain situations to drop everything, sit down, and read fifty pages in a pinch to find the answer I need.

Regrettably, I recall suffering *some* tech support experiences in which I'd imagine reading fifty pages may have been faster.

I was literally alone in my kitchen weeks ago performing that lovely task we all so cherish: deveining a pound of shrimp, only to think to myself, "Well, at least I'm not at the DMV or on the phone with tech support."

Everybody who's gone through the experience can surely relate to the most common elements of dread and loathing during those first few minutes of the call.

The more elements that are involved, the less pleasurable the experience is — for all.

<u>Common Elements Of Dread And Loathing</u>

1. Your Account Number

"Thank you for calling [company name], may I have your account number?"

To never hear that phrase again would be quite the pleasant fantasy. Whether it's for a utility bill, a statement from a doctor's office, an online retailer or any other service, no human I've met keeps a reference list of their account numbers for every company they've done business with. Yet, it's often the first question asked.

One might expect companies to make an effort to better showcase the account number within their correspondence.

Verily, this appears to be but a futile request as most every invoice I've received from utility companies, dentists, chiropractors, et cetera, appear to feature the account number in the most inconspicuous manner possible.

It's neither bold, italicized, underlined, enlarged, nor is it placed in a prominent location compared to any other densely plastered information.

Any **one** of these would be a game-changer.

Thus begins your tech support experience with this inquiry of frustration as you scrounge around your desk and file cabinets with a justified huff.

As a tech support agent, I'm not too jazzed about asking for account numbers either, as I know very well of the above reality.

Customers just want their issues fixed. That's all I really want as well. I get my thrills from solving problems, not prodding people for account numbers.

It's especially confounding when Caller ID isn't exactly new technology, which brings us to the next element.

2. Your Name and Phone Number

"If you don't have your account number, that's OK. May I have your name and phone number?"

This is perhaps the fairest question to be asked when calling for tech support. People generally know their own name, and they might even recall their phone number.

Cell phones have spoiled us rotten with the ability to save contacts by name. I myself went from remembering about twenty phone numbers of friends and family in my youth to only mine and my wife's numbers today.

That being said, customers will still on occasion have Caller ID Blocking activated, and when we request a valid phone number where they can be reached, we'll hear them shouting across the room at their peers that they can't remember it.

As much fun as that is, *far* less than 1% of the customers I assist these days actively use Caller ID Blocking.

Call centers have used software that traces the customer's account number by the Caller ID for decades, so there's no logical reason to defend popping the question by default in the 21st century.

There are exceptions, mind you; it's not a *perfect* system.

When a customer calls from a different phone number than one on file, complications occur. This frequently affects those calling from larger business offices that have multiple phones and extensions.

If a call center hasn't been informed of every single number and extension in an office or household, their software won't be able to automatically locate your account number from Caller ID. There's no way around that other than to ask more questions.

"I see you're calling from a different phone number than the one on file. Would you like to update the phone number associated with your account?"

This is where the support agent quietly gulps hard knowing that if an optional survey happens to be offered to the customer, the scores *probably* won't look all that swell.

We never know which of our calls will be recorded and reviewed for quality assurance purposes; if we *don't* ask these questions, we're likely to enjoy a condescending earful from multiple supervisors.

I've had as many as seven supervisors in the same department trying to micromanage my every move. This practice is still as common in the workplace today as it was decades ago when Mike Judge hilariously berated these despicable practices in his 1999 film, *Office Space*.

Most every agent I've worked with in my life loves that film as I do, and drops quotes often — right over the cubicle wall to their neighbor during their shifts.

It bolsters one's sanity.

3. Your Address.

"Could you verify your address for me?"

Sure, it's feasible that a utility company or online retailer may want to verify your address, but when tech support asks, it could come off as illogical, intrusive, and unnecessary.

It often is.

Many companies do this for two reasons. One is for an additional security measure to verify the identity of the caller.

You know, in case somebody broke into your home, turned on your computer, guessed your startup password and ran into an error message when using said software.

The other reason is for demographics. These days it's unlikely that a software company will send you something through the mail, but your ZIP code will be the key information utilized to make future development or marketing decisions.

That of course also depends largely on the nature of the product.

If you refuse to provide your address, some companies *do* allow the agent to proceed with troubleshooting, but some will require them to obtain it before providing support "for security purposes," lest the agent be issued another wave of verbal lashings.

4. Your Email Address.

"We need to ensure we have your current email address on file..."

It's not over yet. You haven't confirmed your identity with a digital fingerprint and retinal scan in order to be provided tech support.

This is a big one.

It's a sore subject.

People don't like to give their email address to strangers, and they have over time grown to mistrust businesses as well. This is because many unsavory companies have exploited it for marketing.

Many people know this, thus the irritation.

The bottom line is, if you're doing business with a reputable company on a regular basis, it's probably going to be a benefit (or even necessary) to provide your email address since chances are you really **do** want to be kept in the loop.

On the other hand, if you purchased a new peripheral or accessory and it isn't properly functioning as designed, then you probably won't want to give up your email address to a company whose brand new product is now providing a touch of misery in your life.

That's completely understandable.

Regardless, please remember not to personally take it out overmuch on the poor sap at the other end of the line.

They weren't the ones who produced the piece of junk.

5. Your Ticket or Case ID Number

"I will go ahead and document that your issue has been resolved. Would you like your ticket number?"

Congratulations. You've sat through a potentially painful hold time, and several minutes of being grilled for personal info before getting to the meat of the problem.

After anywhere from five minutes to several hours later, your computer issue is fixed and all you want is to get off the phone from this one-time issue.

Logic doesn't exactly denote that you'd like to document a ticket number, go to the company's website, register, log in, then search for your ticket to see the word "Resolved" next to it.

It's the icing on the cake of this adored ritual. Be that as it may, we can't neglect the sprinkles...

6. Repeating the Company Name.

"Thank you again for calling [company name], have a wonderful day."

This is one of the most difficult segments of any script for many support agents to comfortably sneak into the conversation. It must be *fully rattled off* before the customer hangs up the phone to stay their torment. If not, the quality assurance recording may potentially stop prematurely, thus ending in the agent getting disciplined.

The final fifth and sixth elements very often work together (for the customer and employee alike) to make their experience all the less pleasant if they've had a rough time with a product or software.

You **know** exactly who you've called. Their brand is mentally burned into your noggin after having blown money on their product, encountered a frustrating issue that should not have been, and enduring a less than convenient phone call trying to re-solve the issue... only to be *thanked* for calling them?!

If it's one thing you didn't need, it was to be reminded of the brand name of the product in which you're now eager to give a less-than-flattering review.

Your tech support experience is hereby concluded, and you're left with an unwanted souvenir of a bitter taste in your mouth.

Bon Appétit!

Not every call center enforces these completely, and some may in fact craft their own original elements of dread and loathing.

Nevertheless, those most common which have been men-tioned above will henceforth be referred to simply as:

The Big Six.

Constructive Destructives

Nobody enjoys suffering the routine of The Big Six.

As agents are customers *themselves* outside the workplace, we often feel uncomfortable to patronizingly jab callers with redundancy.

One also learns to quickly gauge their level of patience.

Throughout my career, the only times I recall a customer actually requesting a ticket number are following the most *disastrous* calls as to be sure to lambaste the agent and company alike through an online survey.

The fact that the agent didn't manufacture the product, write the code, or cause the defect at hand is neither here nor there.

Antacids are popped like candy by many of us.

From an inside perspective, I am glad to share the most effective measures to take if you're unhappy with the procedures of a call center.

I've seen what works and what doesn't. I've witnessed what successfully changes companies' policies and what gets laughed at by managers when the customer hangs up.

I've even seen some of the Big Six removed from practices due to overwhelming customer demand.

There are *effective* methods to achieve such victories.

One of the most fruitful is to take any available survey regarding your experience, taking care to leave fair and honest feedback about which elements were offensive or unsatisfactory.

Fabrications and exaggerations, as well as profanity-laced diatribes will be easily detected by those reviewing your feedback. If that's your strategy, it will likely be dismissed by management as the rant of an angry child exhibiting their immaturity.

When a well-written survey submission clearly indicates that your experience has affected your decision whether or not to purchase company products or services in the future, it will most always be taken into consideration.

If it's a reputable company, you might also receive a follow-up call to smooth things over.

When a survey isn't offered, there's nothing that gets the attention of a company faster than a respectfully phrased online public review.

Some would rather not take the time with either of these options. If that's your case, ask the agent to speak to a supervisor or manager at the end of the call to give your feedback.

One of the biggest issues with technical support surveys is the lack of polite, honest feedback devoid of pure rage and spite.

Daily, I would hear the same harshly worded comments and complaints regarding the Big Six, but there is far less impact made when an agent relays complaints to a manager versus them hearing it directly from the customer.

Companies know that people aren't calling for tech support because they're having a great day, so some level of *generic* complaints are always expected; a personal interaction with management involving specifics will always make a stronger impression.

The absolute *worst* action to take of course is personally berating the agent for elements out of their control. They didn't establish the policies, and don't own the company.

They don't deserve to be disparaged, and doing so is a tried and true method of accomplishing absolutely nothing to improve your next experience, or that of other customers.

There's also a certainty that the agent you've finished deprecating is going to ridicule you amongst their co-workers when the call is over.

People have feelings, and if you don't acknowledge theirs when on the line, they'll return the favor upon disconnect.

How strictly employees are held to the scripts and policies is widely varied. I've worked for some companies in which next to nothing is enforced; agents are permitted to behave like flesh and blood humans, scripts are treated as loose guidelines, and even leaving out a couple of the Big Six is acceptable depending on the situation.

I've also worked for companies that if during the assessment of your randomly recorded call, you fail to meet any of the criteria or stray a single syllable from their introductory and closing scripts...

Per their policy your employment shall be instantly terminated after three strikes.

It's a cut-throat industry.

FOUR

Welcome To The Machine: The Shipping Company

Getting Ripped

College debt wasn't something *I* felt necessary to embrace, meanwhile droves of young adults all around me began judging each other by their chosen mascots and colors.

Many people I'd graduated with had either enrolled in city college with a part time job on the side, or went straight into a university to rack up tens of thousands of dollars in debt to kickstart their first year of adulthood.

It wasn't for me.

Later in life, I did enroll in *some* college classes to obtain specific skills. Digital audio recording was one. Another was a self-paced IT Certification.

I paid cash for both.

After graduating high school at age 17, I pushed myself diligently to get where I am today. In fact, I've worked full time ever since, never being unemployed for more than a few days between jobs.

I'd taken some **lousy** minimum wage jobs to get started, though...

I learned more about people, business, government, budgeting, driving, cooking, and life in general within the first two months of working full time than I learned throughout all four years of high school.

One of the most unpleasant early experiences was my morning shift working as a "ripper" at a large-chain grocery store in the Santa Ynez Valley.

Juggling it with another part time job, the shift was from 2 a.m. to 8 a.m. five days per week.

I had the delightful chore of mindlessly breaking down the boxes left by the active stock clerks in every aisle, and carting them to the cardboard baler behind the store.

After stacking the bales of cardboard on pallets to hand off to the loading crew, I would repeat the process every 20 minutes for the six hour shift... all the while being harassed and cursed at by one of the stock clerks.

There were entertaining defects discovered in management as well.

Several times during my first week, I was called and woken up at midnight, being told I was late to work. Double checking the copy of the shift calendar I was given, I replied that it showed me starting at 2 a.m.

They insisted someone must have made a mistake, demanding I come in as soon as possible.

Confronting the on-duty supervisor, he told me that I was correct; the shift calendar *was* accurate.

As if stuck in an episode of The Twilight Zone, the same song and dance happened three times the following week as well, but that wasn't the worst part.

Look, I don't mind gettin' chops busted every now and then as part of traditional initiation or in the context of camaraderie, but the offense being dished out from that stock clerk was excessive, and coming from me that's saying something.

I'd gone through the public school system as a mixed race Yaqui-Iberian-German-Irish, simultaneous band geek *and* computer geek who'd been overweight since the 7th grade. I was also one to two years younger than the student body average.

That made for a lot of social targets on my back; I had thicker skin than most anybody I knew.

I took it so well, several of the other clerks even confronted this guy and told him he'd crossed the line. Some would even fire insults back at him in my defense throughout the shift, as they respected my attitude and hard work.

Nevertheless, he wouldn't quit.

The constant hazing hit the threshold for me after my second week, and I'd taken enough harassment, personal threats, cracks about my weight, lewd comments toward my Mother, my Father, and random senseless insults about my intelligence.

I shouted to get his attention, waiting for eye contact.

"HEY. You don't like me? Fine. YOU can fucking rip."

After releasing a flattened cardboard box from my grip, I tramped headlong toward the front door of the store as the offending clerk ran after me suddenly asking "please" not to leave, and that they'd had issues finding a ripper to keep on staff.

I wonder why.

When he promised he'd lay off and shook my hand, I decided to stay to see if he kept his word.

He did not.

The following day, one of the other stock clerks encouraged me to go directly to the night manager because this was a pattern the rest of them had grown tired of.

When I finished my shift I tracked down and spoke to the night manager, Stan. I let him know of the unacceptable behavior and stressed firmly that it had gone on too long.

Displaying no interest in addressing my mistreatment, he casually replied that it was likely all jovial, and it sounded like *I* probably wasn't fitting in. I was let go on the spot.

This being a union job, he didn't refer to it as being fired; he used the term, "placed on probationary release."

I've... preferred shopping elsewhere since.

A couple of years later, I was nauseated to learn that Stan had been promoted to Store Manager.

I'd grow to learn that being sickened by what went on at large companies wasn't an uncommon phenomenon.

I soon took on another joyous position working for a retirement community as a file clerk. I did nothing but tediously organize and scan hundreds of neglected stacks of tax forms and legal documents for days on end until my brain turned to mush.

The center was being self-audited by new management for suspicion of having a large number of illegal aliens on staff.

They indeed had many.

Over 70% of their 200 employees had no identification on file and hardly spoke English.

Of *those*, over 20 of them had claimed they developed carpal tunnel syndrome caused by carrying serving trays in the restaurant.

Some were even shown to have filed their claims *weeks* after being hired, and having milked the system for over a year since.

Witnessing acts of mooching and exploitation detests me. They are alternate forms of blatant thievery.

A thief is a pathetic waste of life.

I left that job after a month when I could stomach no more, as it was both mind-numbing and sickening.

Bussing tables here or there and working at a couple retail stores kept me busy until finally landing my first full time tech support job a year after high school graduation.

My parents had moved out of California, so I moved a few miles north, found a room to rent for $250 a month and took a position at my first call center.

The job was with a major international shipping company looking to hire tech support agents for their label printing software.

It was the strangest hiring mechanic I had yet seen.

The company had contracted a temp agency to permanently operate in-house to screen and manage all hires.

The workplace was a large, single-floor building with a massive grid of cubicles, and two small computer labs on one side. These were used solely for putting new temp hires through a two week training course before assigning them at a cubicle to take their first live call.

On day one we were given what would be best described as a "reverse pep talk" by our instructor, who spoke very frankly about the nature of the job.

This was a very strict, script-oriented call center. The building housed a staff of 400, less than 10% of them being permanent.

It had only been open for 16 months, and within that time, the location had already experienced a turnover of nearly 2,000 employees.

All temps were put on a three month probationary period. Our incoming calls were recorded so that one could be scored at random every week. If we hadn't been terminated from failing to abide by the ruthless call procedures or the harsh attendance policy, our performance would be reviewed and we'd be considered for permanent hire if deemed worthy.

Starting pay was fifty cents above minimum wage. There was no vacation pay and no benefits despite all temp positions being full time.

The training was thorough, and we were soon familiar with every single function of the software.

We became proficient storing mailing addresses, organizing them into groups and lists, importing and exporting them. We learned how to properly measure and enter dimensions of letters and packages in accordance with company guidelines, and how to connect and configure a compatible scale with the software.

Finally, we were taught the ins and outs of printing the actual labels, and troubleshooting the company-issued printers.

That's when we were thrown to the dogs.

Failure By Design

Every week, one of our recorded calls would be selected for review by a panel that leaned slightly sadistic.

Our mouse and keyboard actions were recorded as well, and points would be quickly deducted for every infraction.

We were required to follow the introductory and closing scripts verbatim.

By the first ring of each call, account numbers had been already traced by Caller ID and populated on our screen before we even answered.

That was a relief for both us *and* the customers.

Our scripted intro was, "Thank you for calling [the shipping company] technical assistance center, my name is [first name], how may I help you today?"

After hearing them out, we were to repeat an acknowledged summary of the customer's support request *back to* them. If we tripped over any words, stuttered, hesitated, or failed to understand any part of their request, we lost points.

The next step was to type the customer's issue into our call logging software, then click a series of corresponding drop-down menus to reflect the symptoms described. Upon doing so, the documented solution would be displayed at the bottom of our screen. If we *failed* to locate the correct solution or did so in an untimely manner, we lost points.

There were well over 100 documented solutions for known problems, so it was easy to end up at the wrong one. We were also forbidden from using the words "known" or "problems" with customers. As quoted by our instructors, "We don't have known problems, only issues that can be resolved."

If we were caught using either word, we lost points.

If we failed to clearly state any verbatim steps of the documented solution, we lost points.

We were also to recite a scripted disclaimer every 20 seconds of dead air: "I apologize for the wait, there may be another short delay while I'm researching the issue."

If over five seconds of unannounced dead air lapsed at any time during the call without reciting or refreshing the disclaimer, we lost points.

If at any moment during this delightful experience we'd failed to maintain an infallibly cheery inflection as subjectively judged by the panelist, we lost points.

Finally, once the issue had been resolved we were to close with the script, "Thank you very much for calling [the shipping company] technical assistance center, have a great day."

As with the intro, if we strayed a single word from the closing script, we lost points.

Our reviews had a maximum possible score of 5 points, and we were required to obtain one score per month of at least a 4 to be eligible for permanent hire.

Though it was technically possible to lose *more* than 5 points, the minimum score generously remained at 0.

Failing to earn a 4 wouldn't necessarily result in being let go; if management determined that you still showed the potential, you could be granted an extension of your contract to retain the honorable privilege of working for $6.25/hour as a temp without benefits.

As for the attendance policy, it was *absurd*.

The company didn't pay us for the time it took between arriving at our cubicle, powering on our computer, logging in, and launching all required software.

Completing this procedure would take an average of eight minutes due to the sluggish performance of their outdated computers.

We'd usually get to our cubicles 10 minutes before our shift to play it safe. That would give us enough time to complete the above ritual before signing into our landline phones with our personal five-digit employee code.

This served as our time-clock stamp and allowed the incoming calls to start rolling in.

We weren't paid for any of our time until then.

The instructors referred to this model as "butt-in-seat, phone-in-ear."

Eight unpaid minutes each work day adds up to a lot of money. With 400 employees in the building, that's over $86,000 a year the company was pocketing at the *starting* rate of pay.

Thankfully, many call centers in California have since been required by the labor board to pay for this time in more recent years.

We all had a 30 minute lunch, and two 10 minute breaks during our shift. We were allowed three unpaid sick days per year.

If for any reason we were *one minute late* clocking in to the start of our shift, or returning from lunch or breaks, we were given one attendance demerit for tardiness.

If we ever clocked in at any time more than one minute *early,* we received an attendance demerit for unauthorized overtime.

If three demerits were accrued in a quarter, we were to be terminated instantly and escorted from the building.

It was no mystery as to why the high turnaround.

The place was a warehouse of anguish with policies designed to fault employees with ease, or breed enough displeasure in the environment to encourage them to leave on their own long before three months passed.

This was an incredible method of operation that empowered the company to cover their call volumes without having to pay the majority of their employees benefits.

It was also a great way of keeping a steadily rotating, unskilled, unhappy staff. Of the 20 people in my training class, less than 10 remained after the first week in the cubicles.

The Help Menu

My own reviews often earned low scores. I never received a 0, but had plenty of 1's and 2's. Many times, it was due to longer calls over 30 minutes which by nature, were easier to slip up from the stiff robot-like inflection required.

The memory of one call in particular stuck with me as comedy gold. It's one of those calls that could have been a sketch in a sitcom or a stand-up routine.

The customer was a woman with a thick, raspy Brooklyn accent who spoke very frankly. She was impatient, irritable, crass, disrespectful, inappropriate, used profanities and crude expressions.

She personally berated my own skills, the department, and the company itself over the course of the call.

Unfortunately for my review, I'd found her attitude and accent hilarious.

One of the challenges was riding the mute button on my phone to hide my frequent laughter. This made for several moments on the recording that had longer than five seconds of dead air, so I got dinged repeatedly.

She called because she was tired of seeing a message telling her to update to the latest version of the software, but she was *certain* she already had.

You already know where this is going.

Naturally, one of the very first steps of the solution was to verify the version of the currently installed software. This would reveal if the customer had successfully run the latest update.

Always verify.

Naturally, it was a great offense to her that I would even *imply* she'd failed to do such a thing, and a barrage of verbal obscenities were fired across the country from the east coast to California — right into my headset.

After several minutes of combating this logical step and repeatedly assuring me that she was *"not stupid!..."* she finally relented and understood that this was what needed to be done; I could not proceed otherwise.

The version was listed in the same place the majority of software usually displays it, right under the "About" option within the Help Menu. This is typically the rightmost menu at the top of a program.

Getting her to *spot* the Help Menu took about 20 minutes.

I first walked her through maximizing the window. She didn't know what that meant, and had trouble listening to basic instructions such as differentiating "upper right corner" from "upper left corner."

After achieving that miracle, I asked her if she could locate the File Menu that should now be in the upper left corner of her screen.

At the cost of my sanity, she barked that she didn't know what a menu was, and the word "file" was reportedly nowhere to be found.

Taking a different approach, I finally asked her what she **did** see in that corner.

"Well I've got a bunch of those yellow sticky notes on my monitor with my passwords on them. I can't remember all of them so I keep them written down..."

Yah. That'll help.

After fumbling a few minutes more with futile attempts, I tried instructing her to use a keyboard shortcut to expand the File Menu, (Alt+F), hoping that might get her attention to see it when it pops down.

This only proved to open up another can of worms, as she had never heard of the Alt key and didn't know where to find it.

Giving it that school try, I directed her to start by looking at the bottom left corner of the keyboard and slowly move right, asking if she saw the Control key, Alt key, or the Space Bar...

"I know where the space bar is, but I don't have anything else there."

Due to her impatience, trying this method backwards by starting at the Space Bar and having her move left one key at a time was equally successful.

Grasping at desperation, I went back to asking her to look near the top left corner to locate the File Menu, and for an unknown reason that I was grateful for, she spotted it instantly that time.

I muted the call, exclaiming, "FINALLY!..." before continuing:

"Great, that's perfect. To the right of the File Menu, you'll see several other menus. The Help menu will be the last one on the right."

She still didn't see it, so I went a littler slower.

"Okay, let's go ahead and find that File Menu again. Got it? Great. What do you see immediately to the right of the word 'File?' Do you see the word 'Edit?' Wonderful, let's keep going to the right. 'View' is next, correct. A couple more? And what's to the right of that one? The next? And the next? 'Help?' Yes, that's the one! Go ahead and click on it."

Her painfully inappropriate response was icing on the cake — or rather, the twist of the knife.

"OH, well *pffft*. Yes there it is, HELP. Of course I see it, it's right there. I mean, I'm not retarded, you could have just *told* me to look right there at that one spot..."

She was dead serious, oblivious, and far too stubborn to realize that it took her 20 minutes to find one word that was in the same place the entire time.

At that point the primary obstacle had been tackled, and she was able to then locate and click "About..." to find that she had indeed been mistaken, and was using an outdated version of the software.

She proclaimed she was comfortable enough searching her office for the latest update that was mailed to her, and would proceed to run it on her own.

Ending the conversation, I hoped for my co-workers' sake she was right; I wouldn't wish a return call from her on anybody.

Though that was the most exhausting call I remember from that job, these types of calls are *far* from uncommon in the world of tech support.

Agents either quickly develop extreme levels of patience and pacifism, or eventually get fired for being caught audibly swearing at customers when failing to accurately engage the mute button.

By the end of my three month probationary period, I had zero attendance demerits, but hadn't a single review with a score of 4 or higher.

No worries, a quick meeting with management, and I was granted another three month contract to try, try again.

...but it was not to be.

Micro-shaft

Soon after my fourth month as a temp, I was a quarter mile away from the office on lunch break with two co-workers, one of which had offered to drive us.

We'd been handed our steaming bag of grease from a fast food window and were approaching the edge of the driveway to head back to the office.

What happened that next moment sealed my fate with the shipping company.

Our car was struck by another young driver's vehicle that was exiting the lot. They'd run a parking lot stop sign and plowed right into the front left fender of my co-worker's car at 10 miles per hour.

Anger and panic abound, 911 was called and a police report was filed. Both drivers were told that since they were on private property and no other witnesses were present besides the passengers, no fault could be established.

This was in spite of the other driver's brilliant exclamation to the officer, "I didn't even *see* them there!"

Insurance companies would need to be contacted and dealt with... yet another of everyone's favorite pastimes.

We were livid returning to work, the three of us making a mad dash to HR to explain why we were on lunch break for 75 minutes instead of 30.

Pardons were given to no one. All were issued an attendance demerit even though the reason for our tardiness was having been victims of a traffic accident.

That's how the company played:

Dirty.

Having tolerated over four months in that toxic cubicle jungle, I ended up taking a sick day the following week as I couldn't shake my stale, negative attitude I held about the company. Just thinking about entering that building one more time made me ill.

The day after, I called in before my shift and quit my job without giving any notice. I felt no remorse.

I'll never forget how hard it was restraining my inner laughter at the HR rep's feigned surprise, asking me with a dramatically inquisitive, pseudo-innocent tone: "Why *is* it that you have decided to leave our employ?"

Gee.

I ended up exercising tactful restraint, and mentioned that I'd found a better position elsewhere, leaving it at that.

Sure, I was tempted to gush forth with a righteous tirade, but something told me that a company with a turnaround rate like theirs had *no* interest in growing a conscience, and I'd only be wasting my breath.

Looking back at the entire experience is still angering. As the vast majority of their hires were fresh out of high school, it's clear it was one big operation designed to take advantage of inexperienced youth — by a large corporation that knew *exactly* how to pull it off.

Disturbingly, these conditions are the stuff that employees working for corporations in some *other* countries could only dream of.

That puts things in a very different perspective.

Regardless, I will never again work for a company that adopts such practices.

Companies that intentionally cut corners, micromanage, and embrace immoral methods to save a few bucks will always lack a knowledgeable and loyal staff.

Furthermore, customers will feel it.

Embracing policies so strict as to discourage sincere human interaction between agents and customers is a cardinal sin of tech support.

It's a routine that's practiced by many large companies today.

There are reasons tech support has been well known by everybody as a predominately unpleasant experience, the butt of jokes, and source material for countless internet memes for decades.

Though it only boils down to one main reason, really.

That would be greed.

FIVE

Getting Chewed Out In Person: The Electronics Store

Hands-On

After enduring a less than ideal tech support job, I elected to distance myself from the large-scale environment of corporate buildings and embrace a position that *didn't* involve adopting the behavior of a mindless drone.

I returned to Solvang, and rented a room from a good friend, Jay, for $150/month.

I hit the pavement, ready to score some job offers...

Selectively.

There were a few offices here and there looking to hire administrative assistants, but I didn't want to be stuck in a chair all day again so soon.

I wanted to find somewhere I could be passionate about my work, enhance my existing skills and acquire some new ones. Fortunately, I knew just the place to target.

I tuned up my resume and applied at our local electronics store. Though the name was that of a large chain, this was an independent *dealer* location.

That meant all the fun of their products and services without the mess of corporate policies.

Two days later I got an offer, and accepted the position as a sales associate starting at $8.50/hour. Minimum wage was still $5.75, so I was making decent money being less than two years out of high school.

I was the only employee aside from the proprietor and her brother; it was a comfortably independent franchise, and that meant freedom.

I had the freedom to think, and the freedom to speak and behave like a real human being.

My self-confidence shot sky high during my very first shift.

The store inventory consisted of products representing every bit of geekery that I'd been tinkering with my whole life.

Televisions, boomboxes, audio/video equipment, portable cassette players and CD players, headphones, cables, adapters, batteries, telephones, cell phones, satellite dishes, remote control cars, scanners, a variety of Amateur, CB and Two-way radios, electronic components...

You name it, they had it.

To my dismay, the only thing they didn't stock was computers.

There was a good reason: selling an $1800 computer once a month wasn't worth the profit. Being a franchise and not a corporate location, their store's *cost* of that computer was $1780.

Solvang is a Danish tourist town, so selling AA batteries at the rate that 1990s digital cameras drank them dry was a far more profitable transaction.

The next most commonly sold items were replacement cables, headphones, and audio/video adapters.

I had a blast troubleshooting peoples' issues in person for a change. They'd often bring in a small appliance like a corded telephone or a component of their stereo system that had stopped working.

Sometimes they'd even bring in a small television that'd had its coax connector snapped off, needing repair.

The owner's brother gave me my first lesson in soldering small electronic parts, which I took great pride in. It felt clumsy at first, but after practice was like second nature.

Customers would leave the store with a grin on their face, clutching their cherished devices they'd feared were headed straight for the junkyard... only to see them working like new for a few bucks.

It was a great feeling to fix broken devices and breathe new life into them.

The store stocked a few books regarding the basics of electronics, maintenance, and small appliance repairs, so I was able to review and broaden my knowledge as I'd hoped.

Educating myself on the finer points of customizing audio systems for the home (as well as for automobiles) proved to save money for both myself *and* my friends.

Before long, the owner had been so impressed with my performance that I'd gotten a raise to $10.00/hour.

I had made it into the double digits!

Taking advantage of my employee discount more than a few times, a good part of my paychecks went right back into the store to upgrade my own appliances, and acquire new gadgets.

This only increased my familiarity of the store's products, bringing that much more passion and energy right back into the job.

It was a win-win.

I was able to flex my over-the-phone troubleshooting muscles, as well.

People really appreciated hot tips when calling for help configuring their surround sound systems.

I'd even on occasion get to resolve their computer issues; we did offer keyboards, mice, and accessories like mouse pads, wireless peripherals, and more.

Flaunting my skills along with learning new tricks, I was enjoying my work.

Life was good.

Some People

No other customer experiences yet rivaled the hilarity of the legendary Help Menu affair, but I did have a laugh on a few occasions.

One customer who'd purchased a portable cassette player came back to the store a few hours later with a question about the "Mega Bass" feature.

They approached the counter with a perplexed look on their face.

"Hi, I was wondering... what is this little switch for on the side here that I've never seen before: Mee-guh Bass?" (Pronouncing at first it like the fish).

Hearing the question, my brain desperately tried to get a read on whether or not the person was serious.

I couldn't really tell.

An adult who'd purchased a cassette player was either playfully feigning ignorance to terms as common as "treble" and "bass", or wasn't aware that audio features weren't typically named after game fish.

Scanning the store, I tactfully glanced behind me to make sure somebody with a video camera wasn't stealthily filming a staged prank.

The coast was clear, so I took a slow breath and responded as seriously as possible.

"Oh okay sure, the *Mega Bass* feature, absolutely. When you turn it on, it will boost the lower frequencies of anything you're listening to. Many people use it for music, but it'll work for dialogue as well when listening to audiobooks for that deeper, richer sound..."

I rambled on with generic elaboration until suddenly the customer snapped-to and the word finally clicked.

"Oh, BASS! ...Yes, I got it now," they nodded with wider eyes upon realizing.

Aside from such patrons needing a high-protein snack or a good night's sleep, there were other varieties of customers that were always a challenge.

I can't not mention them: Cheapskates.

Most of us know at least one person that's certain *every* manufacturer on earth is out to put the screws to all the suckers born every minute.

They'll swear up and down that their roll of duct tape, bundle of toothpicks, and 500 yard spool of agéd twine they'd scored at a garage sale decades ago is all they need to keep their devices running like new.

It wasn't uncommon to encounter a hybrid variant: The Cheapskate/Know-It-All.

Their practice of purchasing the lowest priced [and lowest quality] generic brands possible often requires having to replace them more often. This only fuels their confirmation bias ensuring they remain convinced that *all* new products are the stuff swindlers peddle.

Some are bold enough to verbally share their certainty in front of their friends at checkout that they're "being had."

There's a thick line between those being frugal and handy, versus miserly and ignorant. It's the latter of which that I'll say were admittedly fun to shut down, pulling the plug out from their thin-walled tank of volatile, viscous, disaster-fuel before they could use it to try nurturing any more of their dim deficiencies.

Electronics stores serving as a potential *danger* to these types, catching them before they could act often served to help prevent them causing damage to themselves, their products, and possibly their homes.

The owner's brother was skilled at being blunt with a smile on his face.

It was for their own good.

I recall a favorite example.

He noticed one customer spending a great deal of time picking up every spool of electrical wire on the shelf, looking only at the price tags on the underside of each.

After loudly and dramatically sighing, they had slowly traversed the store, performing the ritual again with the spools of speaker wire. They moved on to repeat the same price-tag hunt over by the telephone section.

Finally grabbing a twenty-five foot spool of beige telephone wire, they approached the counter.

Upon ringing them up, my co-worker couldn't resist commenting on what he had seen, and with exaggerated enthusiasm.

"All right! Running some indoor phone lines tonight? Do you have all the tools and connectors you need?"

Hook, line, and sinker...

"Oh... no, I'm rewiring an old floor lamp for my office and I won't need that heavy duty wire."

With a grin, the follow-up response was fired off:

"I see. Do you have fire insurance? Because you're gonna need *that!*"

"Oh uh...um, really?"

Catching their attention, he'd made them realize it wasn't worth running the risk of incinerating their home to save a few dollars, so they'd agreed to listen to a rundown of what things *not* to do when dealing with several amps of electrical current.

As it turns out, running them through too small of a gauge wire ranks pretty high up there on the numbskull-ometer.

I believe I learned this in fourth grade science class, but something also tells me being a fan of *Mr. Wizard's World* in my youth may have also played a part.

Rest in peace, Don Herbert.

Looking after the welfare of the lesser logically inclined was slightly exhausting, and potentially insulting.

They were constantly doubting your intentions and trying to reveal an assumed hidden agenda of yours to swindle them out of an extra three bucks — when honestly you're trying to prevent an explosion or house fire.

Ignorance aside, nothing compares to the universally most difficult customer type which as anybody in the restaurant business already knows is *not* exclusive to tech support or retail...

The rude.

Vanquishing Aberrations

In a small town where most people recognize each other in public, the discomfort of dealing with rude customers is increased.

When handling rudeness, it's a generous presumption to consider the person may have recently been cut off in traffic or had an off-moment in their day.

Though when seeing the *same* faces return for additional doses, the residual sediment from their chronic insolence begins to compile, and painfully bore into your psyche.

No matter how much flak you take or how many conversations you spin with positive effort, they'll beat you up repeatedly with their arrogance, curmudgeonry, and spite for the world.

Some folks have grown so negative, their only established goal is to make sure that your life, when in *their* presence, is as miserable as their own.

In retail, there's not much else to do than simply allow their poisonous blathering to float in one ear and out the other, moving them along as quickly as possible.

Not taking things personally is an acquired art.

Ample patience in retail is a must; you never know if an impolite face was that of a tourist you'll never see again, or a *new local* who you might possibly win over in the long-term by killing them with kindness.

Sure, this increases sales by keeping a loyal customer, but may end up something much greater.

People, after all, do possess the ability to shock and surprise when it's least expected.

I encountered a shining example of this behavior after an ongoing set of events that began my first year at the store:

A casual yet well-dressed woman entered the front door, with the steady gait of someone with a clear motive.

Knowing exactly what they were after, they approached me at the register with a posh British accent:

"Hello, I'm looking for a portable CD player, what do you have?"

Rarely receiving such a direct and concise request, (always an easy sale), I instantly pointed into the glass counter below to give a rundown on the five available models we had in stock.

"Sure, we have a range of players starting here at $39.99, which inclu-"

The elegant voice interrupted me sharply upon my revealing of the price.

"That looks like garbage. I don't want *garbage,* don't try to sell me any garbage..."

She then made eye contact for the first time, with an unhappy yet expectant disposition. Having been shut down so quickly into my opening sentence, I was eager to complete this merry little exchange.

I went right for the top.

"I understand. Our very *best* model includes upgraded head-phones, at $169.99. With 45-second skip protection, it's gonna be a nice and smooth-"

"*That's* fine. I'll take two."

"Great, I'll bag those up for you."

With a terse thank-you and her bag in hand, she quickly exited the building as the owner's brother approached from the back room, shoulders bouncing in a silent chuckle.

"Nice job there... so did you, uh, recognize her?"

I hadn't.

I *should* have recognized her name from her credit card when she paid, but I didn't. I was at work. I was in my "business" hat.

My co-worker chuckled at my reaction as I had my ah-ha moment: stunned face, mouth slowly gaping, eyes widening... the only thing missing was a dolly zoom to clinch the scene.

She was an actress who'd starred in a goofy '80s comedy that — surprise surprise — remains one of my favorite cult classic films to this day.

Laughing about the experience, I put it out of my mind until she returned later that year.

She was inquiring about some upcoming toys seen in the holiday flyer, in particular some remote control cars.

Her having shown interest in several, I mentioned it was slightly early for our location to qualify for ordering holiday items, but I would keep her list of requests and contact her to confirm availability as soon as we were able.

A few weeks passed and as expected, our store's franchise status allowed us only a limited supply of remote control cars... as with several other holiday toys which had been prioritized for corporate locations.

When calling to inform her of the limited supply and the date they'd be available for pickup, she replied with a scoff and an attitude.

"You're *kidding* me? That's *ridiculous*..."

Proceeding further into a condescending outburst, it was clear she was less than pleased, and had intended to ensure that by the time *I* got off the phone, I'd be as well.

It worked.

I mentioned the call to the owner and she encouraged me to be firm with her in the future if I ever felt she crossed the line, as *she'd* dealt with her for a while.

Though she was a regular, it was **not** okay for any customers to get away with berating or harassing us.

The following week when my new "friend" came to pick up the order, it was nearing closer to the holiday season and there was a warm jolly energy in the air.

I retrieved her special order and began cashing her out.

"...and you're sure that's *all* that was available? Why is it that other stores seem to have more in stock? I really didn't want to have to drive an hour out of my way when your store is local."

I explained to her the details as provided by the owner.
"Yes, I'm sorry about the limited selection. Since we're a franchise, we aren't provided with as large an allocation for the holiday items as the corporate locations; they have a higher sales expectation, so they reserve a larger quantity for their stores."

She hadn't even tried to lower her voice as a foul-mouthed rant broke out:

"Pff. Well, *bah fucking humbug.* Bloody corporations — *fucking* cocksuckers!"

Body language still completely posh...

Instantly, the festive spirit and holiday cheer had been sapped right out of the air, there in our small Solvang electronics store in the early midst of December.

Now coated in a thick layer of discomfort, I made eye contact with a few other customers... *some with children present*, as we all swapped reactions of jarringly dumbfounded open-mouthed nods from afar.

She didn't even realize, as she was avoiding eye contact as usual.

Recovering from her exclamation with a strenuously stifled stun, I tried my best to move on as if nothing was amiss.

Cashing her out that day was an extra swift act, if I do say so myself.

There were several more visits that soon followed.

She'd once made an attempt at self-deprecating humor. Upon asking if she'd like a bag for her purchase, she replied with her signature scoff, and as usual stared past me at an angle.

"Psh, no I'll just use these bags under my eyes." As her complexion appeared perfectly healthy, and she'd lacked any obvious jovial inflection, it was sad and awkward, if anything at all.

She eventually started bringing in her child during her visits, who was absolutely the one in charge. Trying to coax her young one to come with her as she left was never a short ritual.

When her hands were full from purchases, I'd hold the door for her for uncomfortable periods of time as she slowly kept raising her voice to a level convincing enough to resemble authority.

As soon as the door would close, I'd begin retrieving the products the kid had thrown to the floor in revolt upon being told they couldn't have this or that.

It all eventually came to change a few weeks later in a manner that I would never have seen coming.

Her previous visit had been in late December, and it was approaching mid-January when she entered the store alone for a small purchase.

I'll never forget what she said to me after cashing out, and it's something I still respect today.

Making sincere eye contact upon taking the receipt, *she owned up to everything*.

"Thank you so much, Michael. I know I've treated you poorly in the last year and I'd like to greatly apologize. I've been enduring a very difficult time in my life, dealing with finalizing a divorce that has been rough on me and my children... and I feel I've taken some of that out on you. I wanted to say I'm sorry, and I appreciate all your patience with me. Have a *wonderful* New Year, and God bless you."

She leaned forward and offered an authentic hug, and I was ... floored.

No customer had ever apologized for *any* behavior, much less with such real, and profound elaboration.

I was speechless.

"Thank you, and... you have an amazing New Year, too."

I could breathe easier around her after that day. We would on occasion see each other in town outside the store, and she'd greet me by name, with either a wave or a hug.

It's a trite lesson, treating rudeness with patience, but for good reason: people who behave in an inherently rude fashion aren't doing so naturally.

Something hasn't gone well.

Pain or trauma has been a likely factor.

Having gone through that experience and persevered in the manner in which I did isn't something that I would casually call "pleasant."

It was neither enjoyable nor effortless... yet in retrospect I'd absolutely call it rewarding.

I could have easily been more firm, and you can bet I was with others going forward, as the experience did alter my personality to become more assertive.

Witnessing someone else's character develop over time to see them reveal the painful details at the root of their prior misbehavior is a potent display of humanity, humility, and again last but not least — honesty.

One might also take a moment to realize that evil, cruelty, and any other aberrations involved in one's conduct that would fall into the category of "inexcusable" *are* in fact just that.

Inexcusable should never be equated with *unforgivable*.

Remember that next time you encounter this "somebody" whoever they may be, and realize they've likely been enduring a hardship that has left them exhausted, bent, and bitter.

They may only need a little touch of extra kindness, patience and perspective to snap them from their stupor.

Squandered Carbon

Disrespectful attitudes aside, some people require a swift, direct confrontation if their deeds bring about more instantly tangible negatives.

Premeditated exploitation, and theft are some of these acts.

I noticed over time that *some* customers would utilize the return policy to treat us as a free rental service for one-off uses of products.

Meetings during local business conventions, or video presentations at job fairs were common events that would trigger these schemes.

The pursuit was quite obvious as it was always involving the same types of items: speakerphones, extra long RCA and coax cables, and couplers to extend existing ones.

Often purchased in the morning by somebody dressed in sharp business attire, they'd be brought back in the late afternoon with the arguments: "The cable wasn't compatible with our TV" or "The speakerphone wasn't loud enough."

Some were even as bold to repurchase the same item(s) a few months later, using the identical lame excuse to return it once more at the end of the day.

The cables they'd buy all had standard RCA or coax connectors; of course they were compatible.

The speakerphones had standard jacks, sensitive internal microphones and a *sturdy* amplified speaker you could hear clearly 30 feet away; of course it was loud enough.

Over time, our store's return policy was reduced from 30 to seven days, and we had to deem many such items as non-refundable to prevent being taken advantage of.

We still ended up with a regular amount of "ugly" items peppered throughout the store.

They'd be stapled closed in clear plastic bags hanging on the pegboard with a manually printed label, the original clam shell packaging having been destroyed upon first purchase.

The owner had to eat the cost and sell the items at a discount, as they were now used products.

Though it was off-putting to see a minority of customers practicing this behavior, it was always imperative to give *new* faces the benefit of the doubt. This was difficult having grown adept at recognizing suspicious mannerisms, but over time it proved to be good for business.

Eventually, several repeat offenders were in fact banned from our store. We exercised our right to refuse service based on past exploitation, and after several warnings at that.

Though negative experiences will on occasion soil your day, it's important for sales reps to remember that most people who enter a store do *not* walk in with malicious intent to rip the place off.

Regarding blatant theft, it was nearly unheard of in our small town store.

An average month would see no less than 2,000 people enter the doors of the establishment, and the beautifully positioned surveillance cameras combined with our frequent inventory checks would reflect nominal theft attempts.

Confronting shoplifters would usually prompt one of two common reactions:

Most would stop dead in their tracks and melt down into an apologetic puddle proclaiming they "didn't realize" they were in the process of carrying unpaid product(s) out the door.

The other types would play it aloof, pretending not to hear us calling after them and still trying to get away with it. Those boldest would desperately increase their power-walking pace out the front door to be later caught after we'd contacted the authorities.

When *that* happened, there would almost always be a larger stash found in their vehicle(s) from multiple shops in town. All stolen merchandise would be returned from whence it came, with tourists often being more than happy to act as witnesses in identifying the thief for law enforcement.

In my time at the store, only *one* known petty theft (of a cassette adapter), was successful during a holiday season.

It happened when all three of us were busy assisting the dense crowds of customers; none of us realized it was missing until later in the day.

Security footage showed the thief to be a kid looking in his mid teens. I didn't recognize him from our small town, and he was never seen in the store again.

Whether he was merely a bored, rebellious juvenile offspring of a tourist, or a troubled young man suffering from kleptomania was immaterial; it was infuriating to watch a video of your proud place of employment being compromised in that manner.

A thief is a pathetic waste of life.

Scrambling Southbound

Jay had a satellite dish in his backyard — one of those big ugly dishes (BUD) resembling a beastly upside down jungle gym. This enabled me to catch several episodes of what would become one of my favorite shows at the time, *Call For Help*.

Originally aired on the TechTV channel, the show was hosted by Chris Pirillo and Morgan Webb, in which they advised and assisted with live callers' varieties of questions about computer hardware, software, and business trends.

The positive passion and energy they brought to the show with such honesty and candor had me hooked from the beginning.

I'd never seen tech discussed so frankly. The hosts were both professional *and* personable. This later became a style that I'd embrace in my tech support career.

With no short supply of humorous antics and relatable chemistry, they pushed all the right buttons for geeks everywhere to help expand horizons and scratch that techie itch, delivering great entertainment with educational subject matter.

Weird Al Yankovic even called into the show during an 18-hour "Call-For-Help-A-Thon" in 2002, as it was no secret that Chris was huge fan of his.

I didn't catch the original clip, but caught it on a rerun. It was still available online last time I checked, and seeing it surely made every '80s geek shout an unrestrained, "YES!" upon watching.

I sure did.

I've been a Weird Al fan since hearing his tune, "Eat It", in the mid-'80s. I still recall his special appearance on *Family Double Dare* a few years after that, and his unforgettable sway pole act on *Circus of the Stars* in the early '90s.

As I had been introduced early on to Spike Jones, Raymond Scott, and Dr. Demento, Al fit right in to my favorites quite naturally.

After becoming a full-fledged band geek in high school, I slowly stopped listening to the radio as mainstream music wasn't holding my attention as it once did when MTV was in full swing.

As a result, I listened only to enough radio to make sure I was familiar with the most popular hits as to fully appreciate Mr. Yankovic's next album of parodies.

That's the truth.

Call For Help made me realize how much I enjoyed working in a more computer-oriented field, and I've followed Chris's work ever since. He continues to produce quality content always relevant to the industry, while staying true to his credo, "I view technology as an enabler, not a destination."

That's a great way to keep one's head in check. You can be impressed and wowed with the latest tech all you want, raving all day long about how cool a device is, but specs only mean so much. It's what one does with them that counts.

Jay ended up moving in 2002, so my sweet deal of cheap rent had come to an end. I quickly realized that I had to take on a second job to make it in the Santa Barbara county, as the lowest rent I could find with a roommate was $650/month, several miles outside the valley.

Though several raises had me pulling in over $11.00/hour, that wasn't really enough.

My boss at the electronics store was more than understanding, and she granted me a flexible schedule so I could conveniently take a second job for additional income.

For a while, I'd picked up an evening shift at the local hardware store. It was literally right across the street, so after ending my day job, I'd lock up, cross the road and change company name tags.

On top of that, I squeezed in working pizza delivery on weekends.

After several months of this intense schedule, I left the hardware store for a slightly lighter shift at a hotel, filling duties as both a bellman and a reservation agent.

It was there working in reservations that I met the General Manager's daughter, Kelly, who would eventually ask *me* out on a date in the upcoming months.

Enduring 65 to 70 hour work weeks with one day off a month *at best,* I was eventually thrown into fatigue and began to lose steam.

I had no time to pursue any interests, study for certifications, or take any courses at city college. I also eventually wanted to have a place of my own with a couple days off per week.

I made a choice that I don't necessarily *regret* since it was a learning experience, but it wasn't my finest decision: I eventually transferred from the electronics store franchise to the *corporate* location closer to where I was living.

My old boss had warned me that although I did have the potential to make a much higher paycheck within a shorter work week, the corporate locations were all about commission. That meant enduring possible conflicts with my future co-workers.

I applied for a part time shift there, and continued working pizza delivery in Solvang on nights and weekends. I'd hoped to get back some of my personal time so that I could catch my breath and think about my long-term future.

Knocking the corporate interview out of the park, I ended up accepting the position, getting paid whichever was higher: minimum wage of $6.75/hour, *or* 10% commission of all my sales each pay period.

I indeed had the potential to make **big** bucks considering my performance at the franchise location.

Potential doesn't always translate to actuality — a lesson I soon learned well.

The manager at the corporate location was one conniving fella. He had the power to delegate all the store's tasks to others, and was very efficient at assigning the work of unpacking the plentiful product orders between all the employees below him.

By embracing this technique, he had come up with an effective exploitation to keep us busy in the back of the store, or stocking shelves during the majority of our shifts.

He'd kept the place mildly understaffed so that he could make himself ever-present in the front of the store to greet, schmooze every customer, and rake in commissions as he snagged every sale.

Whenever there was a quick rush, we'd come running out to assist in hopes of making more than a battery sale, but it was rare that we'd ever see our commission in lieu of a paltry paycheck.

We'd been bamboozled into a minimum wage trap.

Every time there was one customer left in the store after a busy wave, the manager would never hesitate to ask us if we'd finished checking in and stocking the latest shipment.

Tensions rose after one of the veteran sales associates had called him out. His exploitative behavior was reported to regional management, getting the attention of corporate suits to investigate.

I was much better off at the franchise location.

Not wanting to bother riding out the wave of that corporate mess, I gave my notice and tried my luck once again with local temp agencies.

My parents had soon moved back to the Santa Ynez Valley, finding a house to rent in Solvang. Glad to have family back in town, I took them up on their offer to rent out the fully carpeted basement with private entrance for $450/month.

It was glorious.

That year, the family's Magnavox TV from 1985 finally emitted its last ray, and went kaput after 16 years of loyal service.

They don't make'm like that anymore.

Still being in contact with my old boss in Solvang, she offered to take me back full time, but working retail could no longer satisfy my techie craving to work with computers once more.

I was still making decent money from pizza deliveries, so I gave notice at the hotel to take up bigger temp jobs.

They were all less than gratifying.

At one point I took an assignment 35 miles away from Solvang in which all I did was file papers for a small office. Their permanent assistant had gone on maternity leave a couple months prior, and about eight large boxes of accumulated documents needed sorting.

I thought I'd *never* take another filing job after the retirement community assignment, but money was money.

Finally, I'd spotted a long-term direct hire opportunity that had me more excited than I'd been in years.

I accepted instantly.

That position could have been a potential career job: performing data entry and admin duties with opportunity for advancement to the Tech Support department.

The company was a reputable, post-graduate online university that was one of the first accredited of its kind.

I started at $12.50/hour, in the Admissions office.

Months in, it went south.

I discovered that being the only male in an office was a ripe opportunity to become a target for sexual harassment; the popular belief that only males are likely to harass females at work is a painful inaccuracy.

About two months in, I'd been told by one of the other employees *in private* that my presence made everybody else uncomfortable.

I didn't see how; I remained extremely busy, rarely took my eyes off my monitor, and seldom left my desk which was in the corner facing the wall.

She continued to behave unprofessionally, with her behavior quickly progressing into more uncomfortable forms of harassment involving attempts at flirtatious teases.

They failed.

After deprecating my work performance and threatening to report that I was behaving lazily on the job upon refusing her advances, I decided to inform Human Resources of her actions that very afternoon.

It seems that wasn't the first time she'd been reported for unsavory conduct.

HR confronted her, causing her to quickly be reduced to guilty tears.

She came to me with a blubbering apology and a confession that my work performance had intimidated her, causing her to lash out.

I accepted, but when the university revealed they'd still planned to keep her on staff after her repeat offenses, I gave notice and walked away from that place, infuriated.

Nobody should be made to tolerate harassment.

Following that ordeal, I would see more instances of sexual harassment throughout my many short-term temp assignments, from both female and male co-workers. All were swiftly reported, and I personally saw one of them fired.

I would strongly encourage anybody else to do the same.

In welcomed contrast to my experiences with unwanted advances in the workplace, it was around this time I had recently started dating Kelly.

Later that year, my parents announced they had plans to move up to Oregon. Kelly and I decided to try making a long distance relationship work, as she'd registered to attend college in Northern California.

As the new year came around, I realized I had nothing really keeping me in Solvang other than my current hodgepodge of jobs, which would be easy to replace anywhere.

My older sister had recently moved south to San Diego, and could do nothing but gush about the opportunities. She offered for me to crash on her couch for a couple weeks if I ever wanted to visit the city.

After toughing it out in the valley until summer that year, I took my sister up on her offer and drove down to check out the job market in San Diego.

It was a staggering contrast to Santa Barbara. The scope of San Diego County's temp job scene proved to be vast, and I had no problem quickly becoming a favorite of several agencies.

In a matter of weeks I'd found a room to rent for $400/month, and established myself comfortably in summer of 2003.

Not owning much outside of game consoles, a TV, computer, and work clothes, I bought a metal futon for $200 and started my new life.

Kelly had soon transferred to Point Loma University and was living on campus, a ten minute drive from where I lived.

Taking every temp job that was offered meant mostly data entry requests and basic admin tasks, but once in a while to my delight, a computer-based assignment would come along that I'd always blow out of the water.

I'd been so hungry for computer work that I'd regularly complete all the tasks at hand long before the deadline that was originally established by the assignment terms.

Some weeks were better than others, and it wasn't without some hardships. One month saw me trading in about 300 of my audio CDs to pay rent between jobs during a slump, but I quickly recovered.

Some new acquaintances in town told me the reason I was having these dry spells was that I'd been playing the temp game all wrong...

They'd encouraged me to "milk it" by working slower so that I'd be guaranteed steady work the full duration of the assignment.

That wasn't me.

In no way did *I* see that as honest conduct, and I had to sleep at night.

My methods did earn me a hot reputation amongst many temp agencies, but I was still gunning for a long-term position. I couldn't escape my love of resolving computer issues, and it was strongly calling me back.

Fueled by my memories of high school days, and recollections of *Call For Help* episodes, I expressed my desires to every agency that I was all-in and looking *exclusively* for a more challenging technical assignment.

The following week, I was sent an offer from a company that would soon become the place I'd spend the majority of my life in a fruitful career as a tech support agent.

I had no idea of the adventure I was in for.

SIX

The Empire, Part I: Joining The Ranks

The Final Temp Job

Long-term assignments were far from rare during the temp agency years, but I'd always ended up requesting to be reassigned either due to lack of challenge, lack of pay...

Sexual harassment...

This one was different. It was an assignment classified as: "temporary long-term with opportunity for permanent hire."

The agency proclaimed it was right up my alley. The job listing had put an emphasis on browser application experience, and advanced knowledge of Windows. The pay started at $13.00/hour.

"The Empire" was a mere eleven miles from my place in Clairemont, and that meant less than a twenty minute drive to work.

That's a sweet find in a big city.

They'd been one of the agency's most loyal clients for years, and had shown a consistent pattern of taking on permanent hires every few months.

It was a sizable corporation of several thousand employees, which was the only big red flag.

As I'd expressed my distaste for larger corporations upon registering with the agency, they knew of my general aversion to the zombie-cubicle work environment.

That being said, they professed that the working conditions were excellent, and they "weren't like most corporations." Most of the employees that had been permanently hired on by them from the agency were still there after several years.

I took some some time to read about the company online. I quickly happened upon an article on a local independent news website that had ranked The Empire in the top 10 best local companies to work for in the county the prior year.

I decided to give this not-so-naughty sounding un-corporation a whirl, and accepted the offer.

Starting on a Monday in September of '03, I arrived at the provided address, joined by seven others, as we waited outside per our instructions.

Right on time, out walked our trainer, Dylan. He welcomed us, provided us each with temporary badges, and proceeded to give a tour of the property: The Empire's secondary headquarters.

To the left of the main entrance stood a modest cafeteria with a single microwave and a couple of basic vending machines. As was typical, they contained the usual array of high-carb snacks and drinks. A small number of tables and chairs were in the center of the room, with extra space abound.

Soon entering the main two story building, we saw that it comfortably held several hundred people. Tech Support and Customer Service were positioned on opposite sides of the second floor.

The Tech Support department was made up of twelve rows of four cubicles. Manager's offices sat behind them up against glass curtain walls. These offices had large windows and sliding glass door entrances, letting fresh natural sunlight into the entire floor.

The room was crisply air conditioned, pleasantly lit, and symmetrically arranged.

Nearly fifty agents sat within their own cubicles, most all of them smiling as they walked customers through clicking and dragging their way to victory. Those who weren't on active calls were reading, or playing chess or checkers while awaiting their next customer; game boards were strategically balanced on the top edges of short cubicle walls.

In addition to the managers' offices, there were additional meeting rooms offering views of the lush trees and fields lining the outside of the building. It was within one of these rooms we'd receive our training upon completing the tour.

We'd each had a phone and computer station set out for us at an extra long table. Four hires sat on each side, with Dylan sitting at the head of the table by the windows.

After giving a short history lesson about the company, he gave us a rundown of their primary services.

The Empire developed, sold, and provided support for a variety of software titles. Their primary products were used to generate reports involving the assessment of property damage. They were designed for use by both independent appraisers, and insurance carriers alike.

In addition to generating appraisal reports, their software could transmit photos of property damage to carriers, as well as manage the financial aspects involved, such as product orders, accounting, and payroll.

Their hours were 5:00 a.m. to 5:00 p.m. Pacific Monday through Friday, with all employees working eight hour shifts.

They were also open for four hours every Saturday morning, staffed purely by veteran volunteers. Their call volume was reportedly nominal on Saturdays, so there was never a shortage of willing participants. Straws were usually drawn each week to see who scored the easy overtime.

We'd all been brought on board to join the small team that would be providing support for The Empire's first web-based software release.

Looking back and remembering the sizes of photos, and average internet speeds in late 2003 reminds me how far technology has progressed.

There were still many businesses using dial-up internet, and the average JPEG file was about 50 kilobytes. Nowadays, everyone's enjoying high speed cable or fiber optic internet connections, and most high quality photos taken with our mobile devices can easily exceed 2 megabytes.

Forty times larger. That's nuts.

In the mid '90s, my friends and I would frequent a popular website called "Lord Soth's Games On The Internet", a child site of happypuppy.com that offered DOS and Windows game demos to download. They were referred to as "shareware" because they were legal to copy and share with friends to promote the full game.

We'd be waiting for them to download through half the night with our 28.8k bitrate dial-up modems, which depending on our connection speed often took up to an hour to download every megabyte of data.

Dial-up used in 2003 had long been twice that fast, but a typical high speed broadband connection could pull down a megabyte in a couple minutes.

Today, most home internet connections can download over 10 megabytes per second.

Awesome.

The industry was aggressively urging clients to embrace high speed internet, as DSL and cable providers had finally approached undeniable affordability.

I had upgraded to DSL at home myself, for $42/month; a mere $17 increase from my dial-up provider was all it took to enter a world of luxurious browsing and impressive download speeds.

I was *ecstatic* to leave my 56k modem behind.

Up until that year, the only software The Empire had available for uploading photos was called "PhotoLink."

It had a mild limitation: A direct dial-up connection was required.

This forced customers with high speed internet connections to hang on to their dial-up modems *purely* for the sake of uploading required photos.

As developing a replacement for PhotoLink was a timely endeavor, the ease of developing a website served as an affordable alternative in the meantime.

That was where we came in. We were the third wave of temps brought in for The Empire's latest growing project.

The website was called, "PhotosFirst."

It started with a username and temporary password being delivered to select customers via email.

After logging in to the website and creating a permanent password, the users could search for and open specific folders for each insurance carrier claim in question.

Clicking the Attach button allowed them to browse and select photos for the claim, and click OK.

Thumbnails of selected photos were shown to ensure everything was in order, and upon clicking the Send button, they were uploaded to the website.

The insurance carriers would then be notified via email that there were new photos submitted for a property damage claim. The carrier could then use *their* PhotosFirst login to view and/or download them.

It was as easy as posting photos for friends to see on social media apps today, but back in 2003 this was a complicated enough maneuver to *destroy* the patience of many customers who upon calling, would refer to themselves as "computer illiterate" - a term that we technical support agents equate with another word:

"Lazy."

After all, even in 2003 it was rather dumbfounding if you took a job in which you sat at a computer for the majority of the day, and still referred to yourself as "computer illiterate." The term was, and still is undeniably, a benchmark cop-out.

If that seems harsh at first, imagine how disturbing it would sound to hear a large number of professional taxi drivers proclaim to be "not all that great at operating an automobile."

It's not expected of taxi drivers to be able to rebuild an engine or replace a fuel pump, but it's expected that they're proficient in operating that vehicle.

Therefore when people who work a desk job with a computer as their centerpiece call tech support and sheepishly disclaim, "Sorry, I'm computer illiterate...", they usually get an over-the-phone-eye-roll from agents.

As the first week of training came to an end, we'd become well-versed in PhotosFirst. We had only to learn of its "known problems."

Bite my tongue...

Practicing mock-calls and taking pop quizzes to prove our competency took up the majority of the second week.

By the time early Friday rolled around, our team of eight had only five remaining; two had been dismissed after the first week, and one had since left by their own accord for another job opportunity.

We were ready to begin "shadowing" the existing PhotosFirst team before taking the calls ourselves.

"Shadowing" in the tech support industry means sitting next to another employee and listening along to their calls with a secondary muted headset. This gives an up close and personal look at real-time troubleshooting.

You can also see how the agent balances working with the customer and logging the case notes at the same time. It's a great way to bridge the gap between textbook learning and taking live calls.

We weren't expected to start shadowing until the following week, but due to our group's collective aptitude, we got to start a day ahead of schedule.

As Dylan let us in on management's elation with our accelerated progress, we were all excited to meet the other team members and see what the hands-on experience was really like.

Mid-morning, we proceeded downstairs to...

"The Dungeon."

The Dungeon

The Dungeon was a dimly lit room in a far corner of the first floor. It was said to have been designed and previously used as a small server room; the walls and door itself were extra thick for insulation purposes.

The independent humidity and temperature control had long been removed, leaving the room with no central air.

A tower fan at each corner provided plenty of circulation, and the room stayed comfortable enough. It fluctuated from the mid to high seventies.

The reason for the everlasting duskiness was that the only light fixtures were two small 40-watt fluorescent ceiling lamps on either side of the twenty by ten foot room. They were so dim and yellow in color, they were unanimously preferred to be left off. Consequently, the glow of the monitors served as the strongest light source.

Thus, The Dungeon was aptly named.

I loved it.

Since we had been told we were the third wave of employees on the project, I was caught off guard upon seeing that there were only twelve partitioned seats in The Dungeon: six on both sides of the room, facing each long wall.

What's more was that only five were occupied, to leave only two available after we joined.

Were there that many that hadn't made the basic cut... or had they all been taken on as permanent hires upstairs?

Bringing this question to Dylan, I learned that several of the temp employees had indeed been let go as they'd had an overly difficult time in training.

That amazed me to hear. Internet browsing had been readily available for a decade, and PhotosFirst wasn't exactly complex.

Honestly, if a person was familiar with how to attach a file to a new email message before sending it off to a recipient, they were *absolutely* qualified.

Did that many people still have an issue using a mouse? Did they really have trouble clicking buttons and finding menus and words on the screen that required no more than a fifth grade reading level?

Yes.

Yes, they did.

They still do.

To this day, it's fascinating to me that when people are asked to look in the bottom right corner by the clock, they might panic and look instead in the lower left. It's surprising that some people are completely stifled when you direct them to click on the Start button, or press Ctrl+C, or Alt+Tab.

The Start button isn't new.

The Ctrl and Alt keys aren't new.

They've existed for several **decades**, and have been in plain sight on the Windows Desktop and every standard keyboard respectively.

Their mention can be found in most any introductory book about using Windows, as well as in several help files and in-product tutorials.

Humans by the droves are willing to attend courses, take tests, and apply for government permission to operate motor vehicles which possess great and terrible potential for destruction and harm.

Lives are at risk there. Public and private property are at risk. Yet, the pursuit of conquering the challenges in order to become a skilled and educated driver are embraced by most every able member of society.

This suggests there's either a widespread phobia of computers... or a prevalence of laziness.

I'm a strong believer in the latter, but there's truth in both.

Something about operating computers deters many — with undeniable bewilderment in their voices, and a glimmer of trepidation in their eyes when clutching a mouse.

There are no loud sonorous noises, no objects traveling at high velocity, no loved ones in danger, and no lives or property at stake when navigating Windows.

Well, unless one screams obscenities whilst chucking a laptop off a balcony...

Regardless, the distance intentionally kept by many from learning the fundamentals of computer operation today is still astounding.

It's a phenomenon that tech support agents observe daily. I often imagine the hilarity of a public service announcement designed to ease the panic and alarm of a supposedly terror-stricken user:

"No power grids will be shut down, no aliens will be prompted to invade the planet, and no natural disasters will be triggered by clicking on the wrong menu or button within the operating system or browser."

Generally, the worst thing that happens these days with computers is that you lose some documents or photos, and for the most part, it *will* have been all your fault.

The computer isn't sentient, it isn't evil, and it isn't going to randomly lose or delete your data under normal operating conditions.

Not dropping your laptop or mobile device in a body of water is a plus, as is not subjecting a computer to power surges. These are both simple maneuvers to master.

If more people would take the plunge and RTFM, perhaps they might realize how the investment of a *few hours* of their time might provide *numerous years* of relief.

They may experience an abatement of confusion and even streamlining of performance at their own job, bringing peace where there was once helplessness and frustration.

My grandmother recently celebrated her 90th birthday, and she is as proficient using Windows as some people I've done business with.

I once asked her if she'd found learning to use computers tedious, or particularly challenging.

She answered that like most new experiences it was of course very different at first, but that she couldn't call it difficult.

Going at her own pace, she in fact found it fascinating — and it was incredible how much she found it to increase her quality of life by embracing it.

She concluded that it was, in a word, "Wonderful."

She then laughed, reminisced, and wished modern technology was around back when she had worked as an accountant in her youth. She recalled the many hours spent and plentiful office space that was taken up while having to manually record, keep, and maintain massive stacks of ledger pads with loose carbon sheets.

"I can't imagine going back to that."

If only half the population were as proactively adventurous!

But I digress... if there were no lazy people in the world, *many* of us wouldn't have a job.

For that, I suppose, in a twisted and uncomfortable manner, I thank them.

Speedy Shadowing & Holiday High Jinks

We were scheduled to be shadowing the entire third week, but most all of us felt ready to start taking calls on our own by Wednesday; that seemed like plenty time to observe the process and learn the ropes.

Logging the calls was a piece of cake. There was no exhaustive list of drop-down menus to select, and we didn't have any required scripts to follow as long as we provided our first name and the company name upon answering.

The Empire had also done the unthinkable and presented their account numbers in **large bold type** on every correspondence, so most every customer provided it upon calling. When they didn't, our system was so well maintained with accurate data, their full name or company name would always bring up their info.

It felt great to all but nearly nix the Big Six.

To document each call after pulling up the customer's account, one would click on "New Case," then type in the reason for calling in the "Reason" field.

Any troubleshooting notes would be entered in the "Notes" section.

The only drop-down menu required was the product name, PhotosFirst.

Other choices were the previously mentioned "PhotoLink", as well as "ReportsPro", and "Specialty", but we didn't support those products in The Dungeon.

When the issue was resolved, steps taken were entered in the "Solution" field, and finally the large "Save and Close Case" button was clicked when the call was over.

It was straight-forward, and nearly mastered after the first time being shown.

Listening in on sufficient varieties of issues over several days, we'd each grown confident enough to head back to the meeting room with Dylan. There we would take our first live calls so he could coach us on the spot when necessary, or jump in if we got stuck.

Shadowing taught us that the subject matter of incoming calls was fairly routine.

Many users first had difficulty after logging in with their temporary passwords, as they were required to create a permanent password with the inclusion of a "special character."

Scads of users didn't know what a special character was or where to find them, so we gave them a rundown of what those funny little symbols had been doing on the number keys for the last century.

Not knowing where to locate their photos was *the* most common call. People would connect their digital camera to their PC and successfully copy the photos to their hard drive, but would fail to take note of *where* they'd copied them to.

We would teach them how to search their hard drive(s) for JPEG files, then sort the results by date to display the latest photos at the top. From there, the customer could view the folder location so that they'd know where to browse for them when attaching to PhotosFirst.

Some customers would also experience issues with their digital camera itself. We weren't permitted to provide direct support for their own camera hardware as it wasn't issued by The Empire, but we *could* offer general troubleshooting advice. Our usual tip of the day was reminding people that the camera did actually need to be powered on. That's all it often took.

Occasionally stunting their progress was their company's security settings being configured too strictly. This could block certain prompts from popping up as designed, or even prevent the entire website from loading.

Adding the necessary security exclusions with permission of their internal IT fixed it in a jiffy.

There were also certain hilarious calls that we'd receive nearly once a week — *far* more often than one would presume to hear of in the workplace: users would call in because their browser was infected by a computer virus that caused it to exclusively load pornographic websites regardless of the web address entered.

Those issues of course were most always caused by the user having visited salacious websites in the first place. As this was outside the scope of our support, we'd simply hold the mute button, have a laugh, then refer them to their internal support team.

Finally, customers who'd pressed the wrong number intending to speak with Sales or Billing would request a proper transfer.

Without exaggeration, that sums up what was about 90% of our calls. Though they weren't necessarily challenging, we all loved the fact that we were able to handle them in a personable manner due to The Empire's practical policies.

I remember one time an elderly gentleman called in with a unique request: he didn't have any issues with PhotosFirst that day, but he was looking for pictures of his grandchildren and had forgotten where they were saved.

Though that was a general computer knowledge question and had nothing to do with the company or their software, I still gave some tips over the phone on how to search for JPEG photos and sort the results by date. The guy was overjoyed after successfully finding the photos on his laptop, and thanked me wholeheartedly.

Felt great.

I would never have been permitted to do that back at the shipping company without getting chewed out for wasting company time and money.

On the contrary, I saw it as an *investment* of time and money in the form of proactive customer service.

The Dungeon team would typically be waiting about ten minutes between our next incoming calls, anyway.

Since we had that time to spare, I took the initiative to represent the company as an authentic, down-to-earth human instead of a snippy support agent rushing to get the customer off the phone.

You know, like the sad majority of them do.

A touch of empathy proved to be an appreciated gesture with the customers often voicing gratitude for patience and kindness.

That's something *I* didn't encounter as a customer very often, so I always tried to do what I could when feasible. Regardless that it *personally* baffled me that people generally weren't more familiar with Windows or the most basic aspects of computers, I was there to help people, not judge them.

My own poor experiences of calling tech support and being stuck with either a condescending know-it-all or an outsourced oblivious trainee were no doubt another driving force to serve the position well.

After a few days of smooth sailing, Dylan began to send us each down to The Dungeon, assigning us our own cozy partitions.

Though I was just a temp, I instantly felt accepted and comfortable with others in The Dungeon. The Empire provided a high level of morale I'd not yet seen in a tech support environment. In every department, people were friendly, outgoing, and showed no semblance of suffering.

The workplace was even open to mild levels of holiday shenanigans.

One memory that stands out those first few months was going into work on Christmas Eve. It was a Wednesday, and though an average day would see over 200 calls routed to The Dungeon, only two had come in by noon.

The word around the office was that employees were allowed to go home early on those holidays which yielded an extremely low call volume.

I was normally a closer, as my shift was 8:00 a.m. to 5:00 p.m. with an hour lunch. Asking Dylan if the rumors about leaving early were true, he said it was possible, but to plan to work the day through just in case.

Since the call volume that day was so low, I asked if he'd be okay with me bringing in my small 13" color TV and Nintendo Gamecube for some entertainment after lunch. He said he'd have to clear the idea with a supervisor to ensure they'd be OK with it.

Minutes later, one of the supervisors from upstairs, Jerry, came down and introduced himself. He told me it was perfectly fine to bring in a game console for the afternoon, adding with a laugh that we looked bored to tears.

Besides, The Empire's *primary* headquarters down the street had a ping pong table for employees to use on slow days, so they were no strangers to blowing off steam.

When it was time for my lunch break, I stopped home and grabbed the gaming gear, complete with *Super Smash Brothers Melee* and 4 controllers.

Returning to The Dungeon, it was clear I hadn't missed anything; not a phone had rung in the last two hours.

We fired up the Gamecube and had some beautiful *Smash Brothers* brawls until about 3:30 p.m. when somebody's phone rang after the several hours of silence.

One of the veteran temps, Chuck, answered the phone with a greeting so comical, we were speechless.

"Thank you for calling and — OH my gosh, *why* are you working on Christmas Eve? Go **home** already!"

The room was pin-drop quiet upon all of us having an expectation the customer would be livid... until we soon heard the laughter coming from Chuck's headset throughout The Dungeon. We all then laughed in response, making the customer laugh even harder after they'd heard the roars of the room.

Chuck then professionally continued with the call, resolving it quickly. The customer loved it, and before the call was over, Chuck relayed the customer's wish for the entire room to have a Merry Christmas and Happy Holiday.

That was the final call of the day, and when 4:00 p.m. rolled around, Jerry came downstairs to tell those of us remaining that we could go ahead and leave an hour early.

The Empire was closed for business on Christmas Day *and* the day after. Their employees were given full holiday pay for each.

Though it wasn't in our contract and wasn't required, they paid all the temp employees for both days as well.

Moment Of Truth

The winter season brought on chilly 49°F nights in the San Diego county, which is enough to make some Southern Californians enter panic mode. Fortunately, The Dungeon still remained in the balmy high seventies all the way through the new year.

By mid-January, we had reached a level of complete confidence in our ability to tackle even the most obscure PhotosFirst calls. Many of us had gotten kudos either over the phone or in person from Dylan and other supervisors upstairs.

Then, it happened...

One day after my lunch hour, I heard news of a permanent hiring opportunity for the department, and applications for screening exams were available upstairs.

I took time during my afternoon break to sign up, and was scheduled an exam appointment for the next morning.

I had trouble sleeping that night.

Kelly was elated to hear that I'd possibly found even more stability in a job that I loved, and told me she was certain I'd have no problem with the test.

I was still nervous.

The excitement was overwhelming, the pressure likewise. To work upstairs with the big dogs in a company such as *this*, such a polar opposite of the typical closed minded, heartless and stiffly run corporations that were so well known...?

Yes, please!

After that night of tossing and turning, I skipped breakfast, but packed a small meal to eat during my morning break after the exam.

At 8:00 a.m. sharp, I arrived at the same meeting room in which Dylan provided our training. He passed out the exam to me and a couple other applicants, and we had one hour to complete it.

The exam had the typical format of questions; some multiple choice, some fill-in-the-blank, and a couple requiring written answers.

Everybody from The Dungeon came up in staggered waves to take the exam, some using the full hour, and some of us finishing in less than 10 minutes. I was among the latter, which made me nervous that I'd rushed it, but I kept breathing and reminding myself to stay calm and confident.

I had double checked all my answers, and was certain I'd nailed all but a few networking questions; although I'd put together my own small home network using the RTFM method, I never really messed with it to the point of failure. That put a damper on having much network troubleshooting experience.

Later that day, everybody was told their test scores would be revealed the following Monday, after all tests were taken.

This was either a generous exercise in patience, or a mild form of mental torture, whichever we chose to look at it.

Without delay, rumors started flying. Some temps said they'd heard from people upstairs that only applicants with college degrees would be qualified for hire. Others proclaimed that nobody yet scored a passing grade. Some even said that those who scored too low on the exams would be let go.

After the intense gut-churning weekend, we would find out that nobody was let go, and no degree was required for a first level tech support position, as that would be silly.

All the rumors had been wrong.

It turns out that I and two other temps from The Dungeon, Erik and Daphne, had scored the highest. We had all been scheduled for on the spot interviews that very morning.

Sitting outside an upstairs office while awaiting our turns, we caught glance of other people exiting from their interviews.

Several had applied to the company directly, looking sharply intimidating with crisp business wear that implied they'd been playing the big city game awhile. Merely catching a glance of the other, better-dressed interviewees made me wonder if I even had a chance.

I did. In fact, all three of us did.

Daphne, Erik and I were *all* offered permanent positions starting February 6th, 2004 at $14.50/hour, with a benefits package including medical, dental, vision, and 401(k).

We all accepted.

Corporate... Bliss?

The first day upstairs was neither intimidating nor nerve-wracking. It was comfortable and welcoming with a massive room of geeks that were just like us.

We each got our own roomy cubicle equipped with two desktop computers. One was our primary machine and the other was used strictly for troubleshooting and testing company software. We were also given a key to our locking desk drawers.

Dylan and Jerry introduced us to each of the teams: Reporting, Media, and Specialty.

Having supported PhotosFirst from the depths of The Dungeon, we were all assigned to the Media team, supporting both PhotosFirst *and* soon to support PhotoLink, its aforementioned dial-up predecessor.

We met Marla, the incredibly kind lead supervisor of the department, as well as her assistant Richard. He had a perky attitude that came off as a little tightly wound, but seemed like a nice guy.

Adjacent to Marla's office was her boss Peter, the manager of Tech Support. He had that great balance of being both plainspoken yet respectful.

Most everybody in the department did, really.

With Jerry being *my* direct supervisor, this was an environment almost too good to be true.

After a day of orientation and meetings with HR to welcome us to The Empire, we were given a briefing on how we'd be settling in to the department.

Starting Monday, we'd be given two weeks of official training on *all* The Empire's software titles in a classroom downstairs with several other hires from Customer Service and Sales.

That's right, not only Tech Support, but *all* departments were given in-depth training courses of company software. A practice rarely seen, this ensured that every department dealing with the software would actually have hands-on experience with it.

Most larger companies I'd either worked for or had interactions with would handle separate departments, well... separately.

This was a *much* better tactic that would put all departments on a similar level when communicating with one another.

We felt a strong sense of pride and team spirit as our pictures were taken for *permanent* employee badges, complete with a lanyard patterned with The Empire's logo.

I'll never forget that feeling.

After our first official day of work, Erik, Daphne and I all went out to celebrate at a sports bar and grill on Clairemont Mesa Boulevard.

It was humid, they took cash only and had no heating or air conditioning, but we didn't care.

We'd achieved permanent employment with The Empire, and victory cocktails and fries never tasted so good.

SEVEN

The Legendary Battle
Of The Motherboard

It Still Haunts Me

I suppose this is the most fitting time for me to share this gem, so permit me now to carry you away on wings of inconceivable madness.

Shortly after being hired by The Empire, I took advantage of my newfound income to replace my custom-built gaming PC. Mine had been showing its age one sputter at a time.

I did my research as usual, and properly verified the quality and compatibility of all desired components.

I was yet unaware of a trial most vicious that had been arranged for me by the fates that year...

There are urban legends. There are fabrications.

There are exaggerations, falsehoods, and stories peppered with enhancements to add flair to otherwise boring events.

This tale, like all others in this book is of absolute truth requiring no embellishment or distortion.

The following is my own worst experience calling tech support.

Week 1, Day 1: The Error Message

In early 2004, I purchased several components from an electronics superstore in San Diego for a new gaming PC. All the components were from the most positively reviewed, reputable brand names of the time.

Everything seemed to function beautifully, and upon assembly my PC ran every game I desired without any issues.

That was the case for about 3 months. One fine summer day upon arriving home from work and getting settled with snack and drink, I took a seat at my desk and powered on my computer — and before you ask, no I did not mistake my CD-ROM drive tray for a cup holder.

The BIOS screen showed up and displayed the usual motherboard branding and basic specifications of the hardware detected. That's the only step in the boot sequence that went well.

BIOS stands for Basic Input/Output System. It's a very small program residing on a single chip on the motherboard. It contains a set of instructions to identify and control the main components of the computer. If you look at a monitor when first powering on a PC, you might catch a quickly displayed mess of info indicating the detection of the processor, RAM, hard drives, and other components.

That's the BIOS doing its job.

Generally, it first checks to ensure required hardware is present and functioning, then looks for a drive containing an Operating System (like Windows) so it can hand over the reins. It all happens very quickly upon pressing the power button, usually in ten seconds or less.

That day, my poor computer never got far enough to detect the hard drive.

I didn't see the Windows XP logo as I had expected... I only heard two quick beeps come out of the PC Speaker. The BIOS information had disappeared, now displaying a single message at the top of an otherwise sad empty screen:

"BIOS ROM checksum error."

I had known about checksums but I'd never had the pleasure of seeing one fail in this manner.

In very diluted terms, a checksum is one of the methods used by the BIOS to make sure several parts of the computer are functioning as intended.

It's similar to having your car fail to start and seeing the "Check Engine" light appear: an indicator designed to tell you, the driver, that your wallet will soon weigh a bit less.

After rummaging around the glove box for your car manual, you may end up reading that the warning light could have been triggered by one of several possibilities:

The gas cap may be missing or loose, one of several sensors may have failed, or spark plugs need attention. In some cases, more expensive repairs may be in order.

These days, troubleshooting a computer really isn't all that different from troubleshooting a car.

I was **really** hoping I didn't have to replace any computer parts. They were still practically new.

Not knowing where to start, I searched the internet using my older PC, (which, luckily I had still held onto), to find several forums containing topics posted by many other customers also encountering this error — and with the *exact* same brand and model of motherboard.

I was already onto something! Surely if this was a documented error, I should have a fair chance to find the solution. With my experience working in tech support all this time, I figured it'd be a piece o' cake.

I tell you this: more wind was never taken from one's sails than from those of my own battered, broken little ship over the course of the next twelve weeks.

That's right, nearly three tedious months of seething suffering and bona fide butthurt.

Digging through the forums, it was posted that some people had found one of their RAM sticks was defective, causing the error. They had luck identifying the bogus bugger by booting up with one stick at a time.

I did that, but the error still persisted.

I cussed out the motherboard and the box that brung it.

Though irritated, I had only begun to troubleshoot. I had yet to lose a battle against a new computer that I'd built myself.

I continued full speed down the rabbit hole, following the advice of the next forum reply.

Another situation that was said to trigger the error was if any installed components were to have come loose from the motherboard, such as the CPU or one of many cables. It was recommended to check all the components, chips, cards and cables to be sure all were seated properly.

I did that, but the error still persisted.

A third and even simpler resolution found was the possibility of a dead battery.

Most all PC motherboards utilize a small button-cell battery similar to that used by many wristwatches. The purpose of the battery obviously isn't to power the computer, but to retain the functionality of its onboard Real-Time Clock (RTC) when it's powered down.

When that battery is missing or out of juice, the motherboard gets that signal and reports an error.

I'd run into that issue many times when using older computers, and though there's an error involved, the worst thing to happen was the incorrect time being displayed in Windows. It *never* actually stopped my PC from booting, but... whatever.

Using a battery tester, one can perform a quick check to ensure it isn't dead.

I did that, but the error still persisted.

Enhanced cursing ensued, if only for a moment.

Attempting to mitigate the antagonizing waves of emotion crashing upon my sinking vessel, scotch on the rocks soon found its way into a tumbler and into my hand — providing only a short respite before the dose of dejection yet to come.

There was one final possibility found on the forum, involving the most time-consuming of all proposed solutions to implement: Flashing the BIOS.

I had no idea what that was, but I'd soon become quite familiar.

The instructions stored on BIOS chips are customized by each manufacturer. Not only that, but it may be different for each model of their products depending on the needs of hardware components, and how they choose to configure them.

As many of them do, *this* manufacturer's website generously provided an option to download a file with all the latest data that the BIOS chip should contain.

You could save this file to a 3.5" floppy disk, reboot your PC with that disk in the drive, and load that data onto the BIOS chip to give it a good sorting out in case it had become corrupted.

This is what is called "Flashing the BIOS."

Reading further, I'd discovered that corruption of the BIOS chip is potentially caused by physical damage, overheating, or a power spike.

This was aggravating to learn, as I've always handled my computer components with great care. I keep my home and appliances within it clean and frequently vacuumed. That includes my PC fans. I also use and replace surge protectors often.

It was feeling as if this whole mess was caused by a defect or suspicious abuse of the product prior to my purchase.

Patiently digging my floppy drive out of the closet and connecting it to my old PC, I navigated to the website to begin the tedious process.

After connecting the drive to the new PC and completing the final step, I received a confirmation on the screen that the BIOS update was successful.

This was it! This was boasted to be the surefire resolution if all previous troubleshooting attempts had failed!

Alas...

I did that, but the error still persisted.

Looking back, I should have at that moment taken the motherboard to my local archery range, slapped a feathered cap on my head and had some fun.

I sorely regret not doing so.

Instead of enjoying some target practice, I pulled the receipt out of my file cabinet, and as expected, saw the electronics store's disclaimer explaining they only accepted returns for defective products for 30 days.

Honestly, that **was** a generous window.

Not generous enough to be an option, so I grabbed the motherboard box from the closet, and opened it to inspect the manual and warranty information.

It carried a three year warranty! I wondered: wouldn't the company replace it for me since I'd purchased it only a few months prior?

Eyeballing the clock in the kitchen, it was past 10 p.m. I'd blown my *entire night* researching troubleshooting steps and futzing with this fiberglass doorstop to no avail.

I decided to sleep on it, planning to mention my woes to some co-workers the next morning to see if they'd encountered anything like this before.

I slept well, holding a positive mindset that a friend would have a quick solution. If not, I could file a warranty claim for a refund or replacement.

Nothing too arduous, right?

Week 1, Day 2: First Contact

The next day, I brought both RAM sticks to work with me and had a buddy test them out on another computer to be sure...

Yeah, they worked fine.

By lunchtime, I had no new leads to run with. After learning of my night of hardships, Raymond, a co-worker on the Reporting team, seemed to support the idea to file an RMA request (Return Merchandise Authorization) for a replacement.

"Dude, you bought that thing a few months ago. Who cares what the fix is. You shouldn't have to work this hard when it's under warranty. Just RMA it, and they should approve it instantly since the thing's still new. I've done it a few times before, and had replacements in the mail the next week!"

That sounded like a fair plan, and I decided to go that route. Hey, I'd done everything I could within reason from all available documentation.

I'd spent nearly five hours pulling my hair out in angst the night before, spewing profanities at the computer with the intensity of one livid Teddy Duchamp in "Stand By Me"... though much quieter — we *were* living in an apartment after all.

Enough was enough, and I made the decision to tap out of self-troubleshooting.

Arriving home from work, I embraced a positive attitude, expecting the company to live up to their reputation. I located the number to contact tech support from within the manual, and dialed away.

There was an acceptable hold time of a few minutes, and the call started off well enough.

Of the Big Six, only #2 was requested, (Name & Phone Number), so we were able to get to discussing my issue quickly.

I gave a detailed rundown of the error message I had received, when I first received it, and the steps to replicate it. I provided all the actions I'd taken to try fixing it, also mentioning my experience working in tech support.

The agent was quick to apologize for my inconvenience, and the time I'd spent was noted. They stated that they'd need a few moments to locate the next troubleshooting steps.

Placed on hold, my eardrums were then soaked in sappy synth music for over ten minutes.

Another apology was given for the long hold time upon the agent's return, and they gave me some news that I'd already halfway expected to hear.

I was indeed onto something the night before, but before trying any *further* troubleshooting, I would need to be walked through several steps [that I'd already performed] to make sure I didn't neglect any important procedures. Having explained my years of experience and competency was moot.

There's a good reason I expected this: as an agent, *I* would admittedly have done the same thing.

A most amateur mistake is to trust the customer's word without verifying. More often than not, neglecting to confirm that certain crucial steps were followed correctly will dump the customer *and* the agent into a landslide of catastrophes upon attempting successive procedures that should otherwise have been a breeze.

One ends up brewing up a rancid batch of failsauce because the customer was *under the impression* they had correctly done this or that.

Those situations have paved the way for the most painfully preventable hour-long calls for issues that should have been resolved in ten minutes... all because *things were assumed.*

I'd experienced my share of customers who had been responsible for wreaking such havoc in many situations; a great deal of users often know enough about computers to be dangerous. They may end up floundering about, uninstalling, or even manually deleting important components of the Operating System before they give up and call for help.

Many times when this happens, all of their actions are shown clearly in system log files or the Recycle Bin... complete with date and time stamp reflecting actions mere minutes before they called, yet they'll deny it to the end.

They'll also cite their years of experience — like I did.

So, I understood.

It still didn't make it any less degrading.

I was walked through the same first three possible solutions that I'd already tried, step by step. They failed.

After another hold, the agent returned and rattled off a list of seemingly desperate straw-graspings:

"Has the PC been connected to a surge protector at all times?"

"Yes."

"Have you experienced any recent power outages?"

"No".

"Was an anti-static device used when assembling the PC and all components?"

"Of course."

"Did the motherboard appear damaged upon receipt?"

"No."

"At any point was there any abnormal smell or visible smoke coming from the motherboard?"

"No." (Did they really think I would have withheld that little detail?)

"Have any parts or components on the motherboard been modified in any manner?"

"No." (Again, *really?...*)

I was starting to get the impression the agent had *no* idea how to fix my issue.

At this point, call duration reached the one hour mark, and it was explained we would have to "continue tomorrow" as it was past their closing time of 6:00 p.m.

I was provided the ticket number so that I could call back the next day and pick up where I left off. It was explained that if I were to lose it, any agent who answered would be able to find it using my name and phone number.

Though feeling like my time was essentially wasted, I had maintained civil and professional behavior for the duration of the call. Progress had at least been made on *their* end, and maybe tomorrow they'd feel enough was enough and replace the motherboard.

After the call, multiple sighs commenced. A double Glenlivet on the rocks helped, as did a hug and a dose of empathy from Kelly. I vented my frustration to her for only a few minutes; she had indeed been present in the nearby bedroom, so she'd already had the pleasure of hearing some bits and pieces of the futile call. I didn't want to put *her* through the fine joys of repetition.

After enjoying my drink, I fired up the rhythm game, *Amplitude* on Playstation 2 to help unwind, as it had become a new favorite of mine that year.

Music always improves my mood.

In what turned out to be the predecessor of the incredibly popular *Guitar Hero* series by Harmonix, *Amplitude* featured popular rock, electronica and hip-hop tunes for you to play along with isolated instrument tracks.

The game introduced me to the synth-pop band Freezepop with their tune, "Super Sprøde."

They had a heavy focus on bass lines and harmonies using square and sawtooth wave synth voices. I loved their style, as it pandered to fans of '80s music and video game soundtracks.

P!nk had recently released her second album, titled, *M!ssundaztood*, featuring the incredibly successful single, "Get The Party Started", but I hadn't heard any other songs from her yet, having worked such long days during my mess of jobs before landing at The Empire.

I also wasn't listening to much radio at the time, and MTV had sadly all but nixed the M, so my interest in popular music had long been fizzling.

Amplitude featured P!nk's track, "Respect". Its catchy bass line wouldn't leave my head, and the refreshing lyrics made me an instant fan of hers.

Many popular female artists who need not be named had for years been banking on cookie-cutter tunes they themselves didn't even write, with shallow lyrics boasting how fast and often their genitals would come out for strangers after parties.

This fueled more hip-hop songs boasting about taking advantage of loose women to continue flooding the market.

Not my thing.

With her motivational lyrics and positive tunes encouraging *self*-respect, P!nk quickly earned a spot alongside Billy Joel and Janis Ian as my favorite lyricists.

After playing through some fun tunes, I'd recovered from my sour hour, cleared the issue from my mind, and enjoyed the rest of the evening.

Week 1, Day 3: What Ticket Number?

There's nothing like laughing about a poor tech support experience with your friends to take the edge off. Since we were all partners in crime, my work buddies were especially able to relate to my experience and that was a huge boon to stress relief.

Come day three, they had all wished me luck as my story had started to become a hot topic in the office.

Ah, but the material of this tale had still only begun to be woven, and lunacy had yet to ensue.

Off work, arrived home, dialed support.

It was "Go Time."

I got through without a hold queue, and I provided the ticket number to the agent. There was but one complication:

They couldn't find it.

That ticket number "didn't exist."

I assured them I had verified it by reading it back the night before, so they asked what time it was created.

That didn't help.

I was even told after providing my name and phone number that they could find no proof or history of me calling their department from my phone.

Gorgeous.

Maintaining kindness and patience since the agent had never spoken to me before, I very briefly summarized what I'd already been through.

Being as though no case documentation was found regarding anything I had mentioned, the agent explained they were required to create a new ticket number and start from scratch.

That was where I drew the line and broke out the monotone aggression.

"I have spent over 6 hours struggling with a 3 month old motherboard purchase, and spent half my evening last night being walked through many of the same steps I had already tried with no progress. I don't want to be on the phone until 6:00 p.m. tonight without resolving this error. Is there **any** way I can request an RMA since I've already called?"

They didn't budge, as no ticket was found.

"I'd like to speak with your supervisor, please. This is ridiculous and I can't afford to have my time wasted again."

The agent went into script-recitation mode, telling me they'd be happy to contact a supervisor and asked me to hold.

One soon came on the line and I gave them an earful. No profanity or rudeness, but a stern-voiced recap with an inflection of exhaustion.

After more apologies for my inconvenience and a short hold time later, my issue was finally escalated to a second level agent.

Upon being transferred and catching them up on my saga, it was clear from their responses that *this* agent was more experienced, and completely understood the details of my situation.

You can always tell from their inflection, and the absence of that dull rhythm of their words that we all know — when somebody on the phone is clearly reading off steps for a solution they themselves don't really understand.

After hearing me out, the agent explained they would still need to try a couple more things before allowing me to request an RMA. They wanted to walk me through flashing the BIOS step by step to ensure I hadn't skipped any part of the process performing it on my own.

They did that, but the error still persisted.

Even though it was a little past 6:30 p.m., I was grateful this agent stayed on the line with me. The flashing of the BIOS was the **last** item on their troubleshooting list, and since it didn't resolve the issue, they believed the physical BIOS chip itself to be defective. They would be sending me a replacement in the mail via standard shipping.

The BIOS chip wasn't soldered to this model of motherboard, it was easily separated from its socket by doing so gently with the proper tool, applying even pressure all around to remove it.

Crudely prying it up like the lid of a can of beans could risk bending or snapping pieces off from the socket.

Letting them know I *had* no such tool, they mentioned they'd include a small plastic extractor.

After verifying my mailing address, I was provided the agent's full name, as well as a "special" second level ticket number containing all the details of my issue.

I was to call them upon receiving the new chip. With my special ticket number *and* the second level agent's name, I would be instantly transferred to them to continue.

I soon also received an email with the tracking number. That served as some small facade of company competence.

My brain cells fizzled. My heart sank knowing I'd have to wait 5 to 7 business days for another shot in the dark at getting my rig back up and running, but at least it was something.

Week 2, Day 1: Another Scotch

The package arrived exactly 7 calendar days later. I'd spent my lunch break going to the post office, and I was never so eager to rush home after work and dial tech support.

Calling back proved another headache. For a second callback in a row, my ticket number was unable to be found.

When providing the name of the second level agent, I was told by the first level flunky that they weren't permitted to transfer me without an existing ticket...

...and they'd need to go over some basic troubleshooting first.

That was **not** happening.

Another chat with a supervisor, another sharp-tongued spiel, and I was finally handed off to second level with yet another apology.

The second level agent was able to find my ticket number without any issues, and they apologized that the last representative had failed to find it.

They promised they were the best person for the job, and this would be the last time I'd have to call.

We proceeded.

Removing the BIOS chip was not exactly done by the book. Having neglected to include the extraction tool as promised, they directed me to use the plastic cap clip of a ball point pen.

By using the tip and gently lifting one corner, the chip was easily set free and I was able to snap in the new one with careful, even pressure.

At that time, I made a point to tell the agent that I'd noticed the BIOS chip they'd sent me... had a different brand name, logo, and model number than the old one.

They told me not to worry, assuring me that they use several different brands of BIOS chips, and it should still work with the motherboard.

The last step was to flash the new BIOS chip to resolve the issue.

We did that, but the error still persisted.

...Glenlivet.

I started to stew after spending the better part of what was left of the hour being walked through flashing the BIOS not once, twice or even thrice; five times I was asked to repeat the process using different versions of BIOS updates being emailed to me without any change in behavior.

I was certain I'd wear out the cables from swapping the floppy drive back and forth so many times.

The agent apologized *sincerely*, and began to speak a bit more frankly as they were now sharing a decent fraction of my distress. They ended up placing me on hold for an extended time as they consulted their team, checking back every so often to assure me they were still researching.

Finally, returning to the line wasn't the same agent, but one of their co-workers who'd had more experience with this particular error message.

I halfheartedly accepted their apology, and told the new agent something that I myself never liked hearing while working a case... but my patience had dwindled.

I calmly yet firmly told them that because of the reputation of the company, I had expected that the product would have been replaced per the warranty, but I'd now been strung along for more than a week without my issue being fixed, and that this - (wait for it...) - was the worst experience with tech support I'd ever had.

It was true.

I didn't feel *too* bad about giving that line, because I was often given it myself after a measly twenty minutes at times from impatient customers. Thus, I felt my several hours of mental pain sustained in chunks for over a week *more* than justified this level of candor.

Pushing again for the company to honor their warranty and replace the motherboard, they refused, but said they'd contact me within 24 hours after further research.

If they hadn't found a resolution by then, my case would be escalated to the third and highest level of tech support. That department alone had the ability to approve an RMA request.

I was told if I didn't hear from someone by 5:30 p.m. the following day, I should go ahead and call back with the ticket number.

Well, then. *That* didn't scream confidence.

Reminding them of my magnificent struggle to get back through to second level, I asked if I could have a direct number.

"I'm sorry, there is no direct extension to second level support."

What a **crock**. How'd they transfer *me*... telepathy?

They clearly didn't want to provide the direct extension, so they lied to me.

I'd have to go through the main number again.

Week 2, Day 2: What A Load Of Bullship

I dialed support at 5:31 p.m. the next day since nobody had reached out.

Luckily, somebody at the department had grown a brain, and the ticket number was located with ease. I was speaking to second level in a few minutes, and they had some fabulous new information to wreck my night.

They determined after reviewing the case notes that the BIOS chip mailed to me was *not* in fact compatible with my motherboard as I had suspected, and they'd be mailing me another one.

Hopefully the correct one this time...

It was to be mailed with standard shipping again, 5 to 7 days; despite *their mistake*, they were not willing to drop the money to expedite it.

Rinse and repeat, see you next week, good night, pleasant dreams, and piss off.

Week 3, Day 1: Reinsert THIS

With a single eyebrow raised with Vulcanian fascination that I was spending my month in such a manner, I again reached out to second level upon receiving the *additional* replacement chip.

I announced, "It appears they actually decided to send the correct brand and model of BIOS chip this time..."

I had earned that, thank you very much.

With an uncomfortable laugh and what little confidence the agent could muster, they again asked me to follow their provided steps to replace and flash the BIOS.

I did that, but the error still persisted.

When the agent started to ask me to reinsert and try flashing the *original* BIOS chip again, I sternly interrupted.

I held them to their word that I would now be sent to third level support to request an RMA. I'd been *more* than patient, and this was a poor way to treat somebody who had clearly encountered a defective product that was well under warranty.

They submitted, and after a short hold they confirmed that a third level agent would be contacting me the next day.

I mentioned I'd be at work all day and wouldn't be home until at least a quarter after five, so they entered a note for third level to reach out to me after that time.

Week 3, Day 2, 1st Call: Mr. Smarmypants

Discussing the drama with my co-worker Raymond was still good fun. We continued to berate the motherboard company with our banter, both of us still in shock that with such a good reputation in the industry, they'd drag a customer through the gauntlet this mercilessly.

Returning to work after lunch that day, my cell phone buzzed.

It was a third level agent calling to troubleshoot.

Mid-day. While I was at work.

He had the sickly fake tone of a smarmy used car lot associate.

Presuming he must have been too busy eating paint chips to read the notes in my ticket, I mentioned it should have been documented that I would be unavailable until a quarter after five because I was at work.

He said he *had* seen that note, but decided to reach out to me sooner to be proactive.

Proactive? Had he thought perhaps I'd have called in sick or quit my job?

He explained the number he called from was his business cell number. Stating he'd try me back later as requested, he added that since he was working a couple other escalated cases, I may want to dial his number if I didn't hear back by 5:30.

I've gotta say, for a department that apologized as often as they did, one would have thought they'd try a shred harder to embrace punctuality.

Week 3, Day 2, 2nd Call: Foolish Pursuits

Dialing the number, I wasn't counting on this clown answering his phone.

He did, apparently deeming it acceptable to be snacking and chewing in my ear for the duration of the call.

Applying that well-known used car lot tactic, he teased that he *would* be able to grant my request for an RMA, *but first...*

He wanted to walk me through installing the original BIOS chip and flashing it with a *special* BIOS version that he would provide to me via email.

As I still wasn't confident he'd thoroughly read my case notes, I summarized my hardships over the phone once more, with record time.

Practice makes perfect.

Like others, he performed the routine of apologizing and promising that he'd fix my issue if I let him walk me through *just a few more steps*.

In a shocking turn of events...

I did that, but the error still persisted.

The agent quickly got deeper under my skin with his pseudo-friendly tone and poor attempts to empathize with my situation.

"Wow, I don't get it. This usually works so well!"

"I'm as surprised as you are, man, this doesn't make sense!"

"I'm right there with ya, this shouldn't be happening!"

I finally interrupted him during one of his many saccharin responses.

"Enough."

I would troubleshoot no more. I would tolerate no more.

I asked him if this company made a habit of taking several weeks to fix a single error. I questioned if it was normal practice for them to dodge honoring their warranty and avoid replacing a clearly defective product purchased 3 months prior.

After a short silence and another scripted apology, I **demanded** an RMA.

He updated the notes for my ticket, and would consult his co-workers one last time to see if they had any other ideas. He assured me he would get back to me at 5:15 sharp the next day, adding another piecrust promise of satisfaction.

When the call ended, Kelly asked me at that point if it was even worth battling it out anymore.

It wasn't.

The company clearly wasn't dealing with anything in a serious or professional manner. The amount of time I'd spent on the phone, and the weeks I'd been left to stew waiting for standard mail packages were truly not worth my time, my effort, or my loss of sanity.

Part of me tried to accept the fact that my issue probably wouldn't be resolved, but the other part couldn't let it go.

I still had some fight in me.

I decided to play the game longer for sheer curiosity. *How long* could I possibly be strung along for the company to avoid replacing one of their $130 retail products?

The funny thing was: even if their agents were all paid minimum wage, the company had already lost far more than the manufacturing cost of the motherboard between the hours on the phone, and shipping charges for two items.

Who *knows* what else had yet to come...?

Madness, that's what. Utter madness.

Week 3, Day 3: Progress, Kind Of

I wasn't as angry anymore. I had surpassed the phase of rage and frustration in a manner I had never experienced; I felt pure disbelief.

I *almost* saw the sick twisted element of humor in this appalling disaster.

It wasn't over yet.

Mister Smarmypants explained that no other suggestions were made by anybody else in his department. Therefore, my request for an RMA was approved — but as he went on, it wasn't as fair of a deal as I'd expected.

Covering the shipping costs *myself*, I would need to mail the defective motherboard to one of the company's return centers, and they'd have to process the return before mailing me a replacement within 7 to 10 days.

One thing more:

It also wouldn't be a new product, but a refurbished motherboard of the exact same model.

Hey, as long as it worked, I didn't care. All I wanted was for my gaming computer to be functional again.

As all of my faith in the company had been *long* since obliterated over the past weeks, I grabbed a pencil, and sharpened it to a fine point. I then made several nearly undetectable dots in a small corner of one of the bar code stickers on the motherboard. That way I'd know if they decided to send the very same product right back to me posing as a replacement.

I had indeed developed trust issues.

Spending nearly $20 in materials and postage, I shipped the motherboard off to the return center, and tried my best over the next couple of weeks to forget about this nightmare.

Playing *Amplitude* helped.

Week 5: All For Naught

The replacement motherboard had actually arrived at my post office at the end of the prior week, so that extra tease of waiting for it to be sorted over the weekend and delivered first thing Monday was a nasty element soiling my mood.

I unboxed the refurbished motherboard, quickly proceeded to install all of my components, and reassembled the case.

Delirium would soon kick in.

Firing up the computer, I didn't get a BIOS ROM checksum error.

In fact, I didn't get anything.

Power *was* being fed to the computer.

Fans *were* spinning, and the monitor was working fine...

A black screen with a blinking cursor was all I had.

I tried restarting and accessing BIOS settings, but it wouldn't respond.

I shut it down and double checked all components, confirming they were all seated and installed properly before powering it on again without any change in results.

Something inside me said to quit. Go outside and run the sucker over with my car and call it good. Buy another one.

I *should have...*

Instead, for an illogical reason that can only be categorized as gluttony for punishment, I called Smarmypants and informed him of the situation.

When letting him know the replacement motherboard wasn't working at all, he began to laugh at the ordeal.

"Are you *serious*? Hahaha! *Wow*, Mike you gotta laugh at this situation by now, huh? I mean, *nothin'* seems ta' be workin' for us here. Can you *believe* that? It just doesn't make **sense...!**"

I interrupted his counterfeit tone before he could continue.

"No, I **don't** find any of this hilarious... that I've been held hostage by three different levels, waited for weeks of several shipments that were stabs in the dark to correct an issue that **nobody** in the company seems to be able to resolve? I don't find that funny at all. I'd like a rebate, a replacement product that works, or a gift card to the electronics store from where I bought it so I can grab another new one. They still have plenty in stock, I just checked this week!"

I really had.

Smarmers responded that he couldn't carry out that request, but he *would* arrange to have my original motherboard mailed back to me; he'd been in touch with the staff at the processing center and they'd proclaimed to have discovered a solution to get it working again.

I couldn't **believe** he suggested that.

Confident that the original motherboard was beyond hope, I demanded to speak to his supervisor, but was met with a reply that — to this day, when recalling it — still amazes me.

"Hah! I don't *have* a supervisor, Mike. *I am* the third level support, there's no one else!... but I promise you, we will get your original motherboard right back to ya and get it workin'."

We argued for several minutes more, accomplishing nothing.

I clearly had to accept, or give up; I didn't have the time, the money, or the will to bother with small claims court.

I **needed** to see how this would end.

As a "favor" due to what I'd gone through, I was to be emailed a return label to ship the refurbished motherboard back at their expense, and Smarmypants offered to have my original motherboard returned to me without waiting for the center to receive or process the refurbished model.

Like Ralphie Parker hypnotically nodding to Santa, I agreed.

Week 7: Running The Clock

With my original motherboard in hand, I was able to verify its authenticity from my secretive pencil markings.

I assembled everything and was back to square one with the checksum error.

Smarmypants hadn't contacted me at all since our last conversation, and I didn't mind; everything about him defined insincerity, so I enjoyed the hiatus.

Alas, now was the time to reach out to the phony fellow and see if there was anything he had for me to try other than flashing the BIOS for the umpteenth time — because I was done with that.

Honestly, any attempt after the first was simply to indulge these morons to reach the point of requesting an RMA... but that ship had sailed and it was clear they were not willing to honor the warranty in a reputable manner.

As he answered his phone, my shoulders tightened upon hearing his voice.

"Mike? How have you been? I'm guessing ya got your board back?"

I was as cheerless as one could be, embracing my monotone, spirit-lacking pacing as I awaited to see *what* manner of rubbish it was that I'd be walked through this time.

What happened next was finally the last straw.

I was directed to enter the BIOS settings by tapping the Delete key immediately upon boot as usual. He then navigated me through a few menus to reach the controls that adjusted the performance of the CPU.

These settings are most commonly tweaked by users who like to heavily customize their PCs for extreme performance, usually by *very serious* gamers.

They often choose to "overclock" the CPU, forcing it to run faster than the default rate selected by the manufacturer.

Though increasing performance, this creates extra heat, and in turn requires higher quality fans and larger heat sinks.

Some will push the envelope by overclocking to a *substantially* higher amount and installing a liquid cooling system to prevent their computer from overheating and incurring permanent damage such as, oh, catching fire.

It can become as extreme and expensive as one's budget allows.

What *I* was being directed to do here was to *decrease* the speed within these settings by about 30 percent, and reboot the machine.

I did that, and the error was no longer encountered.

The error. Was no longer. Encountered.

The Windows logo was shown following the BIOS information. I soon saw my Windows Desktop. Mouse control was present, and the booting had successfully completed.

The error had been vanquished.

There was only one problem:

Checking System Properties, my 1.8 gigahertz CPU was now shown to be running at a clock speed of 1.3 gigahertz.

1.3Ghz wasn't the *slowest* of speeds at the time, but I'd paid for an on-par decent gaming-caliber CPU.

Not knowing or expecting that I was bright enough to check the clock speed, Smarmypants burst forth with a self-righteous exclamation:

"All RIGHT! We FIXED it for ya, Mike! It's bootin' up, isn't that great!?"

I was silent.

I *remained* silent as the sleaze grew nervous.

"Are you... there, Mike?"

"Yes, I'm here. And sure, my computer booted, but I'm viewing my System Properties and I see my clock speed is now 30% slower. It's not running at the proper speed anymore. You slowed it down by a huge amount and you call that *fixed?* Dude, nothing **about** this is fixed! The motherboard still isn't operating as it should!"

He laughed off my reply, and said that I have to understand that not all issues can be perfectly resolved all the time, and sometimes compromises need to be made.

I shut the machine down and reverted the BIOS settings I'd been asked to make, and the error returned.

It didn't matter, Smarmypants had established a "functional workaround" and was standing his ground.

We had reached a stalemate.

I'm not proud of what followed, and I generally don't condone shouting profanities at, berating, voicing wishes of employment termination of any and all co-workers of an entire department, but I can't lie...

I came unglued, and did all of the above to that pathetic joke of a technical support agent, Mister Smarmypants.

Following my tirade, I asked him directly if he had any pride in himself when he went to work.

I asked him if he was out to sadistically provoke and string customers along only to arrive at no resolution.

I asked to speak with the department that processes his paychecks as he was unfit to direct me or anyone else through any further troubleshooting processes.

I demanded he honor the company warranty and ship me a brand new replacement motherboard as mine was clearly defective, and I was done being jerked around.

What chilled me to the bone was how calm and collected he was once I was done.

It spoke volumes.

It proved he'd done this before.

It told me what kind of human he was.

He was not honest, he was not honorable.

His answer was golden:

"Mike, you see, I can't send you a *new* replacement because we no longer manufacture that model. We don't have any more; it's from late last year."

He continued, circling back around to his classic car lot tactics...

"We do have our *current* model available, so what I'm willing to do is give you a credit if you'd like to purchase the updated model and pay the difference to-"

"I will *never* spend another dime on this company's products as long as there is another manufacturer to choose from. I'm going to write a detailed letter to the CEO of your company explaining my incomprehensibly miserable experience with your entire department. I will explain that you failed to honor the warranty after nearly two months of stringing me along. I have *never* had such a terrible experience as a customer in my life, and I doubt I ever will."

To this day, I haven't.

More saccharine apologies commenced, followed by a nauseating array of generic excuses right out of a handbook.

"Mike, you have to understand, these things happen."
"We can't be expected ta fix all the problems with every single product we have out there."

"We tried our best, and sometimes things..."

I could hear no more, so I ended the call as he continued to spew his verbal putrescence.

There was only one thing left to do.

I kept to my word, and wrote a one page letter addressed to the office of the company's CEO.

Maintaining 100% professionalism, it included an explanation of my issue, the date it started, the names of every agent I spoke to, all ticket numbers I was provided, a list of the dates and duration of every call, a list of shipped items, the amount of money I'd spent on materials and postage, and the final proposed resolution.

The letter ended by stating my experience was inexcusable, and if a failure of this proportion had occurred within a company in which *I* held an executive position, *I* would want to know, so that I could ensure no other customer suffered likewise.

I sent the letter via international mail with tracking, also requiring a signature upon delivery.

I honestly didn't expect anything, and held the belief that if this were only for catharsis, and the CEO or his staff threw the letter in the trash with a sadistic chuckle after reading it, that was fine.

I just needed to write and send it.

Week 11: The Answer

Several weeks had passed since I'd mailed the letter. I'd still been playing games on my "new" PC for over a month. Suffering frame loss and choppy movements on what should have otherwise been my high performance gaming machine had permanently set my bitterness toward the manufacturer in stone.

I didn't think I'd ever hear back from them.

I was certain my letter would be used as kindling.

I was wrong. .

Several weeks after sending the letter overseas, I received a reply from the office of the CEO in Taiwan.

The letter explained that although the CEO himself was unable to personally address my issue, a colleague opened the letter and offered an extremely professional apology for the way my issue was handled.

To bury the hatchet, their reply also contained a special code. It was a coupon code to enter upon checkout from their own website. The code would allow me to directly order *any* motherboard from them free of charge, also including free standard shipping.

They were trying their best to finally make good on this astronomically embarrassing flub.

I could have easily exploited the situation and spitefully ordered the most expensive motherboard on the website, but I didn't. All I wanted was a working product that I had paid for.

I found the current model that had most closely matched the specifications of the product I had purchased. There was only a $40 difference in price. I selected it, continued to checkout, and entered the code.

Honorable behavior aside, this was also the *wisest* move, as the more expensive models weren't compatible with my CPU and Graphics Card; I would have had to spend hundreds of dollars more replacing those components, too.

I confirmed the order, and awaited my new mobo.

Week 13: Tapout

A couple weeks later, I received the new board.

Eager to put this weary issue to rest and swap over all my components for hopefully the last time, I carefully cut open the package and pulled out the product box.

... but it was the wrong product.

Could it be? Was it really?

I ran to my PC and viewed the confirmation email that showed the product number and model that I ordered. I had indeed ordered the model I intended.

It wasn't the product they shipped.

Somebody had screwed up and sent the wrong motherboard. It was slightly nicer than the model that I had actually ordered, but having a different sized CPU Socket and Graphics Card Port, this rendered the board completely useless to me.

I did the only thing my sanity allowed.

I put it right back into the shipping box, carefully and securely taped it back up, and wrote with a bold black marker on both the front and back of the package:

RETURN TO SENDER

The next day, I took my lunch break to drive to the post office and slipped the package into the drop box. Noting the date, I couldn't believe it was one day shy of three calendar months that I'd first started dealing with this issue.

It wasn't the perfect end to such an epic battle, but I was content knowing *that* was the last time I would ever lay a finger on that company's products.

To this day, that has remained true. As long as I can help it, that won't change.

I never heard back whether or not they received the return, whether they lacked the competency to follow up with me or didn't care, it no longer mattered...

I no longer cared.

I continued using my underclocked PC until I'd saved up to shop around for new parts.

I settled on trying out an MSI brand motherboard.

It performed beautifully, and I've preferred MSI motherboards ever since.

Even my current gaming PC today is sporting an MSI. I've matched it with an Intel CPU, an EVGA Graphics card, and a beautiful 144 hertz widescreen monitor from Acer. I've not experienced any disappointments, difficulties or issues as of this point with any of these companies' products, and I'm extremely happy with all of them.

So... next time you deal with tech support and the agent takes a few hours, or perhaps even a few days to fix your issue...

Count your blessings. It could have been much, much worse.

EIGHT

The Empire, Part II:
Settling In

The Fancypants Vending Machine

I had overdressed a bit for the first day of official company training; I was sporting classic black slacks, a white shirt, black tie, and black dress shoes.

Hey, when in doubt, right?

Though I didn't get any snide looks or any mentions, the majority of others were in neutral slacks, colorful or white polo shirts and blouses, and for the most part, sneakers or even comfy canvas slip-ons.

There was a high school reminiscent chill that was present inside the training lab, and though it kept my wrapped neck from overheating due to my seldom-worn tie, I still followed suit on day two and switched to more comfortable apparel.

The dress code was "mild business casual," allowing jeans, but no shorts or anything that would be considered beachwear — except on Fridays, when a t-shirt, shorts and sneakers were commonplace.

I loved working at The Empire already.

The trainer, Sean, absolutely loved *his* job, too. He was the sole individual when it came to generating all course material on The Empire's software to provide to new hires.

After each daily segment, an entire two hours was left open for questions, and not a single one was shirked. He even stayed past end of shift when there was anybody that needed additional clarification.

It's not often a company sees people with that level of passion about their job, and it's an especially beneficial quality for a trainer in particular to have.

The entire class would become quite comfortable with all three of The Empire's flagship products by the end of the two week course.

The content for ReportsPro took the longest to cover, taking up the entire first week. Creating basic appraisal reports was self-explanatory, but the program contained a multitude of options and preferences that could serve to make one's life easier... or more difficult if used improperly.

There were several menus available upon launching the product, and several *different* ones appearing when editing a report. Some menus had over fifteen items, and those items contained multiple layers of sub-menus within.

On top of that, many of the menu selections would prompt a dialogue box, potentially containing several tabs chock-full of even more additional options.

By well-thought-out design, for the most part they were all very logical and intuitive; it was the very quantity of features that would take time to become familiar with.

PhotoLink's course took up three days of the second week, and it was nearly identical in concept and function as Photos-First. The main difference was that since it was an installed application as opposed to web-based software, PhotoLink had an entire section to configure a direct dial-up connection.

For computer geeks who had played games through direct dial-up for over a decade, it was nothing foreign. For others, it was an overwhelming task seeing it for the first time.

There were hundreds of phone numbers listed by ZIP Code for the customers to filter and select to dial The Empire's servers for the first time. Upon doing so, the program would then download an updated, *more* extensive list in hopes of finding a local number to dial.

Back in the day, charges added up quickly when uploading large amounts of photos through a long-distance number; an average upload at the end of the day would range from 5 to 20 minutes.

Thank goodness those days are behind us.

Finally, PhotosFirst training took only a day and a half, as it had been greatly refined and condensed compared to the entire week-long course the temps had originally been given.

I was grateful for that since it was still a boring recap of what I'd already been doing for the last several months.

After lunch on the last day, we finally found out what the Specialty team did!

They were a team of only six agents, and handled the software family of add-ons, miscellaneous utilities, and older, lesser-used software titles from years past.

That software was in use by niche markets and fewer insurance companies. Their smaller demographic meant only a nominal team was required to provide support.

We were given only a brief description of each Specialty product, being told that depending on future trends, we may be offered to join the Specialty team after gaining experience with the core products.

To polish off the last hour of the day, we were given a tour of The Empire's larger, primary headquarters a couple blocks away.

The Empire stored their servers there, and it was an impressive sight! I'd never seen so many hard drives all in one place. Hundreds and hundreds of drives were arranged beautifully to store all customers' uploaded data.

I didn't envy the poor sap who suffered the tedious task of installing all that hardware. What was an expected tangle of cables was neatly channeled along the edges of the room.

It was a crisp and clean, yet artful implementation of zip ties and tubing to both hide and protect the thick mass of wires feeding electronic life to the gently humming servers.

Primary headquarters served as the meeting place for clients and potential customers, so the outside grounds had more plentiful, and excellently kept landscaping compared to our tech support headquarters.

Pristine concrete walkways lined the building amid peaceful foliage and freshly watered greenery. Benches and small tables were found sparsely placed for employees to enjoy a lunch break or short respite in the lush company of nature if they pleased.

Returning to our own headquarters, we stopped by our cafeteria which had recently been reopened after having undergone several snazzy upgrades.

Though no cafe or staffed food service existed at the time, the older mid-'90s vending machines were being replaced; we'd soon have more options other than cola or a bag of chips to nosh on during break.

Brand new microwaves were being installed in a new kitchenette, and additional tables and chairs would be delivered in the upcoming weeks.

As sufficient as the facility had been, it hadn't seen much active occupancy, as many of us had the habit of going out for fast food or takeout from one of many local places.

Only a select few were seen frequenting the cafeteria with a sack lunch, and looking back I wish I'd have been one of them.

Six or seven bucks never seems like much at the moment, but over the course of a year, that's more than $1500 spent for one meal a day. One can easily cut that in a third by taking a few moments at home prepping a lunch that actually provides *nutrients* to the body, rather than a mouthful of deliciously synthetic fat and salt fumes.

Live and learn.

Besides, another temptation had entered the realm: one of the brand new vending machines had already been installed, and it was unlike *anything* any of us had seen before.

It dispensed frozen foods of several varieties. There were desserts like frozen juice bars, ice cream sandwiches, and cheesecake on a stick.

Selections of microwavable meal entrees were also aplenty: mini hamburger sliders, burritos and enchiladas, sausage sandwiches and more.

Upon inserting your cash or card payment into the corresponding slot and pressing the button for your selection, a mechanical lever would open the lid of a large chest freezer behind the window, revealing all the frozen foodstuffs stacked within respective columns.

A moment later, a large previously unnoticed apparatus descended from above that only at first resembled a claw arm from one of those stuffed toy arcade games that we all love or hate.

In place of a claw attachment however was a long round-tipped vacuum hose that was lowered with precision over the top-most item of the selected snack stack.

Once the vacuum attachment sensed it was directly touching the item, the exact measured suction was issued to grab the snack as the arm then relocated over top of the retrieval compartment.

Suction was released, dropping and sliding the treasure gently into the hands of its new owner.

The first unison, "Woooaaah...!" from the small crowd watching the machine do its thing was followed by the expected mass chuckle and trite wisecracks.

"Isn't it always the simple things..."

"That machine really *sucks*."

"Not a bad way to inhale 500 calories."

I'd secured a job at a company with friendly, like-minded employees who were quick to learn and thrived on it. I was making above-average pay with full benefits at age 24 without a college degree, and pun intended: we had the coolest vending machine I'd ever seen.

Life was great.

Quality Assurance

Taking calls on the official Tech Support floor was identical to the workflow we'd followed in The Dungeon: greet the customer with our first name and company name, pull up their account number, cut to the chase and resolve their issue.

PhotosFirst calls were of course a cinch; being the *exclusive* software title I'd supported in The Dungeon, I was more adept at using it than many of my co-workers upstairs. Due to this advantage, I was able to easily focus on PhotoLink as the only new software to fully familiarize myself with supporting.

Getting acquainted with all the solutions to common issues customers had with PhotoLink was simple, but not always easy.

Occasionally it could be time consuming, and for a common reason.

We'd been trained on how the software was *designed* to function. How it *actually* functioned in the real world was an entirely different matter due to, well, humans.

It isn't feasible in training to cover every situation or question about the software, not to mention the many methods of how the user might have screwed things up with a frenzy of frustrated clicks.

Reading any instructions, or even calling The Empire for help *before* unleashing their bombardment of button-mashing buckshot was a rarity.

Humans still seem to not have the patience to read first and act later.

Job security, this.

If we didn't have an idea of what to do next when on a call, The Empire kept a large Knowledge Base within their intranet that contained articles on just about every frequently reported issue, error message, and question that had been called in over the years.

The causes and resolutions were all there, but with one caveat: They were a **pain** to find.

The Knowledge Base had been independently designed by internal staff, and lacked a decent search function. There were no convenient features like sorting or filtering, so even when typing a verbatim error message into the KB search field, it *would* reveal the correct article to show up... on the third or fourth page of search results.

What a *mess*.

There was much room for improvement, but the cost of designing and hosting an intricately organized KB was expensive.

Since the Tech Support teams were all placed in adjacent cubicle groups, you could easily ask your neighbor if they weren't on a call, and they were glad to help you out.

If they *were* on the line and too intensely involved to be bothered, you would need to place your customer on hold and walk over to the respective "team lead."

Employees who had been on each team the longest were often designated as the team lead, as they were presumed to have the most experience, and therefore best advice on finding the solutions needed.

This wasn't optimal, but worked well enough.

The Empire was one of only four primary competitors in their industry, and they'd been number one for years. Customer feedback consistently stated that although their software wasn't perfect, the efficiency of Customer Service, and knowledge of the Tech Support staff was excellent — and that always earned their repeat business.

From an inside standpoint, it was easy to see why our team was so well-rewarded and our performance so appreciated by our customers:

The nature of our Quality Assurance program resulted in seeing that our morale was always through the roof.

Customers and employees alike, nobody normally *enjoys* having their calls randomly recorded. It always has, and always will impart a feeling of privacy violation... as if some stranger is listening in on your conversation.

That's because they absolutely are.

When customers would call tech support, one of the first things they'd hear was a message explaining that their call "may be recorded for quality assurance."

I'm sure this dance is one that sounds familiar.

The thing is, calls were rarely recorded. The Quality Assurance department consisted of one person: Betty.

She had been working in call centers her whole life, knew how to remain unbiased, and had the true intention of actually *better-*

ing the agents' performance instead of penalizing or threatening termination due to low scores.

This was far superior to the staff of scoundrels at that dastardly shipping company, whose presence was solely intended for *preventing* promotion. Criticizing unmet call quotas and the occasional too-quiet single syllables of script were their bread and butter.

One thing The Empire's QA department clearly proclaimed was that they would *never* be using the quantity of calls taken as a method of grading an employee's performance.

This was truly unorthodox for call centers, and they took time to explain to all new hires why this decision was made.

The trouble with holding agents responsible for taking a minimum number of calls per day, or even weekly, is that when dealing with complex software issues, the agent is often at the mercy of the customer's level of familiarity with using a computer.

Some amateur users may in fact take twenty minutes to be coached through a solution that has a five minute par time, and it's largely unfair to penalize the employee in those situations.

The Empire *had* previously incorporated call quotas into performance reviews, and it was an absolute disaster.

The obsession of quantity superseded quality, and many employees were found to be rushing customers off the phone to finish calls, and skimping out on their call log notes, rendering the tickets useless.

Without sufficient info for those reviewing the call, it was unlikely to understand what the issue was, or how it was actually resolved.

Once the quotas were nixed from reviews, the entire department's performance went up, and The Empire instantly saw a drastic increase of positive customer feedback.

Management vowed to never incorporate them again, a decision greatly respected by all.

Instead of quotas, "wrap time" was the element the department used to measure agents' efficiency.

A performance spreadsheet reflecting wrap time was pinned up on a bulletin board displaying results for every agent. The only details listed were our names, and a percentage value indicating how often we'd met the wrap time goal.

Every time a call ended, our phones automatically entered "Wrap" status which prevented another call from coming in. At that point we would need to verify that all pertinent details had been clearly entered into the case, including all troubleshooting notes and a short and sweet resolution summary. When we finished, we'd press the button on our phones to return to the incoming call queue.

The goal was to stay under a two minute wrap time for 80% of our calls. There was a moderate learning curve growing comfortable entering partial notes while still on the call, but it was a cakewalk after the first couple weeks.

Most all of the employees in the Media and Specialty teams were over 90% at all times, and I was frequently in the top three. The Reporting team was usually right behind us in the high 80% range; having the primary flagship product to support, they had the highest call volume and more complex issues.

That makes for an intricate case log at times.

It was never to be forgotten that the whole point of logging a case is to allow the reader to understand what on earth had taken place. Sometimes leaving a single word out of the case notes will leave the reviewer completely lost on the resolution.

For most shorter calls, it's easy to skim through your notes in under two minutes, but for longer troubleshooting sessions, you really had to be editing and proof-reading your work during the live call to make good use of your time.

It's a unique skill set, and that's where the importance of QA came into play.

Once a month, we'd receive an email notification to come in to Betty's office for a QA review.

Betty was first and foremost a motivator. She was full of positive vibes with a genuinely energetic smile, and *loved* talking to people. She was a great reader of both individuals and crowds alike, and was as comfortable speaking one on one as she was a large audience.

There was no feeling of judgment when being presented with your review.

Using special software, she went through a list of all tech support agents every month, recording one of their calls at random. If the call was longer than 30 minutes, or if it involved an irrationally behaving customer, it was usually dismissed.

Highlights from the call would be played back to you during your review, and Betty would chime in here or there to give praise or constructive criticism — *always* doing so by relating to the situation, as she'd had first hand experience dealing with most every type of difficult call throughout multiple industries.

She knew what it was like.

She never quoted stiff verbiage from a quality control handbook or threatened with penalties, because she knew the nature of the tech support position and the pressure involved when dealing with customers who were having a less than stellar time.

Let it never be forgotten: nobody calls because everything is going as it should. They're calling because something is wrong, and like all of us can relate, it's fairly effortless to find one's self in a rotten mood when battling it out with a computer.

After receiving their reviews and exiting Betty's office, everybody would leave having learned a few more tricks of the trade, acquiring an easier method of reaching resolution the next time the same scenario was encountered.

Positive reinforcement, proactive measures, logic, and understanding were four elements that held great significance by The Empire's tech support management at the time, and was one of the most effective underlying combinations for success I've ever witnessed.

The Subtle Art Of Nullifying Sanctioned Swearing

By March of 2004, I felt I had really settled in to the department. I'd grown comfortable with the flow of calls, the questions were for the most part entirely familiar, and I'd excelled at resolving issues with a level of efficiency that QA had deemed impressive.

Annual performance reviews were held every January, and I was encouraged by Betty to keep up my pace to see an almost guaranteed substantial raise in pay.

I did exactly that.

I've always excelled when given the freedom to operate autonomously. A project is a playground for me to explore, imagine, and implement different machinations that will enable me to arrive at something much more than just a basic endgame.

Recalling my experiences of suffering team projects in elementary and even high school, what stuck out most was being forced to work with many other students that would sit idly while others on the team carried their weight.

It was both depressing and demotivating because over time, the idlers would catch on to which students actually cared about their grades, and they'd strategically scramble to get at *those* tables so they could leech off the hardest workers' efforts.

That behavior is sadly also seen practiced by many adults in politics, in sports, and absolutely in the workplace.

Those early memories have no doubt served as fuel for my own motivation. I never want to be that pathetic slacker on the team intentionally sponging and bringing everybody down.

I'll always be the first to offer knowledge and a hand up to anybody who asks for it and shows initiative — but when assistance is refused and responsibilities fudged, I'll be first to reveal the vermin sucking the life out of those genuinely expending their blood, sweat, and tears.

Though we each had our own cubicles, our individual outlook and willingness to play well within the department as a team was crucial. We all took pride in honing our craft.

We grew to learn when and how long we could mute our headsets between exchanges with customers during live calls. This talent was priceless as we'd be able to maintain focus when simultaneously listening to co-workers' questions.

Before long, we were calmly whispering hot tips between our cubicles to help each other out amidst the sharply echoing flurries of mute buttons being skillfully tapped within our fabric box forest.

Alas, as it is with any forest, there is on occasion unrest.

There were no acts of brush fires or natural disasters here, neither customers acting as predators nor interdepartmental outsiders usurping the peace, no-no-no.

This unrest I speak of came from within. A livid fellow cubicle dweller a few units down my row, there sat Ron.

Ron was a weathered curmudgeon of a man that loved to vent his burnout from the excessive years he'd suffered in tech support by performing a masterfully fluid little ritual.

"The inhale" was the first and most important hint we'd be tossed, and far too often it was of an unfavorably low amplitude. Thus, this potential warning for what was to come went occasionally unnoticed.

This wasn't preferable.

Luckily, the dramatic flair of the inhale was optionally enhanced by the sucking in of air through the teeth, and it segued beautifully into the second step of the ritual: the sigh/growl phase.

Ron's sighs were always loud, and clearly intended to be heard by the entire row of cubicles. To ensure maximum audible distance was covered, he'd occasionally throw in a groan which *could* be skillfully graduated into an increasingly loud growl if the drama called for it.

If we hadn't already muted upon hearing the inhale, the sigh/growl combo would have a fair chance of being heard by our customers.

It wasn't always acknowledged by them, but once in a while they'd either laugh, or inquire if somebody was having a rough day, as it was clearly audible through our headsets.

Now, if we hadn't muted at *this* stage of the theatrics, we were — or rather, our customers — were to pay the price with what followed.

This was the apex of the tantrum in which Ron would pound one fist [at minimum] upon his desk, and simultaneously let forth a quick burst of sonorous cursing at never less than 70 decibels.

He'd most commonly let a single word fly, but sometimes we'd get treated to a quick one-two punch of profanity with a syllabically matched quantity of synchronized fist poundings.

On the grandest of occasions, both fists in *unison* would come out to accompany the outburst.

The vocabulary itself was never anything all that creative; they were the typical exclamations that angry sports fans might spew forth at the television when at a pub or in a college dorm.

This was a workplace, however.

The first time I'd experienced one of Ron's performances, I was frozen in awe as several veteran employees all around me chuckled and offered their own little quips in response.

"Is that the best you can do today, Ron?"

"Gee thanks Ron, I almost missed the mute button that time."

Ben was my neighbor sitting in the row to my left over the tall side of the cubicle wall in the Specialty department. He'd always be heard laughing or snickering after an outburst. I grew to join him with this response as it was undeniably hilarious and absurd.

Ben loved to make others chuckle in the workplace.

He'd once taken an incoming call from a customer who'd used the strangest expression to explain their issue. Ben saw the opportunity and couldn't help but to exploit it for a laugh.

As the customer had pressed the button for Specialty instead of Media support, Ben created a case and entered the customer's verbatim complaint per the policy, and placed them on hold before transferring them to the correct team.

It was late in the day, and me being the only available agent on the Media team that hour, he shouted over the wall, "Got a PhotosFirst issue for ya Mike. The photos are all SCREWDEY-WHOMPUS!"

"They're all *what?!*"

Upon taking the transfer and being provided the case number, the "Reason" field on the customer's ticket displayed their issue:

"The photos are all screwdey-whompus on the screen!"

The customer *meant* to say they'd attached the wrong photos...

The entire Specialty team had the strongest sense of humor in the department. They'd hold ridiculous yet well-constructed debates about the most random of subjects which would otherwise be mundane if not for the originality of their banter.

The fact that we couldn't see any of them over the high walls served only to make it funnier; we could enjoy the lone audio of their deadpan dialogues:

"I'm telling you, the guy was walking down the road wearing nothing but assless chaps and boots."

"How is that possible? You **do** realize that there's no such thing as assless chaps because chaps by definition, are assless."

"You're mistaken sir, both varieties exist. Have you forgotten every '80s rock video you've seen? Several styles of leather chaps fully encompassing the ass are showcased."

"That proves my point! Chaps are chaps, and leather pants worn by glam bands are leather pants."

"Oh yah? That's not what I saw you wearing when you were dancing on the table for karaoke last month. I still have pictures..."

Busting chops in the workplace was never so entertaining.

Regarding Ron's outbursts, I never did get an answer as to why management allowed the acts to continue, and never bothered to ask.

It *was* briefly explained by Ben and other co-workers that Ron had been with the Specialty team "forever," and was one of the most knowledgeable in the department

At The Empire, one's level of experience and comprehension clearly corresponded to the tolerated measure of steam blowing.

I found it priceless, and I still chuckle audibly whenever I think about it.

Bathroom Stall Coffee & 5 O'clock Meetings

Though I'd grown comfortable over the first many weeks working for The Empire, I would promptly learn that Ron's conduct wasn't the only quirky phenomenon within the upstairs floor of headquarters.

There were several restrooms on both floors of the building, so it made sense that while I'd been stationed in The Dungeon, I'd not yet been exposed to what I would soon experience.

More than a couple of times, I noticed a short stocky man speaking on his cellphone through a wireless headset. He'd always be slowly strolling down the front of the Tech Support department speaking loudly to — what seemed from the context of his responses — a customer.

I had presumed that the man must have worked in the Accounting or Customer Service department.

Upon hire, Erik and I had been placed in the same row with our open cubicle sides facing each other. I leaned over to him during one sighting and asked if he knew anything about this guy so commonly seen speaking on his headset with such gusto.

Erik shrugged as Ben shouted to us over his cubicle wall with a chuckle.

"Oh ho ho! That guy!? He's somebody from Sales. He's off to the bathroom while he schmoozes another potential customer."

"He is **not**...seriously?"

Erik couldn't believe it. I couldn't either.

I mean, the guy had his coffee mug in one hand.

"The guy has his coffee mug in one hand," I retorted to Ben.

He chuckled before acknowledging calmly.

"The guy's a legend."

Ben didn't offer the man's name, and I didn't ask. I figured it was for the best.

Ten minutes later, the man was seen heading back from where he came, still chatting away on the headset with mug in hand.

Shaking my head, I went about my business trying to imagine how one keeps a professional demeanor on the phone with a customer surrounded by the symphonic sounds of a public restroom.

...and with a cup of coffee.

Wow. Really?

I half-doubted Ben's response, thinking he was perhaps pulling our leg. He *did* love joking around...

That doubt was put to rest later the next week when I myself had stepped into the restroom during a quick break.

After washing my hands and reaching for paper towels, our loud-talking fellow swings the door open inches away from me, with his headset and booming voice in full force.

In one hand was clutched his signature coffee mug.

Trying my best to not appear disgusted, I continued to dry my hands as the guy passed me without eye contact, flipped open the door to enter the one stall in the room, closing and latching it behind him while continuing the conversation with his prospective client.

I then heard the base of his coffee mug touch porcelain, which could only have been the top of the toilet tank.

Another employee exiting the facility noticed me standing there frozen in disbelief. Toward me, they made direct and very **wide** eye contact accompanied with pursed lips and a nod.

From my stunned expression, it had become blatantly obvious to them that this was my first time seeing the bathroom stall coffee guy run his routine, and with their silent gesture they had indeed confirmed three things:

Yes I was seeing this, yes it's a regular thing, and yes — all were disturbed by it.

That very day upon end of our closing shift, our supervisor Jerry joined Erik and I along with a few others. We were headed outside as usual for the "5 O'clock Meeting" in the smoking area of the parking lot to swap our stories about the day's oddball calls or unusual customers.

I've only smoked the occasional cigarette, as I'm much more of a pipe tobacco and cigar fan myself, especially when paired with a bourbon aged stout, tawny port, fine bourbon or rum.

I joined them with a cigarillo.

As we lit up, I couldn't help but mention the bathroom stall coffee guy.

Before I'd even finished my first sentence, the others winced and laughed with mild head shakes and shudders as they recalled their own first interactions.

"Yes, we *absolutely* know him."

"I asked him once how he can go in there on the phone with a customer, and he shrugged and said he doesn't worry because his headset has noise-cancellation."

"Yah, but does it cancel the spray of fluid against urinal cakes and the whoosh of a toilet flush? I highly doubt it."

"Oh, you know they must hear everything in there... how can they *not?* Noise-cancellation does have its limits!"

I was glad to know I wasn't alone, but was also equally disturbed that the guy had kept his routine so long to truly become the stuff of legend as Ben had proclaimed.

I'm fairly certain Jerry *might* have mentioned the guy's name to me that evening after we exchanged laughter, but if he did I never retained it.

Only one thing has come from this: I'll never forget about the short stocky fellow who so brazenly and with infallible conviction carried his Cup o' Joe into the latrines. He who pandered to new potential clients amidst the soothing serenades of plumbing and other unique ambiance of which we're all familiar.

He was, and always will be remembered by me simply as: The Bathroom Stall Coffee Guy.

Unwinding

It doesn't matter how comfortable a tech support agent is with a software title, its kinks, bugs, and how to handle them, the process still eventually becomes exhausting.

As with many service industry positions, keeping a cheerful outward inflection while hearing the same negative complaints from customers will eventually take a toll on the psyche.

We know this going in to our jobs; we're in the Tech Support department, not the Receiving of Praise department.

We're paid to be verbally abused.

A great number of humans are sadly raised to remain self-centered creatures with weak minds, believing it acceptable to rip another person a new one for having suffered a hardship that in all likelihood, probably isn't that individual's fault.

The average indignant mortal wants heads to roll, and it's even easier placing blame, redirecting faults, and venting their own misery upon a faceless voice.

That voice becomes the party responsible for the product or service that caused their suffering, therefore that nominal link suffices *us* to be used as an audible punching bag.

The Empire understood this reality of the service industry, and they'd encourage us to hold our ground when being treated with blatantly belligerent behavior.

We'd be permitted to interrupt the customer with sternness, stating, "We have no problem assisting to resolve the issue, but will not tolerate any harassment or profane, rude language."

If the customer continued to behave like a toddler, we could give a second and final warning that if their inappropriate behavior continued, we'd end the call.

The emotional temperatures of those conversations were so intense, it was an equally rich gratification when the customers made the decision to continue spewing their profanities... permitting us to nudge that disconnect button with a grin.

To combat the marks left by these negative vibes, every few months The Empire would hold an "unwinder."

Unwinders were company-sanctioned quarterly parties that started in the early afternoon of a Friday, taking up the cafeteria and front lawn of headquarters.

They featured on-site grilled meats and veggies, local food trucks for additional snacks, and live musical performances from local bands. Hourly drawings for prizes were held, and we were supplied with local craft beer on tap.

Yes, beer... and during work hours! Two drink tickets were given to every employee who wanted a couple glasses of cool brew on a Friday afternoon as they finished off their work week.

The drawings were no shoddy ordeal, either. A multitude of items ranging from quality hats and thermoses to several restaurant gift cards, and even the latest mobile devices were given away throughout the afternoon.

On occasion, at the end of the day after the last shift had ended, some remaining employees would help finish off the kegs from the unwinder.

You know, so the beer wouldn't spoil.

You can bet that *those* 5 O'clock Meetings were some of the most hilarious.

Nobody ever behaved lewdly or unprofessionally, no legal issues were encountered, nobody drove away drunk, and no reason came up to make us suspect unwinders would ever cease to be.

NINE

Timing Is Everything

Am I Stalling?

When driving home from work on the I-15 southbound one fine evening in Spring of 2004, the engine of my '95 sedan went silent.

No sputtering or spitting, no knocking or rocking, it just... stopped running.

Thankfully the vehicle still had full power, so I was able to collectedly ease toward the far right side of the freeway and onto the massive dirt shoulder of doom before my tires gave up rolling.

The gas gauge indicated that I still had a third of a tank, and the battery was hardly over a year old.

Nevertheless, turning the key in the ignition to try restoring the little beast to life was fruitless. I heard the healthy sound of the starter and what I thought was the turning of the engine, but it wouldn't quite come to.

Years prior, I had run out of fuel due to a busted gas gauge in an '81 coupe, and the sounds and symptoms I now heard were exactly what it sounded like back then.

Bummer, dude.

The vehicle had a touch over 130,000 miles on it, and having bought it used, I'd hardly racked up 40,000 myself.

Back when I was considering the purchase, everybody had *raved* to me about how famously durable and reliable that model was. I'd been assured by many sources that I could expect it to last well over 200,000 miles if I took care of it, so I was really hoping it was out of gas.

In my moment of self-pity and fury, I started to wonder how well [or poorly] the previous owner(s) had taken care of it.

Sighing as I dialed Kelly from my cell, I let her in on the fun, and optimistically said I'd call and give an update once I had a running car again.

Roadside service responded with impressive timing, as a tow truck arrived less than twenty minutes later.

The mechanic gave the vehicle a once-over and tried his best to get it started again.

No such luck.

The Shady Dealer

As I didn't have experience with any auto repair centers in San Diego at the time, I made what sounded like a safe decision and had the car towed to a nearby dealer in Pacific Beach right off the 5 freeway.

That seemed like a sure thing to do.

It was about an hour before closing, so I was able to fill out the necessary papers, and Rakesh, the service manager himself got right to work hooking the vehicle up to their diagnostic computer to run some tests.

Within minutes, he returned to me in the waiting room and gave me the scoop.

"Mister White? It seems our system shows that your battery needs replacing."

I didn't understand. My vehicle still had full power regardless of the engine not starting, and the battery was only 18 months old. I mentioned this to Rakesh, and he was ready with another comeback.

"Yes sir, I understand the battery is powering all the lights but it appears to be an aftermarket brand battery. What happens is that over a short time these lower quality batteries degrade quickly and lose sufficient strength to properly start the engine."

I did buy the cheapest battery I could when I last replaced it, but I'd expected it to last at least a couple years. During my incident, no lights had been dimmer or weaker than usual, the radio was working, and the car still beeped at me when my keys were in the ignition.

Power didn't seem to be an issue at all.

Nevertheless, I wasn't a mechanic, I had limited automotive repair knowledge, and wasn't exactly ready to burn more cash towing the car elsewhere for a second opinion.

Yet.

I told Rakesh to go ahead and proceed, taking his advice.

"Great, my friend, we can have that ready for you by tomorrow morning. Might I also suggest replacing your keys? They are worn out and seem to be sticking a bit in the door when unlocking the vehicle."

He was right about that, too. I'd actually been meaning to replace them for some time. They were so worn in fact, that both needed jiggling now and then to get the doors unlocked, and *one* of the keys was able to be pulled out of the ignition with the car still running. I'd often demonstrate this to friends and co-workers for a laugh.

I gave the go-ahead to replace them. After all, keys were cheap, right?

"No problem, Mister White. So with the cost of two replacement keys and the battery after parts and labor charges comes to two hundred thirty two dollars."

Whew! That seemed a steep price for a battery and two new keys, but my hands were tied. My car wasn't running.

One cell phone call and fifteen minutes later, Kelly picked me up and I arranged to catch a ride with a friend to and from work the next day.

That following morning after my first break, I answered the call from the dealer on my cell to have a wrench thrown into the works.

"Mister White? This is Rakesh with the updated estimate for repairing your vehicle."

"**Updated** estimate? Does that mean the new battery didn't fix it?"

"Yes my friend, I am afraid that is correct. After replacing the battery we were still unable to start the engine, so we ran some advanced diagnostic tests. It appears there is an issue of much neglect taking place here."

Neglect?

Rakesh had some nerve. I'd taken excellent care of my vehicle since the day I bought it.

I'd never missed a single timely oil change or any other regularly scheduled services prior. This being my third vehicle, I knew that it was much more affordable to properly and proactively maintain a car than to wait until something breaks down.

"Your total necessary repairs comes to twenty two thirty four."

"Twenty two hundred dollars?"

"Yes my friend, it is twenty two hundred dollars. You see, there are actually many things that are in need of repair on your vehicle. It is in badly neglected shape."

That word again. That dollar amount. What could possibly be *that* neglected from my regularly maintained economy car that would out of nowhere cost thousands of dollars?

I wanted to speak to Rakesh face to face. I told him I'd be there after work.

A buddy dropped me off at the dealership, and upon locating Rakesh I was given a copy of the suspiciously updated estimate.

Aside from the two keys and battery, (of which the work was already done and charged), there were now seemingly random part replacements and procedures added to the list that the dealer's service center deemed necessary to get the car running again.

All spark plugs and the distributor itself were said to require replacing, as did the fuel pressure regulator, fuel filter, air filter, drive belts, and front brake pads. Other items on the list were a major standard service, fuel injection service, and a carbon induction service.

$2234.00 total. I didn't believe a word of it.

The major standard service had been taken care of right before I'd moved to San Diego.

"So you're telling me that all these parts here simultaneously broke while I was driving on the freeway, caused the engine to die, and are now causing the engine not to start? I have a very hard time believing that."

Rakesh started to retort, and I pointed to the estimate as I interrupted.

"Rakesh, can you tell me which one of these parts specifically are actually causing the engine not to start?"

His true colors finally shone brightly as he went into an offensive and belittling speech.

"Well my friend, you see, like I have said it is a matter of neglect. When dealing with automobiles there are two choices, you either pay little now or a lot later, and my friend, the time is *much* later. You see, all these many things have been neglected. They are *all* affecting the functioning of the vehicle and need to be taken care of to see if the engine can start."

I didn't want to hear the word "friend" or "neglect" from his lips anymore, so I asked for his supervisor.

The reality that I was being played became embarrassingly lucid when I realized my failure to notice that another employee had strategically made themselves present a short distance away in silence. I only spotted him when Rakesh gave him a nod to come closer.

It was a nod that was clearly routine and well-practiced.

Rakesh introduced me to Joey as one of his associates that was there to discuss other options with me.

Joey was dressed sharper than Rakesh, but managed only to accomplish looking even less trustworthy than his introduction served.

A light gray sports jacket and tie over a white shirt doesn't normally scream "sleazy" or "dishonest" to me, but with the way he carried himself, Joey sure managed to pull it off.

It was as if he was a protégé of Mr. Smarmypants, as he followed his handbook to the letter.

"I see you're dissatisfied with the estimate Mister White, and I understand completely. I've gone through my share of used cars and trust me — after you rack up some mileage, you may not feel comfortable *spending* this kind of money on repairs anymore, am I right?"

I tried holding up the "estimate"... that sheet of wool that Rakesh tried to pull over my eyes so that Joey would know what was really going on, but my efforts were shot down quickly.

"Joey, this is ridiculous. They can't even tell me which part is preventing the engine from run-"

He interrupted me as he kept waving me on to follow him across the property of the dealership.

"I understand, I understand, it can be frustrating, I'm right there with you. That's why I'm here. If you don't feel comfortable spending that kind of money on an older vehicle, I can get started *right now* on a valuation for your car in its current state. We'll be glad give you a credit with that value toward a newer vehicle if you'd like make a trade-in and shop around in our lot here."

He gestured toward the dealership's lot of inventory with his clipboard.

"As you can see, we have a great inventory at the moment, and I'd love to getcha into one o' these cars..."

Like right out of a movie, he really used that line.

That was the point of no return.

"I'd like to pay what I owe for the battery and keys, and I'm towing my car home. I'm not satisfied with the service I've received here, and I'm seeking a second opinion. Thank you."

Joey kept talking as I turned and walked toward the service office to cash out, but I had already made my decision.

Furious at having been suckered by a dealership, I informed Kelly of the charming turn of events, then reached out to the tow service once more to bring my car home.

I needed time to think.

Underclocked Bus Speeds

San Diego's public transportation system back then wasn't something to be relished.

To be frank, it was unadulterated rubbish.

Being my second home and quite near to my heart, I *love* San Diego, and if I were forced to nitpick one flaw, the public bus system would be it.

I wanted to chat with co-workers and friends on *where* to get a second opinion about my four wheeled paperweight, and I'd also need to establish an alternative method of getting to work for a few days.

Taxis were too expensive, I didn't want to bother my friends to be my chauffeur as none of them lived nearby, and Kelly needed her car for her part time job when she wasn't in class.

The local transit was the only realistic option, but it meant losing at least an extra hour of my day. No matter — I could easily read a book or bring my Gameboy Advance along. I knew there was no chance of me ever tiring of *Final Fantasy VI*.

For me, many vintage Squaresoft games with a soundtrack composed by Nobuo Uematsu prove to be timeless, magically enveloping experiences that ooze charm. If anything could alleviate the boredom of *waiting for the bus,* it was either that or a good book.

To arrive at The Empire on time for my 8:00 a.m. shift, I'd have to be on the street to leave Clairemont at 7:00 a.m. for the first bus to deliver me up the road at Clairemont Mesa Boulevard.

About ten minutes later, another bus would take me to University Town Center, one of the major transit hubs a few miles up the road.

I'd then catch the final bus at 7:30 to polish off the trip seven miles further to the northeast, arriving two blocks away from The Empire with ten minutes to spare. I was able to jog the rest of the way and clock in on time.

The price was fair, at no more than a couple dollars each way. It was cheaper than the wear and tear on one's own car, but instead of a twenty minute commute, it was just shy of an hour.

Victor, one of the Reporting team veterans and a fellow music lover, had heard me lamenting about how long it had taken to get to work. He had lived in San Francisco for years, enjoying a far superior public transportation system before moving to San Diego, so he had an intense aversion to suffering the local buses. He empathized, and wished me luck on a quick repair.

This short-term travel plan was time-consuming enough on its own — if it weren't for an additional little catch.

Remember, the system was pants.

The buses were punctual in the morning en route to work, but getting home was an entirely different matter.

My first return trip on the bus did not go according to plan.

I was to take the same route in reverse, leaving two blocks from The Empire at 5:25 p.m. I'd arrive at the UTC hub at six sharp, and quickly hop over to the Clairemont- bound bus at 6:05. Swapping again at Clairemont Mesa Boulevard, I'd get dropped off near my home at 6:20.

If it were to successfully work out *in* that scheduled fashion, it too would only have taken one hour.

The problem was that the first bus arrived at UTC six minutes late, at *6:06.* What followed was an undesired reenactment of a cliché movie scene: witnessing the connecting bus pull away moments before ours came to a complete stop.

I had to wait until 6:35 for the next one, as I was still about eight miles from home.

Unlocking my front door minutes before 7:00 p.m. was a nice kick to the face; I had left twelve hours prior for an eight hour shift.

Crap.

I wouldn't tolerate the system very long without losing my mind, so I had to make a decision about my poor car and fast.

I decided on an independent service center in El Cajon that some local friends had suggested. They promised I could trust the owner completely.

It was already closed by that time, so I called them the next morning after taking the bus to work again.

They appreciated the referral, and explained that they locked the gate to the property after hours, so I'd need to drop my vehicle between nine to five.

Luckily they were open on Saturdays. That would be my only chance without taking a sick day during the week.

I rode the bus home that night, and due to lighter traffic, happily arrived at the UTC hub at 6:03!

...Alas, the connecting bus was nowhere in sight. Waiting until 6:10 still without its arrival, I finally asked someone nearby if they'd happened to see the Clairemont Mesa bus.

"Oh yah, it came and went right after six. Were you heading that way?"

They sympathized after our short conversation, as they were a long-time local.

"Yah, the bus system here's hit-and-miss. Traffic's gotten bad recently, so if they don't see anyone waitin' at the benches, they'll pull away early to shave off some minutes to make it to the next stop on time."

Clearly the transit system needed to adjust their schedule, as the routes were blatantly bloated.

Luckily it was a Thursday, so I only needed to suffer this trek a third time before getting my vehicle fixed.

As lady luck seemed to pity me, my first Friday night bus landed me at UTC at 5:58, *finally* allowing me to catch the next connection on time.

One out o' three ain't bad...

A Venture Of Links

After my sedan was towed to the service center and I filled out the paperwork, I hadn't been sitting in the passenger seat of Kelly's car for more than ten minutes on the way home when Tony, the owner, rang my cell phone.

Before we left, he had already given me his two cents after looking at the printed estimate from the dealer.

With a thick east coast accent and great sense of humor, he professed there wasn't a chance that the dealer had any intention of fixing my car judging from the estimate, and that it looked like a classic technique to get me to trade in for an upgrade.

He said he'd be taking a look at my car shortly and would get back to me in a few hours, but there I was answering my cell phone minutes later.

"Hey, Mike? Good news and bad news. Good news is I already found out why ya engine isn't startin'. We hardly rolled it into the garage ta take a look, and right away I see ya timing chain's busted. I dunno how dat dealer missed it... it's toast. Tryin' to start the engine with a chain in this kinda shape can be pretty risky. With some models ya engine gets destroyed depending on how deez tings fail, so it's lucky nuttin' major got damaged."

"Geeeez. Is there anything I might have done, or neglected anything like the dealer told me, to put such wear and tear on a timing chain?"

"Nah, nah. Some models' timing chains are built better than others, but with this make, I seen a lot of'm break after the hundred thousand mark."

"Huh. Well, what's the *bad* news? Is it not worth fixing?"

"Well, the new chain's only a few hundred, but for this model, ya need ta remove the engine ta replace it. That takes maybe fifteen or sixteen hours... ya total's gonna be about eighteen hundred ta get this fixed. I'm pretty slammed, so the soonest I can have it done is a week from today."

Good gravy.

I told him I'd think about it for a few minutes and call him right back.

I wasn't sure if it was worth that cost to keep a nearly-ten-year-old economy car, so I checked with some friends who were more familiar with this type of issue.

They said it sounded legit, and a few makes were infamous for the dreaded timing chain break.

They also said they'd *highly* doubt replacing a timing chain would actually take fifteen hours by a master mechanic, even if the engine **did** require removal, but that it's expected that I'd be charged the maximum allowed labor units for the operation.

That's how the industry works.

Still, it was a reputable make and model, and there was only a couple thousand left on the loan; it was on schedule to be paid off in less than a year.

I gave Tony the OK.

I didn't know which was more painful: the $1,800 cost of repairs, or realizing that if I **had** agreed to go forward with the dealer's plan, I'd have been out $2234 for a bunch of parts and labor that still wouldn't have gotten my engine running.

I tried to put that mess behind me and suck it up...

I had five more days of badly designed public transportation to deal with.

Through The Teeth

"I can't believe this, I *just called* three weeks ago and told the bank I'd have to miss **one** payment because I had a major repair on the car of almost two grand. They said that would be no problem if I made a double payment next month."

"I understand that sir, but there's nothing noted on the account, and our agents don't even have the authority to approve delay of payment without the proper request forms..."

It was Saturday morning, and I was told over the phone that I had 30 minutes to empty my car of any personal belongings before the bank's contracted towing service would be repossessing it for lack of payment.

Like most people, I hadn't read every single page of fine print upon signing the car loan agreement, but you can bet I do nowadays.

The bank had the right to repo the car as they saw fit after as little as a single late payment.

Apparently it's not an uncommon stipulation.

Most banks are typically a little less Draconian, and understand that it's in their best interest to tolerate a late payment once in a while.

Often, it's not worth spending the dough to repo the vehicle after one measly late payment to auction it off for substantially less than its value.

Geez, you'd think that would also be the case for a nine year old economy car.

"So you're telling me the last person I talked to at the bank blatantly lied to me through the teeth, and there's nothing we can work out? I drained my bank account to keep the car running... it was in the shop for over a week last month."

"I'm sorry sir, the collection of the vehicle has already been processed, so you'll have to submit payment in full to collect it as well as pay the storage yard fees."

"I can't make a double payment right now over the phone to get caught up? It's only been a few weeks since my missed payment, and that's the only one I've missed the entire time..."

"I'm sorry sir, we'll need the full remaining balance of your loan which is currently $2600, and the storage fees are $220 per day starting today."

Fantastic.

I didn't have any more room on credit cards at the time, and I had about $1,000 in the bank after catching up from the cost of the timing chain. There were also the three towing fees which were nearly $200 each.

Asking people for financial help isn't something I'd ever done before as a working adult. Regrettably, I'd obviously not been wise with my money, as I was 24 years old and broke after working full time for seven years.

Truly some room for improvement there.

Friends who'd seen my entertainment room walls lined with media might suspect that movies and video games were where my money went, but that's not the case at all.

I've forever been patient in regards to purchasing media; the vast majority were acquired as used titles for a fraction of their retail price.

Eating out... **that** was the problem. Restaurants were always an easy trap for me to fall into, and they've forever been the bane of my budget.

That very day, if I didn't get a loan from family or friends, I was going to lose my car.

Luckily, somebody I'd been close friends with since high school *had* been wise with their money, and was always encouraging others to do the same...

Jay.

"I'm tellin' you. You don't need to make a huge amount of money to be well off when you retire. Live within your means, and don't spend what you don't have to."

He was right. It was very simple.

Not *easy*, especially in Southern California... but simple.

He was familiar with my situation, as he was one of my buddies who was into cars that I'd asked about the estimate.

"Dude, that's pretty frikkin' cold, you miss one payment and they want to yank your car? Hah!"

He really did use the word, "frikkin". He's one of those people who have excellent verbal restraint, rarely spewing profanities.

The only times I'd ever gotten him to truly swear at all was while playing competitive video games. I nearly cry laughing every time he does, because it's such a rarity. I can count the occasions on one hand.

He was only busting my chops because he was more than willing to lend me the money.

Three thousand dollars was deposited into my checking account before end of the hour.

After completing my payment in full over the phone to the bank, Kelly gave me a ride to the repo yard.

Like on all the television shows and movies I've ever seen, it was located in a dodgy industrial area about a mile from the closest suburb.

The lady at the front office, (which resembled a subway ticket booth), was sympathetic when she pulled up my info.

Seeing my young panicked face in a cold sweat, she tried to cheer me up with good humor.

I was even more grateful when she only charged me $80 to retrieve my vehicle, as it was still in their gated front lot, not their long-term storage, having arrived that morning.

I gave her a brief recap of my morning, as well as what I'd gone through with the car: the engine dying, the lousy dealer, what actually fixed it, the price... then I told her how thankful I was for the break she gave me.

"Well, you're sure lucky to have a friend who could spot you. You'd be surprised how many cars never make it back to their owners once they're in here. They auction'm off in this area fast."

I didn't want to think about that. I was appreciating every mile I drove my car home that day, sporting that new timing chain, and now paid off.

These days, my wife and I live debt-free, keep an emergency fund for rainy day occasions, and try not to get into any situation in which we might find ourselves paying through the teeth.

Jay told me I didn't need to rush paying him back, and to try getting it to him by one year.

I paid him back in a few months.

As for that crooked dealership that tried to swindle me, they ended up permanently closing in 2017.

The most recent reviews I had noticed online reflected similar experiences to mine, seeing use of words like, "scummy", "scam", "cheater", "clowns", and "worst" within public feedback.

Though I'm perplexed as to how in the world they stayed in business for another 13 years after my experience, it's a small comfort that they're no longer inflicting their vile craft upon others.

I've held onto the estimate given to me by Rakesh all these years, and still tell the story to new friends and co-workers when sharing ridiculous customer service tales.

It continues to be cathartic.

TEN

The Empire, Part III:
Rise & Fall

Liam Showed Up

The Empire had hired another batch of temp employees in late Spring of '04, and Dylan had taken on a few more responsibilities since I'd come aboard.

He was looking for an assistant to help train the newest PhotosFirst temps.

Jerry stopped by my cubicle one morning and asked if I was interested in taking up the opportunity.

You bet I was! Still a fairly new permanent hire, I was eager to make a lasting impression and earn a promotion when it came time for my review.

The very next day I was going over the distributed training documentation with the new temps, and explaining every page with the strangest feeling of deja vu.

After covering the literal content, I one-upped the material by expanding on crucial areas and offering hot tips to streamline the workflow.

One of the trainees spoke up.

"So... to be clear, we can ignore these useless third and fourth pages, and stick to the nice little outline you gave us, right?"

Dylan was typing furiously in the corner of the room, heavily involved in another project. I shouted at him with a grin on my face.

"Is that good with you, Dylan?"

"Hah! That's fine by me, that section was poorly written, anyway... I didn't even prepare it."

The room chuckled as the pages in question were officially tossed, and they jotted down a few notes.

The gutsy agent that'd spoken up was Liam.

Liam had absorbed every step of training instantly. We both seemed to be on the same wavelength understanding the design and function of the software, but he had the nerve to speak up with that which everybody was presumed to be already thinking — and with humorously dire inflection.

It was exactly what the group needed to break the ice and jump-start camaraderie.

His behavior was infectiously conducive to progress and efficiency, so it rubbed off on those around him who were perceptive to it.

After training was completed, the group was moved down into The Dungeon as I was before. For the week of shadowing, I sat in with the established crew to take live calls as they were short one agent.

Liam was assigned to shadow me for the week, but he wouldn't need that long.

By the third day, he'd familiarized himself so well with the subject matter, recognizing common calls and their solutions, that he was able to take my place allowing me to return upstairs full time.

I'd occasionally email him my latest tips and tricks for PhotosFirst, as well as give him a heads up for changes to expect whenever there were updates to the website just around the corner.

Soon after Liam had settled in to The Dungeon, another of the temps from my class back in September, Luke, ended up also getting permanently hired upstairs. He had nothing but good things to say about Liam.

"I guarantee he's gonna be the next one hired on. He's a step ahead of everyone else down there."

I agreed. The Empire could absolutely use him on their team.

The call volume was on the rise, as business was booming thanks to the success of PhotosFirst.

Even though the majority welcomed it with open arms after their years of suffering dial-up, the occasional new user would call in and blame our software for their own blunders.

"Hi, is this tech support for PhotosWORST? I don't understand how *anybody* can use this thing..."

As usual, most confusion was due to customers failing to RTFM no matter how many times instructions were emailed to them.

Soon Liam was shooting up hot tips to *me* that he'd found to be helpful. He was circulating more keyboard shortcuts to the team and devised several time-saving troubleshooting modifications. I passed them all on to the supervisors too, and Jerry and the others were all impressed.

We were certain we'd be seeing him upstairs before long.

It was about that time that I'd decided to move from Clairemont to El Cajon, and share an apartment with one of my closest friends from high school who had also moved to the county.

As if by fate, it turned out Liam lived a few blocks away, and we ended up often carpooling to work together.

We'd feed off each other's thirst for knowledge, shared our own tech support shortcuts, and became good friends outside the workplace.

Taking Note

Music has always been a powerful force for me that has sparked innovation, provided motivation, introduced new crafts, presented different perspectives, alleviated work stress, and even made me new friends.

Liam introduced me to the Los Angeles rock band, Ra, with their *Duality* album.

I instantly became addicted to their intense driving rhythms and exotic harmonies. I *loved* their use of harmonic minor scales, and have followed them ever since.

In turn, I introduced Liam to some albums from my favorite band, Béla Fleck and the Flecktones. They're still always pushing the envelope with virtuosic solos and irregular time signatures.

Béla plays banjo like nobody's business, and has been nominated for a Grammy in more categories than any other musician. Their bass player Victor Wooten is world class, and his brother RoyEl, (whose stage name is "Future Man"), plays a heavily customized guitar shaped MIDI controller called a "Synthaxe Drumitar" — featuring touch-sensitive keys into which he programmed his own drum samples.

Their harmonica player Howard Levy can make a single harmonica sound like several, and their sax player Jeff Coffin enjoys using multiple horns simultaneously, having been heavily inspired by Rahsaan Roland Kirk.

Liam was impressed with them as well, and was stoked to join some friends along with Kelly and me to catch the Flecktones live when they performed at Spreckels Theatre that year.

I won't forget the moment I picked up Kelly; and Liam had waited in the parking lot as I went to knock on Kelly's dorm room. As she and I walked to the car, she was caught off guard.

"Do you smell something? ... Oh no! Liam, this is a tobacco free campus, you can get in trouble for smoking here!"

He had finished his last drag, so he could only chuckle and shrug.

"Heheh, whoops! Oh well, what are they gonna do, expel me? I don't go to school here."

There was that signature Liam nerve.

We laughed it off as we drove to the concert, and enjoyed an incredible night of talent.

That was my first time seeing the Flecktones perform live, and I can recall moments of that concert like it was yesterday.

My Most Expensive Pair Of Boots

There is no "economy car," really. As a matter of fact, they're all painfully expensive. The only thing that makes it *perceived* affordable is the title.

You can ask a young driver in SoCal how much it costs to drive their car ten miles from home to the beach and back, and they may give the answer, "About a gallon of gas."

Many adults make this mistake too.

I've helped countless friends and co-workers with their own personal budgets and I'm always thrown by this common oversight.

Why is it when calculating costs of driving a car to make a budget, people often only incorporate the cost of fuel?

"Oh you don't *really* calculate fifty cents a mile for transportation costs. Gas is only a few dollars a gallon."

Yes. Yes it is.

Now, go get a bucket and fill it with gas. Did it get you very far? *Ah*, I see: you'd like to pour it into the tank of a vehicle and burn it? Well then, that's going to cost you.

And burn, it shall... a hole right in your wallet.

Even a small sedan costs an average of $0.45 per mile to operate as of recent studies, but even those aware of this true cost are more than willing to pay it. This is because at the end of the day you're in essence paying to prevent loss of your precious time.

Taking a look once more at public transportation as an example, two or three dollars per ticket for a one-way bus or trolley ride in a big city like San Diego can take you 15 miles or further.

Drive your own car that distance and you'll be paying over double the cost.

The thing is, you'll be enjoying a quick fifteen to twenty minute arrival instead of making over an hour worth of frequent stops.

Time is precious.

This is a lesson I was taught a second time when I went back to Tony for my vehicle's next scheduled service, and mentioned I'd started hearing a chunky popping sound when making turns.

He worked his craft and the vehicle was found to have badly worn and cracked CV Boots, housing heavily damaged CV Joints underneath from lack of their proper maintenance.

The total cost would be $600.

Tony mentioned it would take a few days for parts to arrive, but that wasn't the problem.

I was strongly advised not to drive it any further until the decrepit CV Joints were replaced as to prevent some potentially unpleasant mishaps. One such concern would be losing control of the vehicle if they were to completely disintegrate, and possibly render one or both wheels unable to properly turn.

It seemed all the timely routine maintenance services I'd religiously kept up with in *prior* years didn't help to detect the issue earlier, and **that** ate me up inside.

What good did it do me as a customer to exercise careful and proactive measures if the hired services I'd chosen didn't hold similar standards?

Due to the apparently low caliber of these past chosen services, I'd now suffer unnecessary costs, and be inconvenienced for days.

Happy thoughts.

I'd handled riding the bus in the county for nearly a couple weeks earlier that year, so how bad could a few more days be?

From out in El Cajon, exponentially worse.

Less than fortuitous timing had put Liam's ride in the shop as well that week, and he'd been hitching a ride with another full carpool.

In order to get to work for my 8:00 a.m. shift 15 miles from home, I had to hop the first bus at 5:45, and catch a connecting bus after a *25 minute layover* only to meander through University Heights and Mission Valley before heading back northeast to The Empire.

That little route was nine miles out of the way, creating a 24 mile trip that clocked in at one hour forty minutes after all connections and stops.

The cherry on top was me being delivered to headquarters still twenty five minutes before my shift with nothing but fingers to tap and clock hands to stare at.

The exact process was repeated at 5:25 p.m. to arrive home minutes after 7:00.

It was a mind-numbing three days suffering a bus schedule I wouldn't wish on anybody.

It's been sixteen years since that charming event, and I've very recently viewed the feedback for the San Diego Transit system. From the posted reviews, it appears things are still just as fabulous.

Irritating as this ordeal was, it reinforced in me this crucial comprehension: thorough troubleshooting and attention to detail is as relevant in other industries as it is in the realm of digital sand — and if you take pride in your work, you may very well save your customers *substantial* amounts of time and money.

For that, they'll surely be coming back to you.

Increased Amplitude

Kelly and I hardly went a day without seeing each other, and the distance between Point Loma and El Cajon was taking a toll on transportation costs.

After keeping a vigilant eye on available rentals, we found a small 430 square foot, one bedroom apartment less than a mile from The Empire for $880 a month.

That was a great price for a safe neighborhood in San Diego at the time, and saved us a nice chunk o' change. It was also much more affordable than for Kelly to stay living in the campus dorms.

I could also come home for lunch, saving time, money, and the poor health decision of going out for fast food several days a week.

The benefits didn't stop there.

In case you haven't heard, many computer geeks *love* playing video games.

To burn off some steam, several times a week I'd invite some co-workers over to the apartment during our one hour lunch break. We'd fire up the Nintendo 64, Gamecube, or Playstation 2 and play some party games, leaving us feeling rejuvenated for the second half of the work day.

Mario Kart and *Mario Tennis* were some go-to's, as were the mini-games in *Super Monkey Ball*... but on the days I went home for lunch by myself, I still couldn't get enough of playing *Amplitude*.

That game inspired me to take a deeper interest in my music hobby. I ended up enrolling in a few college courses in Digital Recording, and purchasing ProTools LE software with the DigiRack 002 four channel rack-mountable interface. With that basic setup, I started to record my own projects.

Eventually, I would lug that interface to another Flecktones performance, sitting in my seat with it upright in my lap the entire show. The band was generous enough to sign it after their performance with a silver ink pen, including their Sound Engineer Richard Battaglia who was generous with his time, and loved to talk shop.

I still have it today.

Rhythm games and recording software aside, our little apartment complex had begun contributing some amplitude of its own.

A major project to refurbish the property was underway, complete with jackhammers, drills and other heavy duty power tools usurping the silence at 6:00 a.m. during the week for several months.

It still fit the budget, so there we'd remain for a spell.

I continued to stay focused, knocking my projects out of the park at The Empire, absolutely loving the great camaraderie in the department. If I got that promotion after my first year, perhaps Kelly and I could afford a more comfortable place...

Wow

"... I'm not a computer whiz who knows how this stuff works!"

In January of '05, annual performance reviews ranked both Erik and I near the top of the team. We were given raises and had both started to take some calls for ReportsPro software to help out the Reporting team.

I was now making $16.50/hour.

The scale of the software may have been intimidating, but most incoming calls were similar in nature and challenge as those within the Media team.

Weeks after taking on the product, I'd received a real stinker of a call. A customer was having difficulty when trying to run the latest update.

The Empire updated the software on a monthly basis to ensure accuracy of procedural descriptions, material prices, and tax rates for property damage, as well as to ensure compatibility with the latest Operating System changes.

As it was still 2005, *online* software updates weren't completely mainstream yet, so every month the latest software version got mailed out to customers so they could update.

With ReportsPro being subscription-based, this was also an effective method of controlling piracy by having each update expire after a time.

DVD-ROMs were still pretty expensive, so the software was produced on three CD-ROMs which were run like a standard install in order to run the update every single month.

There was always a handful of wacky issues encountered when performing this task.

The media service that The Empire had contracted to print and mail out our updates also had a contract with a record company.

Jerry told me of a story one past month when the update discs *had* been mailed out to our customers with the correct labels, but upon inserting them into the drives were revealed to in fact be Audio CDs of a pop artist's latest album.

Oops.

My customer had started the update with disc one per the instructions, but was stuck at the next prompt on the screen:

"Insert Disc 2 and click Continue."

They had done that, but the prompt kept reappearing.

This was a somewhat common call. On occasion, we'd encounter a customer whose CD-ROM drive had a dirty lens, but the more frequent discovery was that one or more discs were damaged during shipping.

They'd either have minor warping from the heat during their transit, or have scratches, cracks, and other blemishes from suffering excessive abuse during their treacherous journey through the mail.

Damaged media was the number one cause of discs not being detected, and I had gone through the basic limited steps with no success.

The surface of the second disc had been wiped down with a dry soft cloth. We'd tried rebooting the computer to ensure no hardware drivers had failed. The customer had tried starting the update over again several times, and they even found and inserted an Audio CD to test the drive. It was able to play the album fine.

The solution was eventually found only due to a fortuitous routine that *many* customers calling tech support subconsciously practice.

They had started narrating their own steps as they followed my instructions.

After testing the Audio CD successfully, I asked the customer to go ahead and try running the update again.

As with past attempts, the first update disc completed, then prompted to insert disc two and click Continue.

The customer proceeded, "Alright now, open the tray, I'm putting in disc two, close tray, click Continue... aaaaand nothin'. It still keeps askin' for disc two."

With that sentence, he had given me the cause and solution to his problem.

The call time had reached 30 minutes, so it was only a desperate suspicion at first, but with tactful inflection I posed the next question — being so very careful to not sound as if I was speaking down to him.

"Just to confirm, you *had* removed the first disc before putting the second disc in the tray, right?"

"Uh, no, do I need to do that?"

A few seconds of silence commenced as I muted the headset and quietly blurted out, "*Wow. Really?!*"

I continued only slightly louder as I stood up in my cube with the intent of seeking sympathy and to entertain my nearby co-workers with the revelation:

"Yes sir, the first disc does need to be removed from the tray before inserting the second, as the drive reads the discs from underneath. It seems that's what's been causing the issue; the drive has been constantly reading the first disc on the bottom of the two. It's actually fortunate that the drive didn't get jammed from two discs being inserted at the same time."

Jerry happened to be heading down the aisle at the right time to hear this little gem. As he passed, he glanced back at me with stunned oculars before exploding into a muffled guffaw while continuing to walk away.

Meanwhile, the customer offered his defense with an impressively rational argument.

"Well, it didn't *tell* me to remove the first disc... I'm not a computer whiz who knows how this stuff works!"

Especially in tech support, there really is a first time for everything.

I could do nothing but let out a mild chuckle, as the customer had already.

Our chuckling gave way to unison laughter as my co-workers went about their calls with grins and shaking heads.

"Well your company really needs to change that message. It doesn't say *anywhere* to take that first disc out before puttin' the next one in."

"Well, I've gotta tell you sir, you've got me on that one. You're absolutely correct," recovering from my laughter.

I guess that's why I was now getting paid the big bucks.

Upon ending the call, I kept my promise to the customer and indeed *submitted* the request to the Development team asking to modify the instructional message as petitioned.

They laughed and promptly denied the request.

Raymond, along with Sheryl, another veteran employee on the Reporting team, had each heard about my customer and congratulated me on a **great** ReportsPro initiation call, jesting that it was all downhill from here.

Sheryl loved to play computer games, and she and I had recently started playing *World Of Warcraft* upon its release about a month before the new year. Erik also joined in the fun, as did two other long time employees of the Reporting team, Carrie, and their team lead, Gus.

WoW was my first Massively Multiplayer Online Role Playing Game, (MMORPG), and though I don't play it religiously anymore, I still enjoy it to this day.

I tried to get Raymond to join the fun, but he preferred first person shooters and racing games.

Others were deterred from playing a game that required a paid subscription, but for $15 a month I saw it as a bargain.

Being an avid console and PC gamer already, I'd easily complete a game every couple weeks. Though I'd try to purchase used games, the retail price of most new games was between $40 and $60.

If *WoW* held my attention for a while, it would *certainly* be more economical.

Things were a little awkward at first when Carrie tried to constantly commandeer the group while playing, often giving unsolicited advice and critiquing our play styles. Sheryl would always speak up, telling her to relax and stop harassing people.

This mirrored Carrie's behavior in the workplace, which nobody appreciated. We had rarely interacted, as her cubicle was on the opposite side of the department as mine. Still, she was an intelligent computer geek, and was a slightly above average performer in the department. Like Sheryl, she was hired with The Empire a couple years before me.

I did take Raymond up on his invitations every time he hosted a LAN party, lugging my computer, monitor and all hardware accessories to his house. Once all the attendees got their systems organized and set up on a large table, it was an absolute blast.

Multiplayer first person shooters, and driving games were crowd favorites. We'd play from the afternoon on a Saturday into the early hours of the morning fueled by caffeine, taurine, high fructose corn syrup, and crunchy fried processed carbs.

Much like my occasional lunchtime gaming hour, playing games online and at LAN parties with co-workers was great for team spirit. We retained that energy when returning to the workplace.

On our one year anniversary of working for The Empire, Erik, Daphne and I met up at the same sports bar we'd celebrated the day we were hired. We actually kept that tradition up for several years.

As our software kept improving and workload continued to grow throughout the year, everybody in the department kept stepping up their game respectively. Sheryl, Raymond, Erik and I had come forward and volunteered to start supporting the newest product, ReviewPro.

This fancy new product was designed to replace PhotosFirst and PhotoLink. It supported both dial-up and broadband internet connections, making it much easier for our customers to attach appraisal reports *and* photos all in one place to send to insurance carriers.

Having a similar title to ReportsPro proved confusing for customers. They would often call saying they're using ReportsPro but were really using ReviewPro and vice versa.

Not the most wisely selected product names.

Dylan had recently taken a promotional transfer to another department, and a new temp manager Brett was brought on board to oversee new hires for The Dungeon.

Brett had noticed Liam's potential immediately, and informed upstairs management they'd be overlooking a great asset if they didn't soon hire him on as a permanent employee.

Down in The Dungeon by this point was only a staff of seven, with Liam still leading the team. Despite the decreased number of companies using PhotosFirst, there were a few very large clients with many users who were still consistently calling in with a familiar pattern of issues.

Liam had recognized this trend as well as its effect on the team's resources — and they were being worn thin.

As always, he came up with a plan.

The Empire's call logging software still required manual entry for every field. No option existed to store solutions, and there was no function available to easily reflect previous entries for frequent routine calls.

Like veterans in the Media team had taught me, I'd adopted the practice of keeping an open text document containing common procedures and phrases.

This made it **so** much easier to highlight, copy and paste them into different fields without having to tediously type the same long entries every few minutes. It helped, but was less than optimal.

Liam had passed this tip along to The Dungeon team, but he'd formulated a superior method.

He had reached out to Brett and submitted a request for The Empire to purchase several licenses for macro software in order to help automate the logging of familiar calls.

The software request was approved and in a matter of days, Liam had modernized The Dungeon's process for handling a number of routine calls.

After pulling up a customer account, the agent needed only to determine which of the common issues the customer was experiencing, and click on the corresponding button that was set up in the macro software to run the automated scheme Liam had created.

At that point, all required fields, drop-down menus, troubleshooting, and resolution notes were automatically selected and entered, and the case was saved and completed in a matter of *seconds* rather than minutes.

Had The Empire not been planning to upgrade their call logging software later that year, they would likely have utilized Liam's macro process for the entire Tech Support department.

When supervisors saw how efficient and proactive his system had become, they were quite wowed.

Several employees had begun to ask management when they would bring him on to the team, as that kind of energy was exactly what helped the department thrive.

...but it was not to be.

Cold Snap

The Empire would never see Liam hired as a permanent employee.

Ron, along with his fist-pounding curse-splosions had recently retired from The Empire, giving the impression there was an available position in Tech Support, but no.

Brett's position as The Dungeon temp manager had also been eliminated, and a hiring freeze had been temporarily put in place for the Tech Support department due to The Empire having embraced a tighter budget.

They were still constantly pushing improved updates to ReviewPro, and software development isn't cheap.

Liam remained in The Dungeon until mid 2005 when a position opened up in the Accounts department as a data entry/administrative clerk. Though the job wasn't of a primarily technical nature as was preferred, he still applied for the job and listed me as a reference.

Within the week, one of the supervisors from Accounts reached out to ask me personally about Liam's work ethic, project performance, and if he was indeed the fella that had recently made a name for himself down in The Dungeon.

I'd provided them with a brief but bold explanation of how Liam had greatly helped out the team by improving their stagnant workflow procedures, switching things up and boosting efficiency.

The supervisor gave me a pathetic, offensive disappointment of a reply, and it became clear they weren't interested in hiring him.

I was sickened when they elaborated.

They responded that Liam didn't sound at all like a good fit for the Accounts department as they "aren't interested in somebody jamming up the gears" of their procedures. They were comfy with things as they were, and didn't want to put all the employees through learning brand new tricks.

They ended by adding, "Yah, besides, nobody here really likes the sound of being showed up by the new guy."

I hadn't had many interactions with other departments at The Empire outside of Tech Support, and I'll never forget how disappointed and angry I was hearing *that reply* from somebody working at my place of employment.

For this supervisor to so coldly and tactlessly reveal an entire department's laziness, corruption, and abuse of power by dismissing Liam's candidacy as a way to cowardly protect themselves nauseated me.

I brought it up to Jerry that evening at the 5 O'clock meeting, and he understood all too well.

"I wish I could help him out, but Liam's better off not working in Accounts. Their supervisor is a dinosaur who's set in her ways, and been there a little too long. She's grown pretty grouchy a couple years ago and her team is all either like-minded or afraid of her, since she's been quick to snap at people in her later years...

"The thing is: she's set to retire next year, and it wouldn't look very good if they let somebody go right before their retirement; I'm sure the company'd prefer to avoid any lawsuits..."

My guts churned with even more disgust.

The Empire had lost out big-time on a star employee, and I'd lost a large amount of respect for *them*. The amount of time, money, and honest employees' career opportunities being flushed down the toilet in the name of corporate politics had always been palpable — but I'd thought The Empire was above such behavior.

Benchmark naivety.

Liam ended up leaving us that year to work for a competitor in the same industry, quickly finding growth in his career from a company who was wise enough to recognize his potential.

He and I still keep in touch to this day, and he's currently a highly successful Network Infrastructure Engineer.

I could at least be thankful that *my* department was still run by a management staff who embraced and rewarded proactive ideas and hard work.

As long as I stayed within Tech Support, I felt assured I was avoiding any thin ice.

Ironclad Irony

By the middle of that summer, increased call volume began pummeling the payroll budget.

ReviewPro still wasn't as equipped with ample features to impress all of our clients, so PhotosFirst and PhotoLink were still being supported.

The Specialty team was unaffected, but the Media and Reporting teams were beginning to slowly fuse into one large support team, supporting both types of calls.

It was rare to go home without at least a half hour of overtime racked up at the end of one's shift.

The Empire was soon to make a much needed change, upgrading to far superior call logging software that would allow us to publish solutions in a native Knowledge Base with proper search engine. We could finally do away with that old decrepit KB still festering on our intranet!

Upper management decided to throw an *extra* curve ball our way, announcing a new set of procedures intending to help us make better use of our time.

We all spent two weeks with carefully staggered schedules, attending seminars on a problem analysis model designed to quickly and methodically identify causes, and establish solutions.

Though it was a well-known model used in many industries to assist in organizational, manufacturing, and developmental operations, it wasn't the most applicable of models to adopt within our Tech Support department.

The model was created with the intention of finding resolutions to problems.

It wasn't of great use, as the majority of solutions to all of our software's issues were already known. They had already been documented.

Most incoming calls were still "How-To" calls from the customers who still did everything in their power to avoid reading.

We didn't need help *figuring out* solutions, we needed an easier way to *locate* them within our mess of a KB.

The new call logging software would be taking care of that, so why was The Empire wasting big time and money on these seminars?

In the end, all it accomplished was establishing an unnecessarily strict format in which to document case notes and solutions.

We ended up being more strongly graded on the scripted phraseology of our notes instead of accuracy of their content, or our efficiency resolving the calls.

A new column showing average time spent on calls was added to our performance, with those over 30 minutes raising concern. This was absurd, as many of the How-To inquiries for newer customers often far exceeded that.

Additionally, upper management implemented more elements of The Big Six.

Our own manager Peter, along with Marla and Betty weren't thrilled, being made to enforce these new policies.

The very first week they took effect, everyone's performance stats dropped nastily. Most agents who had previously shown to have 95% or more cases wrapped up in two minutes were now showing 60% or below.

My own rate dropped from 98% to 67%, and seeing those results sent my morale to the toilet, as it did everybody's.

Monthly team meetings were filled with negative feedback regarding upper management's changes.

Customer satisfaction had steadily dipped due to longer hold times, as well as now being asked to confirm their billing address and phone numbers upon calling.

To ironically drive it home, Marla ended up using the analysis model to indicate *it in itself* was the cause of decreased performance and customer satisfaction.

Logic suggested the best way to correct the deviation would be to no longer require Tech Support to utilize this supposedly ironclad money-saving model that upper management had so vehemently forced onto the teams.

When the new call logging software finally arrived, the strict policies of the analysis model were temporarily relaxed a bit while we adjusted to the new system, as to allow agents to spend more time writing solutions for its fancy integrated KB.

With customer satisfaction levels on the rise, upper management finally dropped enforcement of the analysis model altogether.

Wouldn't ya know it, we saw continued improvement of customer feedback.

They mentioned specifically that they were much happier with the shorter queues, and that their time wasn't being wasted by being asked for extra account info anymore.

Those Big Six **really** do irk people.

Saturday Shifts & The Unseemly Debacle

I was finally comfortable enough to volunteer for a Saturday Shift. There were no managers or supervisors on duty, so if we were to encounter any major issues, they would have to be addressed the following Monday.

Piece o' cake, that. Clocking out at 11:00 a.m., myself and the three others on the clock had received a total of six calls collectively.

I volunteered often for the easy money, but there was usually a drawing since many people wanted in on the action. As a result, I'd usually only work one Saturday every couple months at most.

That wasn't the only opportunity for overtime, though.

Every company holiday offered the chance to be on a skeleton crew for providing support to those desperate enough to call, and the money was incredible.

If we worked on a holiday, we'd still get our standard holiday pay for the eight hour shift, as well as time and a half for the actual work.

Double time and a half is nice.

As luck would have it, I'd end up getting my way several times working the holidays for extra money, but my first time volunteering that unforgettable year of 2005 ended up giving me more than I'd bargained for.

The December update for ReportsPro turned out to have a nasty treat in store... it broke the software.

The installed program wouldn't launch after that update was run, and all because of a single defect in one file no larger than a few kilobytes.

A couple other elements would make it even more enchanting: as Christmas fell on a Sunday that year, The Empire had closed Friday and Monday to observe and provide their standard two paid days off.

The defect was discovered on the afternoon of Thursday the 22nd when calls started pouring in after lunch.

I wasn't alone working my first volunteered Christmas Holiday, as the entire staff was invited to come in on Friday to address the droves of calls.

Our software developers had worked deep into the hours of the night to have a solution ready by Friday morning. It required nothing more than walking the customers through replacing the defective file with a *fixed* version that had been posted on our support website.

Compared to the daily average of about 600 at the time, the department received over 2,400 calls that fine day.

Luxury Living & Fake Forums

Kelly and I had made some improvements to our budget and spending habits, and by the end of 2005 decided we could afford to upgrade to a larger apartment.

We found a 700 square foot place for $1102/month in a complex just half a mile away. We'd still live in an ideal location for both of our schedules, and were glad to pay a little extra for the breathing room and amenities.

Aside from nearly 300 more square feet of space, the new apartment also had a dishwasher, a washer and dryer in the unit, central air, and very well maintained grounds featuring a large pool and covered outdoor lounge. There were also several generously sized gas grills outside for tenants' use.

To us, that was absolute *luxury*, and it remains the fanciest apartment we've ever lived in.

My annual review had earned me a 3% raise, which for the amount of effort I'd put in to that year was disappointing compared to my previous review.

Marla explained I was doing a great job, and that 3% was the highest any employees in the department received that year due to the tighter budget.

I couldn't help but wonder how much money had been needlessly spent on the blasted problem analysis model seminars, and the steady amounts of overtime resulting from the strict enforcement. Still, I was appreciative to be making nearly $17.00 an hour with a mere one mile commute.

I had no right to complain.

The new call logging software had shown to be everything we'd hoped.

Everybody pitched in submitting solutions to the engineers, who would verify and approve their authenticity before they were officially published and made available in the new KB.

I found technical writing to be fun and gratifying, especially upon seeing how helpful your solutions were to other co-workers. The department's confidence was returning to normal, and the collective performance would fuel the desire for more quality solutions to be published.

By the middle of 2006, there were over 400 solutions in the database. I alone had submitted nearly 250, over 200 of which had been published upon first draft.

My pride in The Empire had been restored to full strength, if only but for a fleeting moment...

Upper management had another bright idea they were eager to pull out of their shorts.

With the newly growing trend of social media eliminating the fear factor of using computers for many, customers were slowly embracing more internet-based methods of support.

Live chat and online tech support forums had started to become popular service models for larger companies to embrace, and studies especially showed forum communities often serving to alleviate a substantial percentage of incoming How-To calls.

The Empire's community support forum was established that year, and it was a complete bust.

Emails were sent, flyers were mailed, and our website was outfitted with banners and marquees to let customers know we now had our very own forums!

All employees were encouraged to create logins with our company email address, and help answer any posted questions between calls, but there was hardly such time to do so.

In reality there wasn't any cause for concern, as our customer base clearly preferred to call for support. They simply weren't using the forums — at all.

Several weeks after release, there were only two customers that had posted their questions on the forum, both of which were answered days later by one of the supervisors.

This didn't go over well with upper management, having spent big bucks on the project.

They should have tapped out and cut their losses, but corporations have investors, and investors have to be pleased.

Upper management had located another study that suggested people were unlikely to use a forum that appears inactive, and *that* convinced them to once again enrage the entire Tech Support department.

In order to reflect an increase of activity of our forums, every employee in the department was **required** to register a secondary login using a fictitious name.

We were then obligated to post a topic, choosing from a generic list of canned questions provided by management. At that point, another member on our team would reply with the answer.

When the activity failed to produce sufficient results, we were all given a quota of *several* required weekly posts using our fictitious names.

Tensions rose, trust was broken, and as usual, both Marla and Betty had our backs.

Together with Peter, upper management was given the real scoop, and after months of the department being beaten up, the forum website was eventually abandoned.

A couple of veterans left The Empire that year, stating they've seen a decline in the quality of environment since "the old days," and they'd had enough.

I as well briefly considered looking for another job due to the scars that these ordeals had left the department with.

It was blatantly undeniable: the upper management of our proud company had started to dabble in decisions that TV shows or comedy films had long poked fun at.

That most dangerous practice of allowing policy to supersede logic has toppled many a company from within.

They never learn.

Still, my wages and benefits outweighed the woes. I had already established a sense of loyalty and pride that was encouraging me to help restore the spirit in the department, and maintain our team's high quality performance.

I decided to stick around, but the funk of upper management's tactics had begun to leave a foul taste in my mouth.

I didn't know it, but I was in for a banquet.

Jane The Schoolmarm

Overly exhausted by upper management, our Tech Support manager Peter left The Empire.

Marla and Betty were still there to root for us, acting as the cushy liaisons trying their best to keep functional relations between upper management, the agents on the front lines, and our new department manager, Jane.

Jane had been promoted from another department after Peter's departure, and she was a perfect caricature of the neutral pantsuit-clad executive that never smiled.

Devoid of any warmth or personality, she viewed The Empire's Tech Support department as an unruly playground — one that needed the strictness of a cold schoolmarm to be groomed and flaunted for dog and pony shows.

Creative buzzwords and methods were brought into play her first week as manager. Expanding scripted introductions and closing statements to include more of The Big Six, and promoting other products and software add-ons were now required.

She could have used a history lesson.

When Marla brought to her concern the recent negative impact such changes had on customer satisfaction, Jane insisted that the previous attempt had been poorly executed.

Betty had extra duties added to her role, and now due to the increased Quality Assurance criteria for our call reviews, there was only time for one review per agent every few months at best. This led to some less seasoned employees losing their edge and falling into bad habits.

It grew more difficult to follow case notes, as details were missing. Repeat calls from customers increased as there were loose ends that needed tying up that were missed during the initial call.

Discipline grew tighter as performance of the overall department began to dip, with verbal warnings and write-ups entering the scene.

The Empire started to occasionally require all employees to skip a lunch break for a mandatory company meeting in which food was provided.

This action was not exactly legal.

Agents began to rebel. A few veterans who had been with The Empire much longer than me ended up reporting the company's lunch meetings to the California Labor Board.

They won.

A small payout was eventually issued to every employee under hire within headquarters during the affected dates.

Aside from general unrest between us and upper management, there was a major issue arising within our call logging software:

It began performing *much* slower.

Jane's strict new policies permitted only so much time on a call for dead air, and expected wrap time was still two minutes. However, after pulling up a customer's account and saving the case, the initial save action which used to take mere seconds was now taking nearly two minutes.

When your mouse cursor is bound that long while you're being recorded and graded on dead air and case efficiency, things get dicey.

Actions like searching the KB, or making the final save to the case after entering the resolution summary took minutes *again*, destroying employees' wrap times and performance statistics.

Some people including myself spoke up, as it was clear that the software was directly affecting our performance.

Unfairly.

Nevertheless, we were told that nothing could be done; all the performance diagnostics the company had continued to run for the software in a test environment showed lightning speed.

The discrepancy that many of us pointed out was that the environment they were using to test it was housing a new, empty database.

Our *live* environment had hundreds of solutions and documentation published, with tens of thousands of cases containing attachments also taking up bandwidth and resources.

The system was sluggish, and *we* continued to pay the price for it.

Only myself and three others had officially come forward, and unless more people spoke up, nothing would be changed.

Speaking privately with many of my peers revealed they were "afraid of what Jane would do" if they complained.

This went on for weeks until I decided to bring up the issue — this time with hard data to submit instead of reporting verbal complaints from others.

At the start of a lunch break, I created a poll via email asking if severe performance delays within the call logging software were being experienced. I also inquired how often it was encountered.

I sent it to every agent in the department.

Though a few never answered it, over 90% responded by the end of the week to confirm severe issues... only one person responding by denying any of course, and that was Carrie.

Regardless that she complained constantly of performance issues, (according to all of her cubicle neighbors), she would proclaim no issues in the poll to both spite me and appear to be the only agent not complaining.

When conferring in private with the agents who *hadn't* responded to the poll, they said they didn't want anything to do with it out of concern of what might happen to them.

The only thing *I* feared was the continued breakdown of open communication between us and upper management. The "open door policy" they proclaimed to hold was looking to be a sham, and I intended to break the department out of this rut of fear.

I submitted my findings to Marla who was very impressed, and she commended me on a job well done of gathering and submitting the data to her. She was eager to show it to upper management.

There was one problem: her assistant Richard.

He had long held an administrative jack-of-all-trades role in Tech Support, very seldom answering calls and taking on more inter-departmental responsibilities over the years.

He'd had even *more* put on his plate since Jane had replaced Peter as manager, as she determined he should be handling more tasks — and he in turn dealt with this newfound stress by way of malice.

Richard embraced the habit of cutting people down and attempting to take credit for others' hard work whenever possible; similar behavior to Carrie's, but graduated to the next level.

I'd never gotten used to his perky, tightly wound demeanor, and true colors had now most definitely been revealed.

Richard was tasked by Marla with bringing important matters to Jane, so *he* was to submit my findings to her.

He also had the opportunity to give it any spin he wished upon presenting.

The following week, I was called into Richard's office. With a gratifying smirk, he let me know that Jane was not pleased to find that I'd wasted company time by creating and sending my poll out to other employees.

When I asked if she had actually *seen* the results of the data and how it's been impacting our performance, I received no answer on the matter.

Richard finished the short meeting (with a toothy grin of superiority) that supposedly, per Jane: if I ever pulled anything like this again I would be let go from the department.

I had never felt so infuriated and threatened at the same time, in or out of the workplace.

Keeping my mouth shut until the 5 O'clock meeting when I spilled the results to my trustworthy peers, I received overwhelming support and gratitude for what I'd at least tried to accomplish.

It was clear that I simply needed to lay low and ride out what was hopefully a temporary hiccup with upper management.

Regrettably, The Schoolmarm's behavior would grow more intense over the weeks ahead, as a new hire was to soon join the ranks.

Jane sent an email to the entire department introducing us to Dave, of whom Jane had personally brought on as an efficiency expert tasked with shaping us naughty little children up.

Overbearing wasn't the word; we felt **gutted.**

We were smart. We were hard workers. We *cared* about our customer base, had pride in both our software and The Empire as a company, and kept pushing to keep our standards high.

Jane didn't see it that way.

As fate would have it, somebody else did.

It was Dave.

Dave took time with every single employee in the department, calling them in one by one to ask how their average day carried out... compared to how it did last year, versus the years before that.

He was direct. He was humorous, and he was personable.

It didn't seem likely that Jane had *intentionally* hired such a cordial, understanding individual.

In less than two weeks, Dave had formulated a plan to improve the performance of the department while simultaneously addressing the growing sullen feedback of customers.

They'd spoken up about the latest policies, voicing that the service had grown tedious.

One customer's survey remarked that it felt as if they were talking to a doctor's office. Others said it wasn't unlike calling a bank being prodded for so much information, after having been a loyal customer for literally decades.

Many other surveys reported similar sentiments.

This consistent feedback had come in droves, and though Marla had always held it as sacred, Jane and upper management had not taken it seriously. She exhibited about as much respect for the customers as she did us agents.

Dave had intentions to trim call scripting and return to a more personable approach to support. He held seeing issues efficiently resolved more importantly than focusing on strict enforcement of case note formatting.

He wanted to encourage speaking to customers comfortably to tend to their needs instead of through coldly crafted criteria.

Dave had been specializing in call center efficiency in both small independent companies, as well as massive corporations for years, and knew exactly what was going on here.

As he called employees in larger numbers back into his office to provide his findings, he spoke candidly.

He explained to us the very real challenge of convincing larger corporations that embraced negative trends such as layoffs, outsourcing, and tightly formulated scripts... to actually loosen the reins and embrace a more human approach to customer service.

Dave then clarified to us one of his career observations that we'd never forget:

It isn't the size of a corporation that leads to their downfall, it's the disconnection from real human interaction. The obsession over excessive quantities of statistics, glorification of temporary numbers, and focusing too intensely on the *short-term* bottom line is the real threat.

Prioritizing the satisfaction of investors who demand instant gratification is what poses the biggest danger of a company's undoing — and if allowed over time, they're **going** to be at the mercy of those conditioned investors who will then burn their company down.

He believed The Empire was nowhere near the point of no return, and was confident they could easily turn things around.

After all, they were still first in the industry among their competitors, just not by much anymore.

We had all been *so* renewed after being called into Dave's office, and so we felt even more incredibly gut-punched when we arrived at work the following Monday to find his office empty.

Jane had been presented with his feedback, and decided she needed him no longer.

The next coming weeks would see a few more veteran employees retire early, while some left to work for competitors.

To replace those lost agents, a couple of temps, Danny and Sarah, were brought in from the last of The Dungeon operation which was then disbanded. All call volumes were now the responsibility of our upstairs department.

Erik had transferred out of Tech Support, and would soon leave The Empire altogether. Daphne was still sticking with me supporting both the Media and Reporting software.

Richard increasingly planted his lips to Jane's backside, firmly establishing himself as upper management's personal yes-man. All the while, Carrie continued to stick her nose into everybody's business, desperately trying to masquerade as a supervisor.

On the flip-side, Jerry's humor never faltered. Victor and I spoke often about our favorite music artists, also finding a mutual appreciation of Mel Brooks films.

Dropping some Mel movie quotes always helps.

5 O'clock meetings continued to provide some release, and strengthen our resolve. Sheryl and I still played *World Of Warcraft* with a few others in the department, and I still had a blast at Raymond's LAN parties.

Marla continued to stick up for us with every fiber of her being. Even in the dark direction that her superiors were pushing everyone, us computer geeks and our immediate supervisors of that battered little department were an incredibly resilient crew.

Our passion and drive was still far too strong to be snuffed out by the likes of Jane The Schoolmarm.

Bottle Bowling & Going Remote

Ben and I had remained cubicle neighbors, still always full of humor to raise the spirits in the office.

We were both on the closing shift, so we enjoyed a few hours a day without Jane's presence as she worked early mornings.

Occasionally in the final hour, he'd blindly toss a toy foam ball over the cubicle wall, attempting to knock down the collection of empty plastic water bottles I'd keep on my shelf before hauling them every week to the recycling bin outside.

"You will never topple this fortress, Ben!" I'd boldly tease his futile attempts.

Finally one day after I tossed the ball back a few times, I thought he'd given up hope as no more attempts were being made.

Sixty seconds later, a phone book came silently sliding over the cubicle wall, dramatically and gloriously *exploding* twenty plus empty plastic bottles like pulverized bowling pins.

A few people slowly wandered over to see what the racket was to find Ben and I silently laughing to tears, crawling on hands and knees to track down every last bottle that had shot out several yards away.

Among them was Jerry, who upon discovering the shenanigans chuckled silently, rolled his eyes and did a one-eighty, shaking his head on the way back to his cube as usual.

Humor was needed in the workplace at the time, as upper management's tricks did a number on more than my morale alone.

Veterans grew bitter the longer they had been there, telling stories of how The Empire had always been the "different" company.

Victor had an impenetrably positive attitude, as he viewed these scandalous tactics as one big game in which to find loopholes, and to play among and around them peacefully.

...The power of positive thinking.

Sheryl was still dealing with it optimistically, while Carrie's demeanor grew darker.

She began to head the direction of the suck-up, the rat. Always passive-aggressively putting people down in and out of meetings, trying to rise up to the top by climbing over all the bodies of which she'd thrown under the bus.

Victor likened her horrific behavior to that of a STASI officer. He and I were always quick to defend our new teammates Danny and Sarah from her jabs, doing everything we could to get them both up to speed with our software's intricacies.

I distanced myself from Carrie and concentrated on my work, as did many others.

I'd found that *distancing* was the best way to deal with petty office drama, but I would never have guessed I'd take it to an extreme when given the opportunity.

The Empire had found another way to cut costs, and it was to everybody's advantage. Real estate was getting more than a little pricey in 2006, steadily building toward the infamous bubble pop of 2008.

Some companies had found success by embracing an optional work-at-home program. As long as employees had a sufficient internet connection, there was no reason they couldn't set up a desk with a company-provided phone and computer to work in the comfort of their own home.

It would quickly free up much precious space in the building.

The Empire began their work-at-home program that year by invitation, and when the offer was thrown my way, I caught it with both hands.

No more upper management funk in the air.

No more having to avoid Carrie The Narc.

No more office drama.

Come late June, I had been issued two company PCs, two monitors, company phone, wireless headset, and an ergonomically approved desk chair. All I had to do was set everything on a desk, plug it all in, and go to work.

Go to work I did. My performance shot back up to the top. I was belting out call resolutions with more relaxed efficiency, and even refining some of my previously published solutions.

I was less stressed, more comfortable, and living only a mile from headquarters — so if for some reason they needed me there in person I could be there without delay, but that was never required.

I could also get in more game time on lunch breaks, and since *Kingdom Hearts 2* had recently released, I *knew* I'd be busy on that front!

What I hadn't realized was that I'd never work inside that headquarters building ever again. I'd no longer smile at a fancy vending machine vacuuming an ice cream bar into a drop slot, never again shoot the breeze at 5 O'clock meetings, or attend any more on-site unwinders.

In fact, nobody else would attend unwinders, either. Jane decided to finally put an end to *that* sheer waste of company money once and for all.

Victor and I wouldn't get to geek out over music in the workplace anymore. Ben had slid his last phone book over the wall. I'd taken my final stroll over to my team lead's cube, and Jerry had chuckled and shaken his head at me in person for the last time.

Northbound

Kelly acquired her Bachelor's degree in summer of 2006, and we now had some decisions to make.

Real estate and rents had been on the rise, and our apartment complex had cranked up their prices as well.

Our rate of $1102 was only an introductory offer for the first year, down from the regular $1250. If we were to renew our agreement at the end of the year, the new rate would be $1400 a month to keep the apartment. That was a bit excessive for our budget.

We loved the area in which we lived, but a small three bedroom fixer upper there was over half a million dollars, and the prices weren't slowing.

My parents and immediate family had still been residing in Tigard, Oregon the last few years. Up there, one could purchase an older four bedroom house on a quarter acre or more for a mere $85,000.

Kelly had graduated with the intention of becoming a teacher, so as soon as we pondered the possibility of moving out of state, she'd already worked some numbers.

The starting salary in most districts in and around Tigard for a full time teacher was $29,000 a year. That was only $2,000 less than the starting salary in San Diego, and for the difference in cost of living it was well worth it.

After phoning several government offices, we were told that the expected time to convert a California teaching license to an Oregon license was just two weeks.

We had no down payment, but I had an advantage of working remotely. I could move anywhere in the country quickly and conveniently.

We decided to give Oregon a try.

Not wanting to spend the time or money to travel back and forth to look at apartments, we were pleasantly surprised that we had the option of applying online for a two bedroom, 900 square foot apartment for $640/month.

I'd never dreamed I'd see rents so affordable again for such a large apartment. Compared to the cost of living we were used to, it sounded like another world.

ELEVEN

Another World

Welcome To The Neighborhood

"Mike wake up! ...there's an ambulance outside and I saw a body on the sidewalk..."

It hadn't yet been a week since Kelly and I started adjusting to the damp weather of the Pacific Northwest, and she'd had a horrifically rude awakening from the siren-chirp of a vehicle pulling up outside our apartment building.

"All I saw was a body on the sidewalk with some blood on the ground, and I looked away as fast as I could."

She was still shaken, as one would expect.

We both stayed inside until the coroner's van left, leaving a few officers who were talking to the apartment manager and a few concerned tenants.

I was soon clocked in and tied to my work phone, so Kelly went out to inquire about the overall safety of the neighborhood to ensure this seemingly peaceful complex was truly that.

Trying my best to listen from inside, I could hear an officer trying to provide as much comfort as possible.

"Absolutely, this is a **very** safe and peaceful neighborhood... appears to have been a suicide..."

Having never been that close to the scene of a crime or fatality, I myself was in a mild stupor without even having shared a glance at the grim scene.

The air remained thick until nightfall, upon joining my parents for dinner.

They also reassured us of the safety of our neighborhood after hearing about our morning.

After remaining wary for a few days, we began to sleep more soundly.

We even grew accustomed to the occasional profanities being spewed from the elderly man who lived in a unit across the parking lot.

The bimonthly ritual of police cars pulling into the complex became ordinary, responding to the calls from the man's irritated neighbors. It seems they didn't relish the codger's unique ramblings being broadcast to their children through open windows.

This was our new neighborhood, and we would remain resolute in seeking to find some charm within its initially soggy, dim exterior... or find another.

I'll allow you to wager how that played out.

Rodents On Lawns

I'd never seen a nutria in the flesh before, much less an entire colony chowhounding on a field of freshly bedewed grass.

Rodents of undeniably unusual size, they have the face of a snub-nosed beaver with brighter whiskers and *massive* pair of dull bronze teeth.

They're not aggressive toward humans, scaring and scattering easily, but being herbivores with seemingly bottomless stomachs, they're quick to destroy entire crops if left unchecked.

Seen here and there all over town by creeks, ponds, and water-holes, their presence was sparsely staggered enough to not be of real concern.

Larger numbers were regularly seen congregating in the early morning on the front plot near the parking lot.

In lieu of a cartoon scene showcasing a saccharin sunrise, full of chirping hummingbirds sipping nectar from dewy honey-suckles, we instead were blessed with this view of mutant beaver-rats tearing up a patch of lawn.

Eyes squinting, teeth grinding...

Something to cherish.

Yet, they weren't alone. Little had we known that another genus thrived with unwavering stoicism merely blocks away.

We'd discovered this specimen while driving home from the grocery store one day. We'd taken an early right turn into the adjacent neighborhood to explore some side streets.

Kelly and I performed a unison double-take as we passed this monstrous being before insisting to turn around for a second look.

Castor Ligneum.

With powerful haunches firmly flexed, there it stood in the front yard of a nearby residence at a staggering seven feet tall.

Examining the creature from the road at a safe distance, it was determined that this beaver was of a thick, presumably oaken build proudly clutching a large display board. Upon it were the meticulously recorded stats of the Oregon State University football team's latest games.

After our fair moment of observation and avoiding direct eye contact, we quietly moved on as to not spook the beast, leaving it in peace.

Truly the proud mammals in those parts.

Kelly and I have never seen anything like it, and we've yet to encounter any others in its class. My only regret was not capturing a photo, but I suppose it really wasn't necessary.

You don't forget a sighting like that.

A Bag, Lady

Succulent slow-cooked bourbon meatballs were a regular item at one of the local grocery store chains, and it was only a matter of time before we realized something else had a common presence:

The sanctimonious.

Quick to find ways of looking down upon you without even having been invited to a dinner party, these folks were quite a treat.

The second time we visited the store, we'd entered the check-out line with a half-pound carton of bourbon meatballs, a small container of fresh cheese curds, and a couple vegetables.

Upon answering, "Yes, please," to the cashier, she proceeded to insert our purchases into a standard plastic bag.

As she handed us our groceries and receipt with a thank-you, our return thanks was interrupted by the squawking of a miserable shrew behind us in line.

We slowly turned away to the exit, but the old hag wasn't through speaking her piece.

Making sure we were in earshot of her audible antigen, she began speaking to the cashier upwards of 60 decibels while strategically glaring at *us* before she'd even set her few groceries on the conveyor belt:

"Well, **I** won't need a bag, miss, and *certainly* not a *plastic* one!"

After grinning upon fantasizing the possibility of her dentures falling out of her loud gob and into her garbage disposal when she arrived home, I tried to put the encounter out of my mind. I didn't want to associate that store with negativity due to the condescending ravings of this one lone grouchy patron.

We laughed it off, and continued to the parking lot.

Later that month after a couple more visits to the same store, that positive effort was blasted to smithereenies when my wife and I had purchased some more groceries, among which happened to be a bottle of craft beer.

I was asked to show some ID. As we were in our mid 20s, it was obviously anything but strange for one of us to be carded upon paying.

Yet, after showing mine, the young clerk who looked like he'd hardly graduated high school gave my wife a suspicious gaze.

"Um... and I'll need to check your ID too."

We'd never yet *both* been asked to show identification when checking out of a grocery store, so it came off as a little strange.

My wife asked in surprise, "Oh! Okay... really? Both of us? But my husband is paying with his card."

She received a condescending reply, with attitude.

"Yes, **everybody** in the checkout party needs to be 21 to purchase alcohol."

That wasn't accurate, as we had already purchased alcohol prior there, and only one of us had been asked.

Kelly mentioned this to the young cashier as he returned a pompous response.

"Well, that *is* our store policy. Someone must not have remembered last time you checked out."

He never even blinked.

Kelly couldn't help herself, holding back her laughter as she popped another question.

"Soooo what would happen if an entire family is shopping — two parents with children? I mean, we have relatives here who have two 5 year old kids... are you saying they can't pick out a wine for themselves to have with dinner if their kids are with them in line?"

He quivered as his eyes widened further, appearing offended that my wife dare mention such an act!

"Ummm... well *yah,* why would you *want* to? That's not something people do, I mean — you don't buy alcohol in front of younger children, that's irresponsible. You just don't ***do*** things like that."

It wasn't a prank; the kid was completely serious.

As he handed us the receipt and we took our groceries, our eyes must surely have been as wide as his were by that point.

Where in the *world* had we moved to?

Shiny

Blankets of thin raindrops fell with a bleak, perpetual despondency. It hadn't let up in several months, and the daily dosings of soggy sprinklings had begun to take their toll.

Only when cranking up the apartment heater full blast would we be granted a respite from the chewy chill in the air; inescapable weight of frigid humidity hung tenaciously like a millstone pendant.

It's a very different type of rain in that part of the West Coast. The droplets came down as if they *themselves* were dejected and sapped of enthusiasm.

Southern California's rain is decisive and willful.

Your skin feels the impact through a sweatshirt when getting pelted by California rain, and heaven help you if you happen to be riding a roller coaster amidst a mighty downpour. It's not unlike having large handfuls of jagged popcorn kernels hurled toward your face by a young child.

It stings.

Ah, but not this rain. This perfunctory drizzle — carrying at best a 2.0 grade point average, served only to turn delivered newspapers into strips of oatmeal, and rob your soul of its warmth and ambition.

Though, a plus was that our car was *never* so consistently shiny.

Before long, we both inevitably entered a mild state of depression. There wasn't much exciting to do outdoors under a constant drizzly rain, so we'd begun spending most of our free time and money exploring local coffee shops, pubs and restaurants.

Happy hour in Tigard and, well, most every city within 30 miles of Portland — are some of the best I've experienced.

Though the usual dollar-off deals, tap discounts, and pitcher specials are as present as anywhere else, no pubs or cafes in any other area I've visited has ever impressed me with such incredibly low-priced food.

Most all of the time, it was *done right*, too.

Everywhere we went, fried foods were light and crispy, neither burnt nor saturated with excess oil. Baked goods were succulent and savory, appetizers were prompt and toasty warm... many at the average price of $4.00 or less.

Upscale steakhouses with normal menu entrees of $50 and up would even participate, offering a medium rare ground chuck cheeseburger and fries for a mere five bucks...

And, let me tell you: public houses in Oregon **know** how to pour a beautiful, sexy pint of Guinness.

Many places in SoCal neglect the importance of taking one's time performing the proper dance with a nitro tap.

The beverage must be respected and not rushed, as a disgraced nitro drink served as callously as one with carbon dioxide will fill a guest with contempt rather than comfort.

Done right, a lovely pint of Guinness resembles that of a fancy liquid tuxedo.

Happy hour and the food scene was the only thing that seemed to stave off my sour attitude, having been born and raised with Southern California's weather.

My body and mind *didn't know* how to handle months on end without sunlight.

As it would turn out, some locals we'd speak to about our recent move had empathized, and they would occasionally complain about it as well.

"It really never stays this wet without a break."

"We usually get all four seasons but summer came and went in a week."

"Yah this year sucks."

It did.

During that year we moved north, all surrounding counties near Portland inclusive had beat out Seattle, Washington for the number of overcast and rainy days. It would do so again for the following year.

Lucky us.

I'm not saying California didn't have some miserable days at times; the Santa Ynez Valley would often reach 110°F for a few weeks every summer, but it's rather pleasant indoors with air conditioning and fresh bright sunlight illuminating the premises with cheer.

Though I didn't relish Tigard weather, I didn't go around verbally proclaiming Oregon was a depressing place. I kept trying my best to stay positive, but at times, society made it difficult.

Learning not to mention we'd recently moved from Southern California was a lesson fully absorbed within the first few months.

To be clear, *some* locals welcomed us warmly, but a couple times a week, we'd get an earful either from the party we were speaking with, or a nearby eavesdropper who'd twitch and convulse upon hearing the name of this location of which they did not speak of.

I'll never forget the first time it happened.

I was shopping for some fine cigars at a local tobacco shop when the middle aged muumuu-clad clerk had recommended some ***great*** local stouts to enjoy with the cigars.

They really knew their stuff, and were very kind-spoken up to that point.

Upon cashing out, I'd mentioned having recently moved from California, and remarked that although the prices for beer and liquor seemed substantially higher in Oregon, the selection and variety of craft beer styles was far superior at the time.

Before I'd finished that sentence, the whites of the clerk's eyes had already grown a shade of red, and begun to enter a squint as she stared into space formulating a real slammer to lay upon me while taking my payment.

"OH. Yes. You mean **PEOP-le's Re-PUB-lic of CA-lif-ORN-ia?** I can't *imagine* living there. It's no wonder the booze is so much cheaper since you'd have to be an alcoholic to ***tolerate*** life in that state..."

She continued with a scoff, rolling her eyes with a sneered upper lip.

Near speechless, a fake chuckle leaked out from my lips in shock. I took the receipt that she'd slapped on the glass counter, gave a quietly nervous thank-you as she remained silently sneering, and walked out of there for the first and last time.

That was by far the most direct and abrasive act of interstate prejudice I'd encountered whilst living in the Pacific Northwest, but it wasn't the last.

In retrospect, due to it being the *first*, it served to moderately desensitize me. I actually grew used to it as time went on and the real estate bubble grew closer to bursting.

You see, droves of other born-and-raised Californians had the idea to tap out and move north before *we* had thought of it. This caused more than a mild economic upset.

A large number of locals could no longer afford to buy a home, thus a minority of Oregonians were quick to insult us once it was revealed where we'd hailed from.

We'd learned to craftily avoid the subject.

Aside from eating out for dinner nearly ever other day, I still found joy playing *World Of Warcraft*, as well as *Guitar Hero 2*, and *Guitar Hero Encore: Rocks the '80s*, with my younger sister.

A few TV shows also helped me escape to a happy place.

Before I had left San Diego, a co-worker had turned me on to the legendary series, *Firefly*, which instantly took its place alongside some of my other favorite TV shows: *The Twilight Zone*, and *The Wild Wild West*.

I must have watched the entire series and the followup movie, *Serenity*, a good five times that first year of our move. It served relatable and therapeutic, observing many characters traveling to distant places in which *they* felt uncomfortable and leery.

It preserved my calm.

I wasn't the only one who needed a change; soon after we moved, Ben, Sheryl, and Carrie had decided they'd had enough of the dreary vibe back in the physical workplace, and they all joined the remote way of life.

Likewise, they all left California and found cheaper places to live.

With gracious timing, a boost to my outlook was found in my next annual review. It was my first one held over the phone, and exactly what I needed.

Getting away from the drama of The Empire's on-site environment was a bigger boon to my performance than I'd expected. It was revealed that many high-profile customers had mentioned their satisfaction of my service skills to management.

Now that January had rolled around again, Marla wanted to make sure I was rewarded for all my hard work. I'd submitted hundreds of published solutions, while there were multiple agents with a tenure double the length of my own who had yet to submit a single one.

I was promoted to Technical Support Agent II along with an incredible 24% raise which brought me to over $21 an hour.

Shiny!

Condensation

Mildew would regularly show up on the bottom frame of our apartment's sliding glass door if we didn't wipe it down with alcohol or bleach every other day. The inescapable humidity matched with an older apartment building served a great breeding ground for spore growth.

That went for our windows, as well.

We never had any serious mold issues, as we were meticulous with our cleaning habits. That's not to say we didn't have any bouts with the apartment management regarding some unaddressed concerns.

Our bedroom window was facing the front parking lot, which happened to be on the receiving side of the steady winds that *always* steered the falling rain directly against it.

For several months out of the year, this caused the window channels to become flooded. Water would fill up and flood the wells, then spill over the sill dripping down onto the carpet.

Steadily, twenty-four seven.

We started going through a roll of paper towels every three days on account of stuffing them into the window wells to prevent overflow whilst we slept.

Of course, windows have long been designed with a counter-measure to combat this sort of situation, called weep holes.

The channels of windows have holes or slots on the bottom and outside edges allowing the welled up water to drip outside and save your inside walls and carpet from flooding.

Upon personally inspecting our bedroom's external wall, I saw that one of the weep holes on the outside of the window had been clogged with paint used to last touch up the building. I was able to scrape and peel it off easily in a single tiny chunk, only to reveal that the inside of the weep hole had been long rusted shut.

The other was all but nearly clogged solid as well with a combination of dirt, rust and debris.

I didn't have the tools to properly clear the obstruction, so I put in a call to management. My request was quickly denied, as I was told, "Oh, that's normal, it only *looks* like they're clogged... that water you're getting inside is probably from condensation dripping down the window."

It wasn't.

During the steadiest of downpours, Kelly and I would dry off the inside of our window and soak up all the fluid in the channel — only to see the rain quickly well up inside, flood, and start dripping down the wall *again* in a matter of minutes.

Condensation isn't such a nimble process.

After the second week of calling every other day, management finally grew tired of our complaints and dispatched maintenance to come take a look.

They happened to come in the afternoon when lo and behold, the rain had completely stopped for about an hour, so there was no flooding for them to see. There *was* indeed however, a small amount of condensation on the windows by then.

How very strategic of them.

Sporting faded blue denim coveralls, in walked a frowning grouch of a being, successfully avoiding eye contact with us the full duration of his stay. He spoke with mild drawl in a deep gravelly voice while delivering the first preemptive jab.

"I'm here ta check your windows for condensation."

We let him in and told him it was only the bedroom window, but restated that our issue was the sill being flooded from active rain, so it wasn't happening at that very moment.

Our comment went selectively unheard.

He took out a cloth, wiping down all four corners of the window, breathed long and hard a couple of times, nose whistling with air and never breaking his passionless, grizzled gaze.

In a picture-perfect curmudgeonly disgruntled fashion with hands on hips, he stood back, smacked his lips, inhaled once more and let that gravelly voice of his blurt out:

"Con-den-*SAY*-shun!"

That was his diagnosis, stagnant and miserable.

Nearly mute with anger, Kelly spoke up asking if he would come back when it was raining to see the actual problem we called about, but the guy wouldn't be bothered. He mentioned that they had many other *higher priority* issues they needed to address on the grounds.

The reputation of property management sunk for us that day, and was a timely match to the dip in teamwork at The Empire.

Keeping up with my submissions of solutions, I'd crafted a 15 page presentation to address The Empire's most glaring and costly call: database corruption.

Occasionally customers would launch ReportsPro to find that all of their saved reports appeared to be either missing, or not able to be opened due to receiving database corruption errors.

This was caused primarily by three common scenarios:

The first was overtaxing computer resources, such as using five or even ten workstations connected to a makeshift server running Windows XP... which wasn't designed to handle that workload.

This would cause delays between the server and workstations, leaving our software figuratively tapping its fingers and giving up. The database would get cut off halfway through its latest save. Hello, corruption.

A second scenario was when customers installed Antivirus software without adding exclusions to allow our software to function uninhibited.

Existing reports could be *opened*, but when the customer tried to make changes or save, the Antivirus software blocked part of the database from being fully written to, corrupting it.

Keep in mind, that *is* an Antivirus's job. It's a security measure. That's what it's supposed to do: protect the files on your hard drive from being written to or modified by malicious software.

They're not perfect, and when leaving them at their default settings, Antivirus programs can only "guess" based on common algorithms, at which programs and files to block or allow.

Nevertheless, these calls would come in, and our software would be blamed.

A comparative analogy would be dropping off your car at a detailing service without leaving the key, then blaming and berating *them* for not being able to clean the inside of your vehicle.

The third main cause was frequent power outages. Some customers were in rural areas in which power outages were common, but they didn't see fit to purchase an uninterrupted power supply.

Using one *would* have kept their computer running for a few minutes to save their work and shut down until power was restored.

These scenarios are all easily preventable by following the most basic of office equipment maintenance practices, but many customers didn't want to spend a few minutes to make a daily or weekly backup, or upgrade their computers to meet system requirements.

Causes aside, these calls were usually no less than an hour long as we'd have to use a proprietary utility to repair the database. After this lengthy procedure, we'd need to manually export every accessible report, then import them to a fresh clean *empty* database to help prevent future issues.

Both the export *and* import procedures would each take about 2 to 3 seconds per report, and most customers had several hundreds or even thousands saved.

If the database was *too* corrupt for the repair tools to actually fix it, the saved reports were toast. We'd then be at the mercy of searching the hard drive for any backups the customer may have made.

Yah, right.

Our software even came equipped with a utility to easily make a backup of all reports in three mouse clicks. Though this backup procedure finished in often less than 30 seconds, most customers rarely used it.

"That takes too much time. You don't realize how busy we are..."

They often changed their tune and would start making backups after realizing that exponentially *more* time was wasted on repairing the corruption.

Enter one of the loudest battle cries of tech support agents: **"Always Make Backups!"**

We're honestly just trying to save you time, money, and heartbreak from loss of data.

My presentation was well organized and easy to follow. It had been designed to be *so* easy to read that for the first time, all new first level tech support agents would be able to handle the calls with a full understanding of the errors, their causes, and simple steps to reach resolution.

Not surprisingly, many of them didn't want to deal with these customers as they were infamously [and quite understandably] the most angry, and unpleasant to work with.

Exploitation was easily found; they'd stall, abuse hold times, and run the clock. After racking up twenty minutes without showing much progress, they'd be instantly approved by a supervisor to escalate a "longer call" to second level agents, passing off the workload.

I found this dishonorable not only to the agents, but more importantly, the customer.

As a result, our overall confidence and trust in our co-workers fizzled a bit, causing a rift in the department between veterans and many lazy first level agents.

This exploitation was pointed out, but wasn't ever addressed, despite repeat behavior.

There in our apartment, Kelly growled in exasperation, struggling to unwrap the stubborn plastic of another paper towel roll to sop up the next flood one room away.

I kept my finger hovering over the mute button, ready to prevent my headset from picking up any of Kelly's potential shouts of rage.

Pair that with the recent echoes of being told by maintenance staff that your trials of window flooding were merely "con-den-*say*-shun" and there you have another fine afternoon in the Pacific Northwest.

With our apartment management having proven undeniably useless, we'd already begun scouting out *other* apartment complexes that weren't run by crooks or incompetents.

We'd soon find one that wasn't overly unpleasant...

At first.

Ghetto Springs

We'd been in Oregon nearly a year, and we'd started to adjust to suffering the onslaught of water spillage into our abode. I was having a hard time with the environment, but was still loving the aspect of sustained peace in working remotely.

Kelly's patience however, was dwindling.

Though being told her teaching license would be converted in a matter of weeks, it had taken the better part of a year.

The county office was inundated with requests in the weeks before we'd moved due to the influx of Californians moving northbound. Both states had started seeing a bloated job market for teachers.

Our spirits were raised when we found a quaint little apartment complex in Northwest Tigard called "Meadow Springs."

We were given a tour of the lush grounds which boasted gorgeously kept fields of grass and flowerbeds complete with active running streams. Recirculated water flowed from five different sources of beautifully arranged rocks with pleasant balance throughout the complex.

The management was very down-to-earth, and the one bedroom apartment we looked at appeared to be in great shape — especially the windows, which we both took great care to inspect.

New carpet, freshly painted walls, washer and dryer in unit, and front and back covered balconies?

Sold!

We moved in for the bargain price of $680/month, sacrificing one bedroom which we didn't really need; the living room had plenty of space for me to set up my computer desk in one corner.

By the time we'd settled in, Kelly had obtained her converted teaching license, and had registered with close to 20 schools within the closest districts. She had made herself available as a substitute teacher for the 2nd grade, until she could find a permanent position.

She kept constant daily communication with a dedicated staffing agency, but was only finding a single day of work once a month at best, even when making herself flexible to cover other grades.

The *one* time she took a slot for a single day to teach Kindergarten on a Monday, those little changelings gifted her with a plethora of germs to bring home, bacterial and viral alike.

We both suffered pink eye, bronchitis, earaches and sore throats later that week, and she vowed never to take a slot for Kindergarten again.

While she continued to do everything in her power to keep looking for a teaching job, I kept doing my thing. I answered call after front line call, and took as many escalations as I could.

It was about that time I'd hit the *sweet spot* of The Schoolmarm Era with The Empire.

I didn't have to speak with anybody face to face in the office or tolerate any stress in the physical workplace. I could focus peacefully without any interruptions or distractions.

I was able to wear shorts and a t-shirt every single day in complete comfort.

Kelly and I had traveled back to Santa Barbara County that June of 2007 to get married, which left us quite rejuvenated after being reminded what the sun looked like.

Our living conditions remained pleasant until mid-Autumn, when the true colors of Meadow Springs slowly came up to surface from beneath their deceptive first impressions.

Empty beer bottles rolling around in the parking lot became commonplace, along with trash and people letting their dogs take a dump on sidewalks and driveways.

I once witnessed our neighbors, (who had moved in about the same time as we did), catching one of said dog walkers in the act. They had let their dog do its thing in the middle of our sidewalk without cleaning it up and started walking away when my neighbor spoke up.

"Hey, uh... are you gonna pick that up, man?"

"Psh. *You* pick it up," was shot back with a pretentiously superior tone.

Reporting the behavior to management proved useless, so one had to watch where they stepped every week until maintenance made their rounds.

It had also become abundantly clear that the beautiful flow of water had stopped on more than one occasion. When inquiring with management, they said it was temporary and that the fountains were under repair.

They were not.

This was a lie, and we soon caught on to their little game.

We'd gotten to know several members of their maintenance staff due to an ongoing issue with our clothes dryer not functioning very well. It would take a good 2 hours for a couple towels and one pair of jeans to fully dry, and during their troubleshooting visits it was quickly revealed that they didn't mind throwing management under the bus.

One guy finally spilled the beans about the fabricated springs throughout the property.

"Oh yah, they've done this for years. They turn them off as often as possible outside of spring and summer to save money, and only turn'm on here and there when they're showing off the property to new renters."

As for the trash and alcohol bottles, the management had become lax on their security staff at night, enabling loud tailgate parties in the complex's rear parking lot to go unchecked.

Some vehicles started getting broken into, so we had to start making sure nothing visible was left in the cab of Kelly's car.

As I'd hardly needed to use my sedan since I was working at home, I ended up selling it to our friendly neighbors for a mere $300, *happy* to get rid of it as it had started requiring constant small repairs. My neighbors enjoyed tinkering with cars, so they said it would serve them as a hobby project of sorts.

We had a few run-ins with *additional* neighbors a few units down that were less than pleasant.

We were outside getting ready to leave with our *good* neighbors to go out to eat one day when one such resident drove around the corner in a Lexus, shouting at us out the window.

"HEY. Have you seen anybody stealing bags of recycling cans off my rear balcony?! I *swear* I saw two girls around my place in the back parking lot eyeballing them and they looked a whole lot like **you two!**"

He pointed at Kelly and my neighbor's wife.

We all chuckled uncomfortably, as we didn't even know how to handle such an accusation.

I shouted back, "Nope, not us. Somebody else must have climbed up there and stolen them."

My neighbor's wife then reprimanded him, pointing out that he had some nerve driving around and accusing innocent people of theft.

He retorted with twitchy body language that he needed those cans for gas money for his car, and she responded again:

"Well maybe you should have bought something less expensive than a Lexus if you can't afford to fill the gas tank..."

She waited to complete her sentence until after he drove off, still twitching.

"...or maybe lay off the drugs, dude!"

The same month, yet another nearby resident had to be told by apartment management to stop using his fireplace in lieu of a paper shredder.

He had been incinerating old newspapers and magazines, prompting several concerned calls to management about the nasty stench and smoke coming from his place.

This was all child's play compared to the adventure we'd yet to endure at that fine establishment.

Things came to an all time low on December 31st at 9:00 p.m. That's right — on New Year's Eve, our neighbors had joined us for a small party in our living room, and the rain had been falling steadily for about its 12th hour when we all... noticed something...

Next to one of our media shelves about six inches down from the ceiling, a small bulge began to form within the wall... the same wall shared with our very neighbors who were presently in the room.

Once in a while, a very small droplet of water would trickle out from a pin sized hole in the growing mass.

It was 9:15 when we finished the board game we were playing, and we figured it would probably be a good idea for me to box up all the DVDs from the shelf in case the growing lump decided to burst.

I made quick work of it, and called to leave a message with maintenance at 9:20. I gave them a quick description of what we noticed, informing them we were experiencing the beginnings of what looked like imminent water damage.

By 9:45, we hadn't heard anything back and were getting nervous as the mass continued to grow. Realizing it was probable that they didn't actively check their messages, we ended up calling the emergency pager number that was provided to us by the office, as this definitely qualified.

Moments later, we got a call from a huffy employee asking *why* he was getting a maintenance call on New Year's Eve, complete with a belittling rant.

I gathered he was perhaps calling back angrily interrupted from a rollicking New Year's Eve party, as his tone and choice of vocabulary was *very* much suspect to having enjoyed one too many.

After clarifying to him that the reason for calling so late was that in fact the drip had truly just begun, and it was *not* an orchestrated stunt designed to foil his New Year's Eve, he changed his attitude and realized he would need to grace us with his presence.

He showed up within the hour, and remedied the situation by opening his pocket knife, puncturing the water bulge that had grown to the size of a deformed apple, and letting 12 ounces of water flow freely down the wall, splashing onto the thick shag carpet.

Lovely.

Well, at least there was **some** water flowing at Meadow Springs once more...

I was glad I'd moved my DVDs.

He apologized, realizing that it could have been handled a bit better, but said there wasn't much else to do at the moment other than to plop a towel on the floor and wait until the morning when the main office was open. He confessed to seeing this happen before in a couple other units over the recent years, and the leak would have to be found by having an expert check the roof and/or possibly cutting open the wall or ceiling.

After he left, my neighbor laughed and told me that he'd gone to high school with the guy, but didn't know him all that well — only that he had a reputation for not being the brightest bulb in the box.

It was days before somebody was available to check the roof and repair the outside leak, which was so large, it had started affecting our neighbors as well. Their fireplace located on the other side of the wall had pooled up about a quarter inch of water.

A nice wide brown spot had formed on our ceiling over the weekend due to the prolonged moisture, and a good sized chunk of drywall would need replacing. Maintenance said they'd send somebody over soon and would need as much of the room cleared out as possible.

I moved out every shelf, couch and coffee table from that half of the living room, storing it and stacking it in the bedroom as best we could for what I was told would be a one day repair.

It was not.

The maintenance crew sent somebody over late in the afternoon on January 4th with a ladder and saw to cut open the affected area. He spoke mostly Spanish, so I tried to follow along remembering as much as I could from high school.

I was able to make out that he would need to cut open the ceiling, let it air out for at least two days to be sure all the moisture had gone, then return to seal it back up.

The makings of the next live comedy skit had begun.

He laid a large black tarp on the carpet, propped up the ladder and ascended. Moments later, the first two long cuts of a rectangular shape into the ceiling were made.

After the third cut, the merriment ensued.

Even with the support of his hand under the sliced drywall, the sheer weight of a saturated pink and gray marbled cloth-like substance forced open the ceiling flap as the maintenance guy let out a cartoon-like, "Aiiiiiiiiiiiiiigh!"

All over his head fell clump after clump of unknown pulpy-stuffs eventually slapping onto the floor in a nasty wet pile.

When the mysterious avalanche was over, a four by four foot mound about two feet tall consisting of a mixture of soggy fiberglass insulation and dryer lint — yes, dryer lint — had made its way out of the attic space and onto the gratefully tarp-covered carpet.

My neighbor had heard the maintenance guy's cry and came over to see if everybody was okay.

We were all three soon laughing in both shock and disgust at what we were seeing.

The maintenance guy called for backup, and it would be another day before the following was discovered:

Several years back when the apartments were remodeled to accommodate washers and dryers, the dryer vent in our unit was supposed to have been installed like all the others, straight up and out through the roof.

Instead, it was all screwdey-whompus...

Without details as to the *why*, it was explained that a thick ceramic tile plate within the walls was right in the way of the intended path. In order to save time and money cutting through the plate, the previous maintenance team had improperly routed the dryer's exhaust hose up into the attic space.

Installing metal ducting, they then ran it above the entire living room ceiling and out the apartment's front attic wall vent.

This allowed for small particles of moist dryer lint over the past decade to have become stuck in the vent, causing moisture to collect in one of the duct joints and slowly corrode it.

At some point in time, this part of the metal duct snapped, and the gap in the duct-work became a convenient exit for the dryer lint to escape and pile up in the attic right on top of the drywall.

The amount of debris trapped above the ceiling grew over the years, and the recent heavy rain over past weeks had found its way into a leak in the rooftop.

The weight of the already damp dryer debris combined with that of the new roof leak slowly swelled the fiberglass insulation until it could simply hold no more, finding the next most convenient points of release...

Our ceiling, our wall, and the neighbor's fireplace.

The ladder, tarp, and pile of slop remained in my apartment for several more days, our furniture still cramped up in our bedroom all the while.

Come the morning of January 7th, I curiously climbed up the ladder myself and took a peek into the gaping hole in the ceiling. I saw there was still a slow active drip coming from the broken duct, and a dank smell of mildew amongst the remaining insulation and bits of lint that had been ejected all over the top of the ceiling panel from past years.

When the same maintenance guy who had cut open the ceiling had been sent back to patch it up that afternoon, I tried my best to tell him that I could still see and smell dank moisture in the ceiling as of that morning.

I couldn't understand him or read his expression well enough to grasp whether my poor Spanish skills were incomprehensible, or if he didn't care.

He patched it up anyway, leaving all the defunct duct-work and moist insulation as it was.

About an hour later, I had a freshly patched corner of living room ceiling. The ladder, messy pile of debris and tarp had been removed. I vacuumed the living room and called the maintenance manager to let them know that though the ceiling was patched, I was concerned about having still seen and smelled musty moisture dripping about in the attic.

They told me not to worry, confident the rest of the moisture would evaporate through the front attic vents of the building. They shared their plans to correctly vent my dryer straight up and out the very next day to prevent a repeat scenario.

They made good on their word, and by the following night they'd finished *correctly* installing the dryer vent.

Its performance had increased substantially, now able to dry a load of towels in 90 minutes instead of two hours.

Out of concern, I did mention the time it still took in general to dry a load of laundry, and the maintenance supervisor wasted no time again blaming apartment management.

"Yaaaaah, they do take foreeeever. These cheap little units are 110s, not 220s, they're pieces o' crap. They know it, but management isn't willing to spend any more on them, so this is as good as it gets."

For all my troubles of having no living room, and a bedroom stuffed full of furniture for a week of inconvenience, we were given no compensation toward our rent.

Considering all our adventures, Kelly and I decided it was probably time to move on from *Ghetto Springs*, and sooner rather than later.

I still have the text file I'd used to document all the events with dates and times from that ordeal, as well as photos and a video I took on my phone of the entire mess.

I got a great shot of the wet slop on the living room floor, complete with a peek inside the hole in the ceiling, dripping with remnants of wet lint from the past tenants of years gone by.

I occasionally break the video out at parties, and it's always a hit.

Mold, Mold, Mold!!!

Looking for a decent place to rent in Tigard and its surrounding cities was challenging in more ways than one.

The entire reason we'd moved north was to seek an affordable place to live and eventually buy a house, and the harsh reality was setting in that prices were steadily on the rise.

With Kelly battling a saturated job market, giving us only one steady income for nearly two years, our future in Oregon wasn't looking stellar.

Kelly's longest temporary assignment landed her in a classroom that happened to have several students that were on the "disciplinary program."

Naughty little kids.

The average for a classroom was only one or two, but she lucked out with a month-long assignment for a class containing eight of these supposed little monsters.

In the end, it wasn't the children that broke her.

It was the system.

At several scheduled times each day, the teachers were to wear a small digital device around their neck that beeped and vibrated like a pager every sixty seconds.

In the midst of teaching, whether she was reading a book to the class, giving a lecture, or tending to individual students' questions, she'd have to mark a chart with 10+ columns to reflect the behavior of each student on the disciplinary program.

Were they distracted? Were they talking without being called on? Were they yelling or speaking too loudly? Bothering other students? Trying to leave the classroom? Were their eyes closed? Were they crying?...

That's a *mound* of questions to answer for each of eight students every 60 seconds when actually trying to *teach*...

Every. Sixty. Seconds.

My Mom had run a day care at home for several years in California, and as a lone operator, the maximum capacity was six.

She enjoyed a higher income than that of a newly hired teacher taking care of twenty-five students.

I can't *imagine* futzing around with a chart to document which kid has which finger up which nostril every minute.

Kelly still tolerated it, and though she knocked the job assignment out of the park for its full duration, with great heartbreak soon tapped out of her dream career.

She ended up taking a job with a temp agency for an administrative position at a drilling company, and she absolutely rocked it.

With her new income, we were secure enough to look at some more expensive apartments that weren't plagued with sordid reviews.

Our alleged *con-den-**say**-shun* problem at our first place succeeded by the hospitality of Ghetto Springs had prompted us to take more time when seeking out our next place of residence.

My home office still required nothing more than a desk and an internet connection, so as long as a neighborhood was serviced by a feasible internet carrier, I was easy to please.

Space was a luxury, but we still didn't necessarily feel the need for multiple bedrooms. We just wanted a place with a roof, walls, and windows that functioned.

After feeling particularly exhausted and quickly approaching the third year of our fight to find happiness up north, we both had started scouring website after website for apartment reviews in different areas.

One complex had caught our eye when we noticed it had been spruced up with fresh paint and beautifully manicured landscaping. We'd passed it often as it was en route to my parents' house, and it had such a nice clean new look to it.

Kelly burst into laughter as she shouted out from the couch after reading its latest review on her tablet.

"Well, I guess we can count that place out. The entire last year of public feedback has the most messed up review titles!"

"What do you mean?"

"'Better off living in your car,' 'Nightmare management,' and the most recent is, 'Mold, mold, mold!!!', with three exclamation points."

"Whaaaat... was that after they spruced it up?"

"Oh yes. They wrote that they had active mold problems in their hallway and in one of the bedrooms, and it was recently just painted over without being addressed."

Unreal.

Sharing that review with friends and family, it was revealed that the practice of landlords knowingly painting over mold was a big problem in the county, and one that never ended well.

It was cheaper and more timely for a tenant to move out and move on rather than try to take a management company to court for mold issues.

Review after review of apartment rentals in Tigard escaped our standards of not wanting to inhale toxic spores, so we took the advice of some distant relatives who had been living in the area for decades.

"Have you checked around in Lake Oswego?"

Lake Oswego was often spoken of as the Beverly Hills of Oregon.

Houses there were expensive — many priced at $500k for a fixer-upper, and properties were large and lavish. It wasn't uncommon to see three and four million dollar mansions in some neighborhoods.

Hearing nothing but words like "high roller" and "yuppie" being associated with Lake O since we'd moved north, Kelly and I hadn't even considered it, thinking apartments were surely thousands per month.

They weren't.

Many one bedroom luxury rentals were available for a mere $1,000; less than those in San Diego.

As we were still looking to be frugal, we took our time, spoke to people about neighborhoods and communities, and spent a slightly obsessive number of nights reading and re-reading reviews.

By 2008, we'd finally found a treasure.

It was a one bedroom with a loft, coming in at over 800 square feet. It had a fireplace and balcony, new appliances, new paint and carpets.

There were no units showing available for several more months, but we'd kept our eye on the place; it continued to be our number one pick after seeking out many alternatives.

We were ecstatic to hear the news when one became available.

Its price was $885 a month.

A 25% increase in our initial Oregon rent withstanding, we were more than willing to take it after all of our experiences with lesser caliber living quarters.

The neighborhood was gorgeous, safe, and walking distance to many coffee shops, cafes, steakhouses, and even a cigar store.

We would end up staying in that complex for the remainder of our time in Oregon, which would be much shorter than we'd expected.

We'd so hoped to have a chance of affording to buy a house and make a good living in Oregon.

...but it was not to be.

Trouble At The Empire

The Empire finally decided to sunset PhotoLink *and* PhotosFirst that year, with all customers now conveniently using ReviewPro to upload their reports and photos together.

Impact from the infamous real estate crash that year was being felt increasingly, and though I was handling escalations with gusto, I'd been given a mere 1% increase in pay due to the impact of the economy on The Empire's budget.

Many others voiced they'd received none, so I considered myself lucky.

Due to these recent changes in our active software products, we saw the main product teams in our department disbanded, with *everybody* now supporting both ReportsPro and ReviewPro.

Second level agents were also expected to learn and take on support for all the *specialty* products as soon as possible. Likewise, the former Specialty Team was completely swamped as they scrambled to get used to supporting the primary products.

This birthed yet *another* element that would gum up the works and plague the department for years to come:

"The backline queue."

As nearly everybody in the department was now expected to support all software titles, several incoming calls were struggled with by many.

To avoid the call queues from blowing out of proportion, if anybody received an incoming call with a question they had *no* clue of how to address after 20 minutes of effort, they were to tell the caller that they'd locate the solution and get back to them within 24 hours.

The agent would keep the case assigned to themselves to address at their next convenience between the incoming front line calls.

The incoming queue was always the priority.

It wasn't long before many had their own pile of unresolved cases in their backline queue, in turn spawning a new pressure to be put on everyone from supervisors and management.

Backline calls were *rarely* resolved in 24 hours.

Stress levels rose, and there was this funk in the air again when I clocked in every day to work.

Though I wasn't physically in the office, I could detect the stiffness in people's inflection as the verbiage of emails grew curt, and cordiality faded from conversations within chat rooms.

People were quoting lines from *Office Space* more habitually via direct messages, and the on-site blight of negativity had become so extreme, it was leaking out and infecting remote employees.

Meetings grew sparse, and open communication with management was waning. Nobody had gotten a quality assurance review all year, and though our customer base was growing, our department wasn't.

We kept having more responsibilities and faster turnaround requirements for escalated calls — lowering our performance stats, and in turn, our moods.

As the cycle goes, it all rubbed off on our call quality, detracting from our chipper demeanor when on the line.

The Empire even held a couple meetings that year about keeping a cheerful attitude when on the phones with customers, which only served to stir the pot.

In more than one of those meetings, agents expressed concern if there was to be downsizing in the near future due to the economy. We were assured there wasn't, but there's something about that...

Employees can smell lay-offs twelve parsecs away.

I was stressed. My co-workers were stressed.

Kelly and I had a long talk one night to discuss our careers' futures, and our prospective living arrangements in the next decade.

As she'd clearly noticed my own stress level increase steadily throughout the year, I told her that I didn't have a great feeling about my future with The Empire.

I was making decent money, but the job didn't feel stable after the dishonest corporate tricks that were pulled over the recent years.

Everything had come together to form an unpleasant work environment, even remotely: the illogical policy implementations, management ignoring customer and agent feedback alike, increase of duties, lack of fair compensation, and all with The Schoolmarm still at the helm.

The delays we had experienced in our call logging software had grown even longer, and it was still being held against our performance if we weren't creative enough to hide dead air and wrap time.

Though I was only mildly forthcoming about my feelings that year to Kelly, inside I had a hunch that this really was the beginning of the end.

Arctic Blast

Kelly still had the majority of her college loans to pay off, and we'd racked up tens of thousands of dollars in credit card debt over a few years between car repairs, multiple moves, and her struggles to find work.

The weather didn't help, either.

I'd gained 30 pounds in the two years I'd been in Oregon. Though it's nobody's fault but my own, I was still not adjusting well to the weather.

Every year was an increasing challenge for me to embrace more than 180 gloomy days per year, (over 150 of those with rain), and 50 more that *didn't qualify as rainy,* but still boasted the likeness of a dimly lit garage with a broken swamp cooler running.

Portland was suffering economic, social, and political issues that put a strain on the quality of life. It had been voted by a popular magazine as one of the most depressing places in America to live, based on factors of homelessness, unemployment, drug use, mental health, and weather.

Constantly scrambling to stay on top of The Empire's frequent changeups, I had recently been elected by management to be one of the first to serve the newly established "Weekly backline duty."

Second level agents were to rotate to fill this role every week. Instead of taking incoming calls, backline duty's primary focus was to go through everybody's personal call queues and address every one they'd set aside as a backline case.

Very quickly, it became clear that many first level agents were quick to exploit this new development by tossing the more tedious calls into their backline queue.

Why work harder when they could let somebody else take care of it?

Management was able to track how many backline calls each agent had, how long it was there, and who actually resolved it.

Still, nothing was ever enforced, and no exploits were stifled regardless of my feedback.

One good thing that came from this was that Daphne had been promoted to level II and was resolving as many backline cases as I was.

I was glad she was still there, as she'd considered leaving the company several times.

Another major change came that year: The Empire upgraded their phone system from POTS (Plain Old Telephone Service) to VOIP (Voice Over Internet Protocol); no more physical telephone landlines and phone jacks.

I was shipped a newfangled broadband phone that plugged right into my router.

This was no new technology, but it was far from mainstream. Hardly over 25% of companies in America were using VOIP phones, and The Empire wanted to jump on the bandwagon.

They'd opted for a service provider from the bottom of the barrel, granting us with poor connections for the first several months.

We'd have calls disconnect, or have such terrible quality of connections that we'd have to try calling customers back due to sounding like we were driving through a tunnel on a cell phone.

One can imagine how lovely this made backline duty. Not only would I have to insert a quick disclaimer that it wasn't a sales call to avoid being hung up on, but the customers were nearly guaranteed to be irritated from every other word cutting out.

I was, too.

The Empire held our repeat disconnects and increased callback stats against us without consideration for the poor phone service.

I loathed our new phones and the backline queue, and this one-two punch exacerbated my already dreary mood.

It didn't help Kelly's either. I still feel guilty for not putting on a happier face to not bring her down.

It's not a proud thing to admit that most of our conversations after work went like this:

"Hey, babe."

"Hi, how was your day?"

"Alright. Glad I still have a job, I guess. What do you want to do for dinner?"

Regardless of who initiated this verbatim sequence, the answer was always the same no less than four days out of the week.

"Let's go out, I don't feel like cooking or cleaning tonight."

We were both in a rut, me feeling extremely underappreciated at my place of employment, and Kelly with hers.

She'd worked for nearly a year at her current temp assignment, excelling to the point of handling the workload of others who had left and not yet been replaced.

Doing everything in *her* power to take on additional duties, she was hoping to make big enough waves for the company to take notice and hire her permanently.

They had already dangled carrots here and there without following through, and it even got to the point that her appreciative department manager said he would threaten to leave the company soon if they didn't take her on.

Idle threats it seemed, as they didn't budge.

I'd begun having three or more beers after every work day to take the edge off, and we were both ordering our own large restaurant entrees nearly every night.

On weekends, I'd enjoy a good five or six cocktails on Saturday without fail.

More timely it could not have been... an enchanting little event that year threw a much-welcomed spanner into the spokes of our stagnant existence.

Snow fell in late 2008!

It was a light powder at first; a mere quarter inch one morning in December.

As my wife had grown up in Jamestown, New York, she found the reaction of the entire county more than mildly amusing.

"Are you serious? The whole town has *shut down* over a quarter inch?! I used to walk through two feet of snow to get to elementary school, and they *still* wouldn't give us a snow day!"

It was unreal. People were smashing up their bumpers and fenders at countless red lights, and sliding off the roads into shoulders and residential fences. Kelly's five mile drive home from work took her 90 minutes due to the pandemonium...

On a quarter inch of snow.

These people *really* needed to play more video games.

I drove on snow for the first time in my life that night, finding most of the town's restaurants to have temporarily closed.

Schools had shut down for the week, and many people had entered such a panic that they'd abandoned their cars on the side of the highway, and *walked away,* leaving them to be retrieved later.

Some hadn't even pulled all the way to the shoulder.

Without any chains on the tires, I drove to a few stores to pick up some food and supplies in case we had to buckle down for a week or two.

I attributed the ease I had driving on snow to those recent years of playing rally racing games with Raymond. Say what you will, but the right video games can *absolutely* serve as an effective simulator.

I knew what feeling of the wheel to expect, how to accelerate, brake, and turn to abide by the new conditions of the road from the light snowfall.

Seeing other drivers' performance was embarrassing; the only real challenge was being wary of *them.*

More than ever, I was craving a Terminator Stout and Cajun tater tots from one of my favorite local breweries to pair with the festive new outdoor environment!

Our old neighbors from Ghetto Springs had the same idea. They had also moved on from the complex, and rented a small house in the area for a great price.

They'd already put chains on their vehicle, so they picked us up, and we headed to the closest McMenamin's restaurant a mile or so from our apartment.

The employees were unfazed by the snowfall, and glad to see some customers.

It wasn't until the next day that I decided I should in fact purchase some chains, as several more inches of snow had fallen overnight.

As I slowly and steadily drove to the store the next day on about five inches of snow, it **still** felt as natural as if I'd done it for years. Still, the challenge of our driveway's slight incline was increasing, so it was a wise idea to chain up.

They proved to be a fantastic $65 value.

The following day, my parents and sisters came over to visit, ending up getting stuck in our parking lot. It wasn't due to the additional snow that dumped down that day, but from the "traction spikes" on their tires failing.

We broke out the bourbon, ordered pizza from one of the few places still open, and met the delivery driver curbside so they could avoid getting stuck in our complex themselves.

Everybody spent the night on our living room floor with inflatable mattresses, and they called a tow company the next morning to come rescue their vehicle.

The dispatched tow truck had ended up getting stuck in the snow itself en route, needing a larger truck to come to *its* rescue.

Snow continued to fall off and on throughout the holiday season, making for a beautiful December.

Come mid-January, there was nothing but large chunks of ice left slowly melting on roadsides everywhere, a reminder of our short but sweet snowy adventure that was The Arctic Blast of 2008.

I wish we'd have gotten more. That white winter was such a welcomed moment of excitement. It distracted us from the string of pitfalls we'd kept traipsing over as we tried so wholeheartedly to make a home in a new state that simply would not have us.

Great Pains

One percent feels much better than a zero percent raise, which is exactly what I was told I'd receive during my review in 2009.

My wrenched guts were torqued tighter still, and I continued to gain serious weight. In fact, I was well over 280 pounds.

Many veteran employees had embraced a minimalist approach, working only as hard as it was to stay below The Schoolmarm's radar.

As we needed the money, I was volunteering nearly every week that year for the Saturday shift, and winning it due to decreased volunteers.

I was never able to sleep at night when even *considering* the dilution of my performance. That's not who I am, and every day I clocked in, I gave it my all even though I was in the minority.

Jerry retired that year, which was a huge blow to what little good humor the department still had at headquarters.

Ben was promoted to the department above Tech Support, which was TSE (Technical Support Engineering), and continued working remotely.

Kelly and I had been paying off credit cards at a stalemate; we were racking up as much restaurant and entertainment debt as the amount of payments that were made.

It's the American way.

As time went on, my health took a bigger hit. Chiropractic visits increased, and my neck and shoulders had been beaten up by the classic sedentary lifestyle that comes with a desk job and 10 months of depressing weather year after year.

The moment we'd long expected had also finally arrived: The Empire announced they'd be downsizing by the next quarter.

This prompted more eating and drinking, and questioning our fickle future.

We were in debt, had no cash for a down payment and the houses hadn't dropped enough for us to afford much of anything with our current financial status.

Banks offering loans with no money down was a thing of the past.

Still, I was making $22/hour working at home without a college degree, and I didn't want to let that go.

Absolutely no local jobs in my field were paying anywhere close to that. We still had full benefits, and were enjoying affordable rent.

We were just depressed; we had no motivation. We needed something... a jolt, a nudge, anything.

Being on edge for months awaiting to see if you still had your job was a terrible feeling, and I never forgave management for inflicting such a thing on the employees. It brought nothing but psychological and emotional unrest.

Months later, the day of reckoning finally arrived.

An "all staff emergency meeting" was called one morning, lasting only minutes.

Upper management explained that those who had been laid off were already notified in private, moments before the meeting.

Wishing everybody well in their future, they ended by encouraging us all to band together during this tough time... yadda yadda, get bent, suck it up, have a good day.

One veteran second level agent, two first level agents, and two supervisors had been laid off that day.

Another second level agent left the company of their own accord later that week.

Other departments were also hit, with some employees of 15 years being let go, regardless of having lead the performance of their teams.

They were chosen because they were the highest *paid* employees on their teams.

The Empire was after short-term savings.

We all know what happens when knowledge and experience is removed from a department's work force, and it isn't pretty.

The Empire had remained number one in their industry for decades. Their programmers and developers had been local, well-educated, and experienced.

Not for long.

In addition to letting go many high dollar agents in Tech Support, Customer Service, and Sales, The Empire had decided to outsource the majority of Development that year.

That rarely ends well.

I couldn't believe they were still following that playbook after all the overwhelming examples that history has taught us about the outsourcing game.

Along with departmental resources having been stretched to their limits, so had the tolerance of my stomach and esophagus.

Later that year, I had what I'd thought was such terrible heartburn, I couldn't lay down due to a bloating, burning pressure in the middle of my chest.

Kelly was worried I was having a heart attack, as the pain I was suffering rendered me unable to fully breath, walk, sit, or lay down.

It was such an odd and *unfamiliar* pain, having both a deep dull throb and a sharp stabbing sensation simultaneously in the front and back of my chest. I couldn't even pinpoint where on my body it was coming from other than somewhere in my torso above my stomach.

It had gotten so bad so quickly that I could hardly speak between struggled gasps. At that point, Kelly felt she should take me to the hospital.

I didn't argue.

Within minutes, we were on the road.

It was one of the most painful and frightening car rides of my life. Not knowing what was wrong with me and being unable to breath without stifling pains, I honestly prayed for death at a certain point.

Upon arriving to the hospital around 4:00 a.m., I was admitted instantly on account of my difficulty breathing.

I was quickly given a couple ounces of gray liquid to swallow containing a couple drugs: one was to help me relax, and the other an industrial strength antacid.

It tasted as if somebody had ground up a fresh stick of chalk into a cup of soy milk and thickened it with a peppered gravy.

It was foul, and didn't seem to help much.

After trying my best to lay still on a bed, propped up by several pillows, the staff determined I was not having a heart attack, but suspected I was suffering either a gallbladder attack, a peptic ulcer, or an abdominal aneurysm.

They hooked me up to an IV drip with more hardcore painkillers and a mild sedative before sending me through an MRI and an X-Ray.

The X-Ray showed no alarming results, and out of sheer dumb luck, a radiologist happened to be on the premises to take a look at my MRI results.

Kelly called my parents with news of the ordeal, and I continued to wince in pain as the staff updated her a few feet away, quietly stating, (and I quote) "We just can't seem to find what's wrong yet."

They took some blood to run more tests, and by then, my Dad had showed up for support.

As I lay there a while, another doctor came out and said it would take some time before they saw the results of the blood test.

The radiologist had also returned the good news that I had absolutely no signs of aneurysms, gallstones, or any other abnormalities that could be detected from the scans.

Since I was now breathing rhythmically and didn't appear to be suffering anything life threatening, I was to go home and rest.

I was exhausted and didn't feel much better, but it was past 8:00 a.m., and that meant that our chiropractor's office was open.

My Dad suggested we stop by, as he could feel that my back and shoulders were as tense as a brick from my body convulsing in pain all night long.

To happen upon a chiropractor who is also trained in physical therapy *and* nutritional science makes for quite the trifecta of care; I was eager to stop by and seek some relief.

This particular Doctor was especially keen on encouraging common sense in nutrition and health practices, and would often drop humorous bits of painful truths.

"Ya know, Mike, if you'd stop eating junk and get outta that chair some more, you wouldn't need to keep coming back HERE so often..."

His words often reminded me of Dr. Sender's advice years prior.

That kind of honesty isn't as common as I'd like in the health care world.

When we arrived, I didn't remember much after greeting the Doctor, thanks to all those drugs that were pumped into me, but I awoke about an hour later after having passed out on a table in one of the exam rooms from good ol' fashioned exhaustion.

Kelly alerted the Doctor, and he gave me an update.

He had loosened up my shoulders and neck with massage therapy before performing a spinal adjustment, then let me stay sleeping on a heating pad on the comfy exam table to relax.

I had woken up much more flexible and incredibly thirsty, but yet still with that painful throb in my chest.

He gave me the straight dope as soon as I was lucid:

"Mike, you're getting older now, and you're gonna *need* to get out of that chair more often and shed this weight, buddy. Sitting that much is literally compressing your body, and your organs are rebelling."

Kelly had given him the details of my hospital visit and everything that they'd suspected was the issue. He rolled his eyes, saying it sounded like they were guessing, and couldn't believe some of the possibilities they'd suggested.

With certainty, he said he believed that I was suffering a hiatal hernia, and to relax in an upright position for the rest of the day.

It was advised to put nothing down my throat except tepid drinking water and bland fluids for the next 24 hours to let my stomach and organs relax, as my body showed signs of moderate inflammation.

Though the hospital's supposedly hardcore painkiller drip didn't actually do much for my pain, it did come fully featured with the generous side effect of vomiting, which was promptly activated upon returning to the car... so that was a joy.

Luckily, my Dad had given Kelly a couple of sickness bags he'd requested from the hospital, suspecting they'd be of use.

They were indeed.

A couple hours after arriving home, I sat only slightly reclined on the couch, slowly sipping a couple pints of water. Eventually, I stood up and stretched tall and long to then feel the strangest sensation:

I felt that final bit of the mysteriously dull-and-sharp throb in the center of my chest travel downward several inches, and fade away... followed by an incredibly loud and almost fictional sounding stomach gurgle as I exhaled pain free for the first time after those many hours of purgatory.

My eyes teared up from the final stab of pain, and my shoulders trembled with waves of soothing relief from the first full breaths of fresh air I'd enjoyed in far too long.

Disturbing, how suddenly the symptoms disappeared within a few seconds.

Whatever this was, I **never** wanted to feel this pain again.

I got a phone call from the hospital later that afternoon with the results from the blood work.

No indications of peptic ulcers were found, my cholesterol levels were perfect, and though being nearly 100 pounds overweight for a 29 year old 6'2" male, I showed absolutely no nutritional deficits outside a mild shortage of Vitamin D.

Unsurprisingly, it was said to be quite common in the Pacific Northwest.

After all the scans and tests performed, they could not come up with any diagnosis other than a generic upset stomach.

I was livid.

Thank goodness we had medical insurance with a $100 hospital copay, because once I received the bill and itemized list of all the tests and their results, the total before insurance for my 4 hour stay at the hospital was nearly $3,000!

All that technology and all those medical doctors never found out what was wrong with me.

At least I knew I had good healthy vitals, but my extra weight had been around for years, and was adding to my depression.

I was eating plenty of quality protein, whole grains, good fats, fruits and veggies. I was also consuming plenty of junk food *right on top* of all the necessary nutrients.

My weight at that time had reached its all time high of 291 pounds.

Good grief.

To satisfy my curiosity, I began reading about obesity & hiatal hernias.

I cross-checked articles from several clinics, including multiple research papers from independent university studies; I made my best efforts to consciously eliminate any possibly biased sources.

I was able to personally identify 100% with every symptom described, and all conditions known to likely cause a hiatal hernia.

I had heard of them before, but had no idea exactly what they were.

A hiatal hernia is what you get when the top of your stomach is forced up through your weakened diaphragm, (perhaps due to obesity from overeating and sitting in a chair 12 hours a day for two decades...), into the bottom of your esophagus.

This allows your stomach acid to easily spray up into it, causing not only intense heartburn, but with the added bonus of swollen, inflamed organs harshly squeezing against, in, and around others they were never naturally intended to.

Many people suffer no pain at all from a very mild hiatal hernia, but depending on the severity of the inflammation and organ displacement, the pain has been reported to be severe.

I've never felt pain anywhere near that level of unbearable intensity, and I wouldn't wish the sensation on anybody.

I recall seeing one young woman's testimonial on one of the forums I'd found when reading up on the subject. She was in her 30's, and stated she'd had a diagnosis confirm she indeed was suffering from a hiatal hernia.

Describing the exact symptoms I had experienced, she also mentioned drinking pints of water and stretching tall to finally feel her stomach slide back down after a miserable night.

The similarity of my experience to her account was uncanny, save for the final detail to which I obviously couldn't relate...

She added that it was more painful than childbirth.

I also happened to read that if the hospital would have performed a CT Scan — or even cheaper — a partial Upper GI scan known as a "barium swallow," they'd have easily been able to find evidence of a hiatal hernia or other possible causes.

I guess they weren't that thorough.

I'm no medical doctor, but if I was wrong, the only side effect I'd endure by following procedures to heal a hiatal hernia would be improving my health via exercise and nutrition.

Regrettably, addiction and habits are powerful stuff. Though pain *is* a great teacher, some lessons really don't sink in as quickly as they should.

Over the next couple of months, I had additional yet much less severe hiatal hernia attacks, learning that some foods were very quick to trigger them.

I could no longer enjoy black pepper or mustard on any foods, and ground beef had sadly begun to tease the sensation as well.

On the flip side, salmon, shrimp, cucumber, blueberries, and watermelon always served to calm my stomach and esophagus sometimes within an hour if an attack started coming on.

I would never have imagined one would have the ability to learn how to *feel* what their stomach and esophagus are doing inside their body to such accuracy, but I assure you: it's an absolute reality.

I felt every time my stomach dropped back down out of my inflamed esophagus with a tight slide of disturbing relief followed by a gurgle.

That year, my Dad helped me build a second level for my computer desk, enabling me to stand up and work rather than sit all day. This combined with avoiding trigger foods and taking walks on my daily breaks helped immensely to stave off attacks.

I wasn't losing much weight as we were still eating out and ordering large entrees, but I was no longer *gaining* weight... I was slowly on my way out of the woods.

That year was one of the darkest in my life, and Kelly and I realized we'd need to make some big changes.

She'd taken all she could take with being strung along as a temp for *well* over a year at her assignment, and neither of us had adjusted positively to the weather.

Rent wasn't much cheaper than living back in California where a fully visible sun existed more than a few weeks per year, and we hadn't made a dent in paying off our debt at all, much less saved up anything for a down payment on a house.

The market was out of our affordable price range, as the average home in Tigard was well over $300,000 even after the real estate crash.

Prices had risen over 300% in three years.

Half sickened, yet half relieved from finally facing the inevitable, we decided to formulate a plan to leave this place.

We tried our best to love Oregon, it just wasn't the right time for it to love us back — and that broke my heart.

Careless Acts

We *really* needed to put a choke-hold on our restaurant spending. Every extra penny we had after our cost of living had been spent going out to eat.

Checking with our friends back home in Santa Barbara County, plenty of apartments were found for under $1,000/month.

Though our entire debt was close to $85,000 including college loans, we needed to save up about $6,000 to move back to California. That would be plenty to cover moving costs, a security deposit, and first month's rent at a new place.

It was time to get a handle on our butchered budget.

The first thing we did was downgrade to a cheaper apartment. We moved into one of the smallest units available in the complex, which were about 600 square feet. They were $845/month which only saved us $40 on rent, but due to its size ended up saving us an additional $100+ a month on our utilities.

We didn't quit restaurants cold turkey, but we kept it at two dinner outings per week instead of five or six. That saved us an additional $500 per month by cooking at home more often.

At work, I had put in a lot of time updating solutions for several high-profile issues that'd long plagued the department, and these ended up decreasing the time spent on many of the top call generators.

I was given a 3% raise from my next review for making strides in saving the company a great deal of money.

The Empire had continued to expand its repertoire by establishing another website suite, "ReportHUB," in which our customers could conveniently view and manage their reports and photos they'd uploaded with ReportsPro. They could also communicate with the carriers to handle and view the progress of each claim.

The website lacked intuitive design, was anything but user-friendly, and required that several browser plugins be kept always up-to-date.

A great number of industries had now *long* since embraced the internet as a primary tool in their business arsenal, so it wasn't exactly unheard of to be expected to install plug-ins and updates more frequently.

Nevertheless, even in 2010, with tens of thousands of subscribers, that meant hundreds of How-To calls per day from folks still too stubborn to take any interest in using computers outside of email or social media.

Victor was still especially tolerant, finding humor in most of the calls. That was another sign that I'd not been myself over the last couple of years.

He'd *still* been able to find something to laugh about from within the walls of The Empire, whereas I'd let them stress me to my breaking point.

Due to our eagerness to return to California, Kelly and I had ended up saving $4,000 by February of 2010, and were rightly proud of ourselves!

Little prepared were we, for the next rotten apple to be thrown into the country's mixing bowl of economic suffering.

The Affordable Care Act would be signed into law that year. Though we'd been following the news, we weren't really worried about a thing.

After all, we'd been given a promise by those in power:

If we liked our current health care plan, we could *keep* our current health care plan.

The Empire had long offered group insurance plans, but they were fairly high priced; we had for the last several years been covered with an individual plan, paying a mere $120/month total for both of us.

The day the act was signed into law, we lost our health care plan that we were promised could be kept.

When looking at the newly established plans that were part of this "affordable" new act, it was clear we were about to be raked over the coals. The cheapest plans started at over $850/month.

That was over 12% of our income!

According to the official ACA website, had we only made minimum wage, we'd be paying less than 0.5% of our income for a *premium* plan.

Why, what a **fantastic** way to reward motivated, driven youth on the cusp of the lower/middle class. We were handed the privilege of paying substantially more for a plan that provided substantially less benefits than we had before the government's involvement.

With the most affordable health care plan now priced higher than our one bedroom apartment rent, we did the only thing we could afford to do:

We went without.

My parents lost their coverage as well, and the new plans for their age range were even more ridiculously priced at $1,800/month.

Since that day, they've also been forced to go without, as have other family members, the majority of my close friends, and a good number of my co-workers.

"*Affordable Care Act...*"

Quite the intriguing name.

Met with the backlash of millions of Americans stripped of coverage being unable to afford the new rates, the President admitted on camera that he *knew* people were misled, and he apologized.

Seemingly, this apology was sufficient recompense, because nothing was actually *done* to remedy the deceit.

The whole ordeal proved only to divide the country further.

I can't imagine anybody being against making assistance available to those who need it, but what happened was that millions of one demographic were given help only by taking it away from millions of another.

The government *really* isn't all that great at their job.

To further twist the knife, and to mirror one California politician's lovely reasoning that the ACA had to be passed to find out what was in it, The Empire adopted this retroactive disposition regarding their monthly updates.

Our outsourced Development department was stretched so thin, that they'd regularly begun approving our software's monthly updates to be mailed out a couple weeks *before* it was analyzed by their QA team.

Customers were granted the pleasure of learning of new bugs and errors firsthand, which they viciously took out on tech support.

Having no information about the latest error messages or how to resolve them, only those with long-term experience were making headway figuring out the solutions.

Victor, Sheryl, Daphne, and I started working more frequently with one of the Technical Support Engineers, Rowena. She acted as our liaison between Tech Support and Development.

Danny, who had joined The Empire in 2006, had also been proving himself nonstop and had recently made level II. He also refused to slow his pace, and worked well with everyone.

It became commonplace to send cases to the backline queue, as we'd often be sending new error codes to the Development team, awaiting their resolution.

The queues had been *wrecked!* It was rare to see less than 10 incoming calls on hold in any product queue, the longest having waited far beyond the optimal goal of two minutes.

Hah! That ship had sailed.

Because of this phenomenon, The Empire decided to implement another factor into our annual reviews:

"Team Performance."

Though everyone was supporting all products, we were to be separated into four teams of about 10 agents each — with newly hired supervisors observing our every move.

Inconceivable. The Empire had embraced layoffs and outsourcing tactics after crying for money, yet scratched up the extra change to suddenly hire several supervisors?!

It confounded us all.

Every day that the department's goals for the queues weren't met, the teams were constantly reminded of how it could affect our reviews at the end of each year.

Lobbing a bittersweet cherry atop this unjust dessert, our department had finally decided to again change the software we used to log our cases.

The latest application in web-based enterprise software had made a name for itself, and among other things promised to alleviate the delays experienced by our bloated local database.

It did!

Alas, this major boon came with a compromise of a *broken* promise...

To ensure we'd still be able to access and attach solutions to our cases, it was guaranteed our existing Knowledge Base that we'd painfully written so many articles for would get integrated right into the new web-based application.

It did not.

The application had many impressive features, offering multiple methods of transferring and integrating data from older software titles in order to help companies get on board with the latest and greatest in web-based enterprise management.

The Empire had skimped on this part of the purchase. In lieu of opting for the certified first-party integration service to handle our KB, they dropped that steaming pile of duty onto our own outsourced, overworked Development team.

By the time we started taking calls with the new application, we ended up with only a fraction of the features and quality of life improvements that had been touted.

To be clear, the hundreds of articles in our KB weren't lost, but were transferred to an archive section accessible within the new web application. This meant they could still be searched for, but we couldn't attach or associate our cases with them in any manner.

To save a buck, The Empire had again prioritized the short-term penny pinch, thrusting Tech Support six years into the primitive past.

We were back to either manually entering our troubleshooting and resolution steps, or painfully searching for an archived solution to copy and paste its content sentence by sentence into our cases.

Oh, well. At least the investors were happy.

Kelly, We're Home

We further decreased our restaurant outings to once a week, often not even going at times due to our ambition to get out of that place.

As we started to shop around for apartments in Santa Barbara County, it seemed the price for rents hadn't changed all that much over the recent years.

Prioritizing affordability and vacancy, we found a two bed-room apartment in Lompoc that was to become available in August for $895/month — fifty bucks more than our current place, which was easily doable.

We had our deadline, and we made it happen.

Though we really weren't going out to eat large meals any-more, we had gone super cheap on our grocery budget, resulting in food that wasn't exactly of the healthiest quality or the lowest processed carbohydrate count. Thus, I *still* hadn't really made any progress losing weight.

I didn't care, as the mere thought of going "home" boosted my confidence and improved my outlook on life exponentially.

Kelly gave a one month notice to her employer, and that really **wrecked** their department. It affected them so intensely that her manager who'd fought tooth and nail to try to get her hired permanently ended up giving notice soon after.

Kelly had also gotten in touch with family and friends to seek out job opportunities before we moved back, and had secured a future job as an assistant at a Real Estate Appraisal company. She'd always had a fascination and appreciation for houses, and she could easily take a couple classes to supplement her teaching degree accordingly.

She established a start date of two weeks after we'd arrive back in California.

The memory I have of loading the moving truck and hauling our few belongings back to the county we missed so dearly was surreal. Every box lifted, every mile driven was another moment closer to happiness.

Sunlight. Familiar faces. Favorite places...

Pulling into the driveway of our new apartment complex to be soon met by many old friends helping us to unload our truck was a sight I'll never forget.

Later that night when the last guest departed from the quintessential moving day pizza party, we sighed in relief, surrounded by an apartment full of boxes and furniture stacked all around us.

Roaming down the apartment walkway and staring up at an unclouded, deep blue evening sky, Kelly and I held each other with childlike grins plastered on our faces.

As we enjoyed steady breaths of calm, we could make out a distant voice far across the length of the parking lot...

A guy who looked like he was hardly into his twenties had walked out onto an upstairs balcony, and was shouting excitedly on his cell phone.

"Dude you'll **never** guess where I am right now. You wanna know? ...That's right! I'm in fuckin' **C.A.** baby! *YAH!*"

Breaking into hysterical laughter, we squeezed each other tightly and didn't even try to wipe the giddy smiles off our beaming faces.

We were home.

TWELVE

The Next Era

The Schoolmarm Vanishes

Kelly's new job started off with a bang. Working a full time shift from the get-go, she loved what she saw as the beginning of her passionate new career.

I was looking at *my* job from a renewed perspective!

Being able to walk outside on my breaks and lunch hour to once again bask in the glory of a flaming sphere in our galaxy was just what I needed, and the feeling defined rejuvenation.

This couldn't have been more timely, serving as a foreshadowing of a brighter tech support age soon to come.

One year was all it had taken after outsourcing the Development team until The Empire was no longer the number one major player in the industry. Only two others had remained, and per the latest market report we'd had our tails kicked by them both.

We'd developed an unsavory reputation in the last year; customers started to think twice about running the latest monthly updates before letting the other guinea pigs discover its bugs first.

They were so wary, that a new trend had even been established. Customers began calling in and requesting to override the expiration date of an older monthly update.

As one of the top 10 department veterans by that point, I'd taken our fall from the top industry slot pretty hard.

I'd yet to sacrifice my work ethic, and still took a huge amount of pride in the department. Though frustrations with some other employees were very real, I held close to the memories of my earlier years with the company.

We were all so happy, so tight-knit back then...

Now we were seemingly all "hanging in there" until better days, sitting it out and hoping upper management might actually realize [or care] how cold the department had become.

Humanity was being slowly and surely sucked out of our Tech Support family.

Then, it happened...

That year, The Schoolmarm was promoted.

Credited with many of the ideas and policy changes that swelled the wallets of investors at the cost of honor and long-term company success, she'd earned herself a place in upper management.

Though her power had perhaps grown, this meant there was a chance for a replacement that may very well add a shred of morality to the department...

A new hope!

Unsurprisingly, as soon as her physical presence in the department waned, the mood of my co-workers who were still on-site had improved *tenfold*.

There was no longer a dark presence patrolling up and down the aisles at random. No longer someone there to sniff about for any ne'er-do-wells that dared step out of line by visiting other cubicles during breaks. Nobody glaring condescendingly from the back of the room at any agents brave enough to glance behind them.

These fears had vanished along with Jane's residence; she'd moved into an office further down the building beyond line of sight, taking her scare tactics with her.

Within the week, we saw yet *another* supervisor brought into the department which was reorganized again to make now five teams of about eight employees each.

Two of the teams were to handle all incoming calls from the independent appraisers, while the other three addressed those from insurance carriers.

In lieu of one manager directly interacting with Tech Support, these five supervisors would now act as our management *team,* reporting to Marla who would in turn report to upper management...

Simply vexing.

The Empire had also adopted some company-wide changes in an attempt to improve the attitudes that had bottomed out in all departments.

The "Empire Values" were soon thereby established — tenets if you will, that boasted some supposed set of respectful traits with plentiful marketing flair designed to attract more investors and customers alike.

They settled on some trite classics:

"Talent" was chosen to boast the presence of skill, "Teamwork" to give the impression of camaraderie, and "Reliability" to convince folks that the agent who answered your call could **always** be trusted to passionately take ownership of your issue until it was resolved.

Some of us did have that level of passion, aligning with these new tenets of "The Empire Way!" as it was marketed.

Regardless, it turned our stomachs a bit, as the values were far from universally upheld.

Carrie was still permitted to behave terribly toward others with frequent upsets. One agent had complained about her so many times over the years to HR that they were literally granted approval to shun her.

They were not required to work directly with her, respond to her in chat, make eye contact or answer her in meetings, or answer the phone if she'd called them.

Carrie wasn't the only cracked rib in the team's chest.

There was another veteran who'd been with the Reporting team since before I was hired, but I'd never really seen much of her, as her cubicle was far across the other side of the department back in the day.

Her name was Mindy.

To manufacture her own self-worth, she had long adopted a most despicable tactic that took years for the department to catch onto:

Info hoarding.

When she'd receive an incoming call that involved an error or software issue that hadn't yet been reported by a customer, she'd quietly and efficiently work with TSE to be provided with the solution.

This could be considered an honorable and resourceful act, if not for her *refusing to document or share* the solutions she'd been handed for the issues.

Her method was smooth and refined.

Mindy would be the first to take calls off other employees' hands when she'd notice them inquiring about obscure issues in the department chat room.

In the heat of the moment, she'd profess to know the solution, but would express concern to the agent of the customer holding too long for the intricate steps to be provided via chat or even cubicle-side.

This easily convinced unwitting agents to quickly hand over the case number. She'd then call their customer back, resolve the issue without fully documenting the clear solution, and take credit for closing the case.

Tech Support Scumbag Tactics 101.

So much for the tenet of "Teamwork" being authentic...

At least we had a fair amount of talent — that was no joke. 70% of the department were still bona fide computer geeks.

As far as reliability, we were getting there...

Fewer agents were shirking ownership of calls by pawning it off to the backline queue, as our supervisors had been directed by Marla to urge agents to take responsibility for their own cases.

Try that they did, a few people still needed a mild kick in the pants to contribute more to the department.

The structure of the five new teams had been designed to do *precisely that*, and despite initially overbearing impressions, it ended up a much-welcomed change!

I was assigned to Jordan's team (one of the newly hired supervisors), and we got along wonderfully.

His was one of the two teams handling insurance carrier calls. I'd been one of the first assigned, as insurance calls required more experience and familiarity with every obscure feature of our software.

Fair is fair; they paid more for support than appraisers, as they demanded shorter queue times and faster resolutions.

We were encouraged to work closely within each team, tossing questions among our own, and offering help likewise. This was intended to be a method of circulating solutions with others in an efficient manner, and it worked beautifully for the most part.

Of my closest comrades, Sheryl and I were on the same team, Victor on the other insurance team, and Danny belting out appraiser calls.

Team meetings were held twice a month to discuss highest call generators, discuss trends, changes in software, workflow tips, any new errors, and how to address them.

Neither Carrie nor Mindy were on my team, and for that I was thankful. They were both said by my co-workers to remain mostly silent during their team meetings, and many had been long fed up with their unchecked behavior.

Those two were seemingly allowed to continue on their lone wolf paths that would be a burden to their teams, and in turn, the department.

No matter... I was to keep my focus, and concentrate on the performance of me and mine.

Jordan thrived off of us embracing the team, and we in turn were fueled by his energy.

He was cut from the same cloth as Betty, favoring positive reinforcement.

We always ended our meetings pumped and rejuvenated, and Jordan was always encouraging us to never feel the need to wait until the next meeting to bring up concerns.

As long as he was in the office, he'd always be answering private chat messages with a link, an attachment, or referral to somebody who could point an agent in the right direction.

He was an *excellent* supervisor.

That was an unexpected experience, as I'd always equated an excess of supervisors to be a nightmare. It truly can, and *is* most of the time, due to the misunderstanding of the concept of management by many.

Those who understand that the main purpose of management is to *help* your team succeed instead of police them will see a checkered flag every lap.

Though the rush I'd get when resolving a customer's issue had never faded, my pride in the department's management over the prior years had previously reached what I thought was rock bottom.

Though The Schoolmarm had been given *more* power, she'd been distanced far enough by her new duties to allow Marla the freedom to once again handle the department her own way: the *right* way.

We were now swiftly on the way up, as was my level of pride in The Empire.

New Headquarters & New Hires

Morale flourished throughout the new year. Though we were still slightly understaffed for the growing workload, we were able to handle it much better than before now that we were basking in positive reinforcement.

Kelly and I had found an apartment for rent in the Santa Ynez Valley for an incredible price of $775, and we jumped on it. It reduced Kelly's commute to work by over 20 miles, so that alone for her was like getting another promotion.

A friend and I both took a break from *World Of Warcraft* to purchase *Minecraft* in its beta stage, which helped save on our entertainment budget.

Rents were a hot topic for The Empire as well. San Diego's rates were on the way up, and prices for both primary and secondary headquarters had been raised substantially that year.

As the remote work program had been embraced by several in multiple departments, there was really no longer a need for such plentiful workspace.

Near the end of the year, The Empire moved to a different community in San Diego county a few miles down the highway, condensing their on-site workforce into a single headquarters.

It was an older building, but the size was a good fit. A humble amount of extra cubicle space still remained in each department.

Parking was reportedly brutal, with tales of those on the late shift having to sometimes park hundreds of yards away.

The Empire was pleased enough for the moment, and they continued their battle plan to regain first place in the industry.

They started to trickle in new hires for trial periods. Despite our smaller team structures and the veterans spoon-feeding the most polished solutions to these new teammates, many didn't last more than a couple weeks and were quickly replaced.

It had become clear there had begun a shortage of qualified, experienced support technicians in the industry. Finding folks truly comfortable beyond the basics of Windows Operating System seemed a challenge versus prior years.

Many struggled with terminology.

Some of us including myself wondered if it was perhaps due to the latest generation of mobile-device users.

Were there really exponentially fewer people using full-sized Desktop PCs, opting solely for tablets and phones?

Maybe the life of a computer geek had lost its luster...?

Other veteran agents and I had clearly noticed we'd been spending a good chunk of our time sharing basic OS knowledge. I related with Sheryl and Victor when they mentioned they'd been teaching the simplest keyboard shortcuts to new hires when privately consulting via chat, as many were in dire need to overcome poor time management when logging case notes.

When shadowing the new hires, Victor mentioned to me in private that some of them couldn't type by touch at all, which was a huge factor working against their wrap time.

The Empire was hiring employees that were embracing the two finger hunt-and-peck. That spoke volumes for their hiring standards; I didn't personally consider it excessively strict to actually expect a tech support agent to know where the letters were on a keyboard.

Still, in an effort to maintain a proactive behavior, I had encouraged many new hires to develop their typing skills using one of many free web-based typing tutor applications available.

Nothing ever came of it.

Exacerbating the difficulty of circulating knowledge, the new call logging application's KB feature was *still nonexistent.*

To dump more fuel on that fire, my reputation had ended up making me a target for the supervisors to pull me this way and that.

I was asked to help out other teams by supporting the independent appraiser calls for a bit until they were able to hire more skilled agents.

Having not supported that aspect of our software in a good while, it took some time to adjust and get caught up to the appraisers' current workflow procedures.

I was glad to help out, and most of the other supervisors shared Jordan's principles of teamwork.

A couple weeks later I was on top of my game helping with appraiser calls, at which point I was... told I could go back to supporting the insurance team again.

The differences in workflow were drastic enough that it took me a couple more weeks to get my head back to my "normal" insurance team routine, and find my groove again.

My performance stats were mildly lower for that quarter because of my chameleon efforts, and I was irked that it was held against me come the end-of-year review.

Marla sympathized as she was aware of every detail; the upper management team was calling the shots.

Another 1% raise was my take. Management didn't even refer to it as a raise, but a "cost of living adjustment" backed by a sob story about how the budget for the department was strained due to the new hires.

There was always some excuse.

Jordan found out about this, and he called me up to mention he'd see what he could do. He knew what I'd gone through and was acutely aware of the quality I put into my work.

That was nice to hear.

Him rooting for me earned me a 3% raise instead of 1.

Now — how on earth one of the newest hired supervisors convinced the The Schoolmarm's team to crack was *beyond* my comprehension.

He truly had my back, and I'd continue to have his and the team's as long as I was on it.

The Problem With Solutions

As months passed, we had retained a small number of hires after persistent efforts of extended training, and we'd gotten a proper handle on the queues and our workload.

We even had some spare time between calls in the early evenings, which served as the most opportune moment for management to drop the most anticipated news of recent years:

The KB feature for our call logging application was ready!

It was *empty*... but that would soon change.

Rowena's TSE team formulated an online certification test to become an approved author for submitting articles to the KB. The test was available to all level II agents.

I couldn't wait to do my part in loading up the KB with easy-to-find solution articles once more. Eager to give the new hires access to all our acquired knowledge at their fingertips, I was one of the first that took the certification test. An 80% grade was required to pass.

I scored 70%.

I knew that couldn't be accurate, as I was *certain* my answers were all correct. To make things even more suspect, only the number score was given; the testing website wasn't designed well enough to reveal which questions were actually missed.

I brought my concerns to Jordan, who was quick to hear me out and offer a retake of the test.

As I did so, *this* time I was sure to grab screenshots of every question and answer, and awaited my results once more.

I scored 70%.

Sending my screenshots to Jordan, I discussed the test questions in detail, hoping he'd relay my findings to TSE.

He took pleasure in doing so, and it was found that some of the questions had indeed been associated with the incorrect answers.

By that time, a few others who had taken the test had actually scored *above* 80%. That meant in reality they'd answered several questions incorrectly... and had been approved as authors while I had not.

That's messed up.

This prompted a moderate upset within the department when management found out, and they really laid into TSE for the mishap.

Well, *that* wasn't what I wanted at all. I was just defending my knowledge of our software.

There was no reason for me to worry. Rowena was a professional with thick enough skin to see the bigger picture, and she held no grudge against me.

One week later, after selecting the exact same answers to the questions on the test, I passed with 100%, as did many other veterans — Victor being one of them.

Now that **that** little problem was resolved, I began submitting articles in droves like before to re-establish our long overdue KB... the one that had been absent for a couple years now.

Better late than never.

I busted my tail, writing new articles for current issues, while also reviving many of the archived solutions that I myself had written previously. This involved a silly amount of copying and pasting into the new system.

Another fantastic boon of the year was the revamping of the backline queue. The role of weekly backline duty was abolished, as our restored efficiency allowed the department to hold everybody accountable for **their own** backline cases.

They were to be addressed or at least updated every 24 hours before supervisors would make an inquiry of its progress.

Most in the department would have multiple backline cases permanently thwarting them at all times, but I'd only ever have one every few weeks, often resolving it the same day.

A backline case hanging around in my queue would pick at the back of my brain, preventing me from relaxing; I was meticulous about closing them out.

Management noticed.

That combined with having again submitted over 200 of the approximate 300 articles that year to the new KB got me another 3% raise in 2012.

Rinse and repeat.

That authentic team feeling of the old days kept growing. Others were motivated as they too began jumping at opportunity's first knocks to pitch in what they could to the KB.

These were a great string of revival years at The Empire, and as I rode them out, I made sure to enjoy them to the nth degree.

Restoring The Thrill

The usual rock stars: Sheryl, Victor, Daphne, and Danny had jumped on the offer to support the latest ReportHUB expansion that was announced, so I dove in right alongside them.

We became the first agents to learn the ropes and create solutions for the *much*-needed upgrades that were finally made:

Supplemental tracking and management features for attachments, and more intuitive communication functions between appraisers and insurance carriers had been rolled out for the product.

We made quick work of it.

Though it would be expected of all agents down the road to support it as well, all new ReportHUB calls would be routed exclusively to *us* until ample solutions were documented.

Our well-oiled machine kept chugging along with gusto, and by 2013, a few of us had been promoted to a newly established tier: Technical Support Agent III.

It came with a cool 5% raise in pay.

Jordan and the other supervisors congratulated Sheryl, Victor, and me at the next company-wide meeting for our accomplishments.

Earning that promotion nurtured my confidence well, finding myself less stressed at the end of the day. I daresay I was even relaxed, come dinnertime.

Kelly had been rewarded a sizable raise at her job that year as well, and we gained substantial momentum paying off our debt.

I truly *enjoyed* my work again. The thrill was back and better than ever.

My damaged calm had been restored.

I'd even been eating far less junk food without realizing it. In fact, I'd gotten down to 240 pounds from nutritional changes alone without having started an exercise routine.

I even picked up a book at home to read *for pleasure* for the first time in years.

Well, sort of...

It was actually the *audiobook* of *Ready Player One* by Ernest Cline — and get this: narrated by Wil Wheaton.

Dude!

I was riveted by the nearly sixteen hour reading, completing it in four nights. That book panders to every child of the 1980s in the best way.

No cheap gimmicks, either; the author is no poseur. Cline clearly has a passionate remembrance of '80s culture that inescapably oozed onto every page.

When **my** regular four hours of nightly video gaming is trumped by the intensity of a book, that's saying something.

That story got me wanting to read again. I didn't even realize how long it had been since I'd habitually read books for pleasure, but it had been far *too* long, and I quickly became addicted once more to the rush of good storytelling.

Voicing my newfound love for books once more to friends and family caught my younger sister's attention, and she promptly mailed me a copy of one of her own recent favorites, *The Name Of The Wind* by Patrick Rothfuss.

Clocking in at nearly 700 pages, I finished it in three nights. I'd stayed up reading until 2:30 a.m. the second night, having had such a difficult time placing the bookmark.

Both of these titles succeeded in roping me back into the world of reading after a hiatus of decades, and I have to recommend them to anybody who enjoys science fiction or fantasy adventure stories. They're up there with my all-time favorites of each, respectively.

EMPIRE WAY

It was a street sign, but it wasn't found on a street. It was planted into the concrete walkway approaching the modestly tinted glass door entrance of The Empire's newly refurbished headquarters.

With symmetrical flags of company colors and logos flying for all to see, "EMPIRE WAY" led one right to the security doors requiring the flash of a badge to proceed past the front desk. Everybody who traversed the walk knew exactly what building they approached.

It was a bit gaudy.

The values defining "The Empire Way" had been touted for years both internally and to customers, but the original three values of Talent, Teamwork & Reliability had now been extended to include Communication, and Praise.

The entrance of headquarters wasn't the only area that had been upgraded.

All appliances in the cafeteria were replaced, and the room itself was installed with a fully functional and *staffed* kitchen. It featured a coffee/smoothie bar with counter service that prepared fresh food and drinks for employees to purchase throughout the day.

New exterior paint along with spruced up concrete footpaths ran throughout the grounds with fancy landscaping to match, like the prior headquarters.

Finally, a multistory parking structure was built to properly accommodate all employees.

As one of the great majority of agents working at home, I would not be taking advantage of these facilities, nor was I ever familiar with the inside of the building.

Since I'd become a remote employee, I'd yet to visit The Empire's new headquarters until that year when on vacation. I decided to drop on by to finally return their chunky old landline telephone still in my possession.

At the front desk sat a new face, and as long as I'd been with the company, I received quite the coldly suspicious treatment for not having a valid badge for HQ.

A guest badge was finally printed for me after two tiers of supervisors in HR were called to verify my employment status. Shortly after, somebody from the Hardware department was finally notified of my arrival so they could check in the company-issued phone I'd brought back.

They took my picture and got me a new *permanent* company badge, explaining it would expire after a few months of non-use like my last one had.

Trying to save them the time and materials, I reminded them I was a remote employee and likely wouldn't have use for it, but they were required to re-issue it to me since I was present.

Policy had superseded logic.

After I was wearing the new badge on a fresh lanyard around my neck, I followed the Hardware tech down a hallway to a small office.

There, the serial number of the old phone was verified, marked "returned" successfully, and then by my co-worker's own hands, tossed firmly into the huge garbage bin in the corner.

"And you're all set! Haha… we already donated the majority of those old pieces of crap a while ago. It's not even worth our time to bring just that *one*."

How painfully symbolic: I had made a detour to The Empire in order to return their equipment only for them to toss it into the trash.

This was now The Empire Way of doing things.

After quickly inquiring if I could stop by and meet Jordan face to face, I was told that he'd stepped out of the office for lunch.

It was probably for the best.

I was really on vacation to enjoy some time with Kelly in San Diego; I preferred not to try visiting with any of the few once-familiar faces of my co-workers remaining on-site.

It was incredibly uncomfortable being there.

Free of my now-discarded old telephone, I walked out the doors wearing my newly printed badge, removed it when I got back to the car, and calmly told Kelly, "It's done… and — I need to get out of here right now."

They're Gonna Wreck It

Due to the money dropped on the expansion of headquarters, the new year's budget was of course, stretched thin. Everybody who was lucky enough to be given compensation after their 2014 review got 1%.

I had taken up the craft of homebrewing, and it provided a pleasant creative outlet as well as a distraction from the creepy corporate vibes recently flaunted by EMPIRE WAY.

It also helped pad the infuriating news we'd soon hear about the Affordable Care Act.

In March of 2014, the President was told at a Town Hall meeting that many families were still struggling to afford the new healthcare plans. He advised that they need only decrease spending on their cable and cell phone bills to afford the plans.

Kelly and I had a nominal cable TV subscription; bundling a 25-channel package actually decreased the price of our internet service to just $65/month, and our combined cell phone bills were only $50/month.

I clearly needed the internet to do my job...

Not only were we trying to responsibly pay off credit card debt, but primarily, college loans.

Kelly wasn't *about* to shirk responsibility by seeking student loan forgiveness, as she felt that was far from ethical to make tax-payers responsible for her personal decision to attend a university.

One can't exactly return an education for a refund.

Bronze ACA plans were still priced at nearly $850/month, so we'd still be $800 short if we abandoned our cell phones.

As if to deliver a cheap groin-kick when we were already down and out with no health care, **penalties** were instituted that year to milk more out of those unable to afford the plans.

Right when we were getting on top of paying down our debt, the government had to stick their boney fingers further into our wallets. All the while, they maintained their front of righteous proclamations for the good of the people.

This promptly resulted in many Americans accusing one of being evil or greedy if they didn't support the ACA.

A side-effect of political party blinders.

Likewise, the front of "The Empire Way" had officially become nauseating, and all employees were now required to take an online company test to ensure that we knew the five Empire Values *and* their subjective definitions.

It wasn't multiple choice; we had to memorize the marketed verbiage directly from our official website.

Everybody passed, but some had to retake the test several times before nailing every tagline verbatim.

The test took but three minutes or less, there was no penalty for failing, and no limit to how many times the test could be taken.

No supervision even took place to ensure agents weren't glancing at other browser tabs to cheat by copying and pasting — yet everybody was required to pass with a perfect score.

Was this all an upper management ego-stroke to give the impression of order and a tight ship to investors? Another chapter being followed out of the classic corporate handbook?

Most felt that way.

We didn't really let it linger on our minds. What **would** be on our minds was the announcement that came late summer that year.

The Empire held a five minute company-wide meeting to present a chart demonstrating a sharp increase of company costs over the recent years.

Aside from the obviously exorbitant cost of turning headquarters into something that resembled a pretentious miniature shopping mall, *one* of the departments in which they'd reflected a large amount of consistent spending over recent years was Tech Support.

Well, *of course* it was. The Schoolmarm was playing with an entire *team* of other invisible managers, and they'd hired five supervisors employed for overseeing roughly forty people.

That's a lot of high dollar salaries right there.

Always having strove to remain one of the top performing employees in the department had earned me an hourly wage of $25/hour. However, as an experienced tech support agent in San Diego County at the time, this was on the low side of the industry average.

The reality was that a remote position was highly convenient, and deep down I loved what I did. I also loved working with most everybody on my team, and the majority of the department.

I merely had a complicated relationship with the company for which I did it.

Our relationship was soon to become rancid.

In the early Fall of 2014, The Empire announced that it would be keeping only insurance support in-house, with plans to outsource the entirety of the appraiser support teams.

Those teams made up nearly 60% of the department.

Everybody felt gut-kicked. We didn't know what to say, or how to even react.

Some who were on-site wept.

Some resigned without notice that week.

The last day of work for the appraiser teams would be in early March of 2015.

At least they had the decency of giving several months notice along with promises of substantial severance packages.

That still didn't make it any easier.

THIRTEEN

The Wreckin'ing

All Time Low Standards

Daphne had transferred to another department before the outsourcing hammer was dropped, as did Betty.

Danny thankfully joined an insurance support team after also being promoted to level III that year. He'd worked hard for it.

Inexplicably, Carrie also made it to level III, making for a total of only five agents in the tier.

Danny tolerated her well at first, but I could hardly stomach hearing her voice after all those years.

Victor and Sheryl weren't thrilled to have her either, but we were all happy to still have our jobs.

The rest of the employees on all the appraiser teams, supervisors included, had been officially downsized as promised.

Marla had been let go, and was replaced internally by a former supervisor of another department, Moira.

Some had left months before the day of "wreckin'ing" out of disgust, spitefully forfeiting their severance packages.

Supervisors included, Tech Support was now a department of less than 20, down from more than 50 upon my hire in 2004.

With Betty no longer in the department, diluted renditions of QA Reviews were now given to us from our direct supervisors.

All of the newly outsourced employees worked offsite, and were from out of state. They were all directly managed by a contracted third party temp agency.

Well, didn't **that** sound familiar...?

They'd been put through a couple weeks of expedited basic training, and all the in-house agents were asked to give them all the help we could in our spare time.

Little did we know we'd be carrying them for years on end.

As it may be known, outsourcing *any* department is usually a raw deal for all. Large well-known companies have been lambasted for the decision time and time again, and many have in turn suffered serious loss of customers because of it.

Satirists and writers have infamously thrived off the topic; it's frequently the subject of ridicule, and justifiably so.

Language barriers, thick accents, poor diction, and inexperienced under-trained staff are infamously painful to deal with.

The customers paying for said goods or services don't usually appreciate it, either. It results in the complete *opposite* of quality customer service on every level.

Still, many companies flock to the trend, as it's a wonderful method of short-term savings, and a fantastic way to quickly please investors.

That is, until the insulted customer base shrinks.

The Empire had selected a very *specific* temp agency for their purposes:

The cheapest.

This agency hired people from all over the world including the USA, but not from Washington, Oregon, California, New

York, and a few other states as to avoid the highest median rates of pay.

The Empire had prioritized cutting costs, and was fully prepared to sacrifice every last ounce of quality to do so.

Sacrifice they did. This temp agency's specialty was locating hires for entry level administrative office positions such as telephone operators, or file clerks. Skippy the lunch boy who gets your order correct half the time would be sourced from such a place.

Now, to be fair, most of these temps were either fresh out of high school looking for their first job, or folks who'd retired and only wanted a simple part time position to bring in some extra fun money.

No harm in that; everybody has to start somewhere.

The great gaffe was that none had actually applied for a position in tech support, nor did they largely show any interest or experience in using desktop computers very much outside of a browser.

Some weren't comfortable doing even that.

One mere week before the layoffs, all level II and III agents were provided a link via email to the temp agency's web-based chat client, with instructions to sign in as a guest.

We were to do this daily upon clocking in.

The outsourced company's managers would monitor our guest requests, and admit us to the chat client as admins so we could answer the temps' many questions.

There were four different chat rooms available, one for each software title the temps were supporting. Most level II and III agents in-house had been assigned to different rooms to spread out the help.

Granted, this was all in addition to our normal daily responsibilities of resolving incoming calls, backline cases, and submitting any articles we could.

There were close to 20 temps initially, and during the very first week, we were bombarded with disturbingly trivial questions that one might expect from somebody who'd never used Windows before:

"How do I get to the Control Panel?"

"What's the Registry?"

"What is an antivirus?"

These were completely understandable questions to be asked by a customer, just as an auto mechanic can't expect everyone who drives a car to know the difference between a camshaft and a crankshaft.

Imagine if you will, hiring somebody who has never looked under the hood of a vehicle to start working as a mechanic.

Probably less than optimal.

The questions and comments got worse as the weeks went on, and I kid you not, these are verbatim:

"Does double-click always mean the left button?"

"How do I reboot? All I can find is restart..."

"Where's the Desktop?"

"I don't really know Windows, I've always used my smartphone..."

These were now our protégés, and we their new mentors.

No QA Reviews were given to temps, either.

The old suspicion of the mobile-device movement putting a damper on Desktop Computer knowledge came back to serve us all with a rock-hard confirmation sandwich.

A tech support agent being stifled by the instructions to double-click something, or reboot a computer in the year 2015 is as embarrassing as a chief auto mechanic who can't perform an oil change.

It should never be.

It should never have been.

Shame on The Empire.

As we struggled to provide the temps with the basics of Windows that we ourselves had obtained decades prior in grade school, the infamous public backline queue had been resurrected, making a triumphant return.

For every case a temp managed to close on their own, they'd dump *four* backline cases into the queue after spending 20 minutes going nowhere for simple How-To questions.

Cases with a par time of less than five minutes to resolve went days without closure, stacking up in the backline latrines as the level IIIs scrambled to plunge them down.

The nature of the outsourced chat rooms didn't help this phenomenon, as it wasn't really designed for this level of communication.

They were free-for-all scrolling chat rooms with questions and responses flying quickly by without clarity of who was replying to who, or which question had yet been properly answered.

It was a challenge to even obtain a case number so that we could review the details before offering a response that the temps often wouldn't see.

Many of them quickly flung complaints to their internal management staff who then relayed them to *our* management staff. *They'd* pass it on to our in-house team supervisors, who finally delivered it to *us* via email to defend ourselves.

This was The Empire Way.

A Nice Friendly Chat

Good gravy, did supervisors have their hands full!

Jordan was still fighting the good fight, but a couple others had tapped out and given notice.

We were relieved to see them replaced with direct hires rather than being outsourced.

Moira remained a quiet lead supervisor, keeping a low profile outside of quarterly meetings.

Teams had been changed up to better incorporate the temps with in-house agents, and I was now reporting to one of the new supervisors, Matthew.

He was very friendly on the surface, but unlike Jordan, he didn't embrace candor when speaking one-on-one, and remained a little stiff. We got along well enough, though.

The only real drawback was now being on the same team as Carrie.

She didn't waste any time initiating daily passive-aggression in the chat rooms. This kept me at the top of my own game with prepared defenses.

It wasn't remarkably difficult to handle her...

Dropping a couple of hard facts about stats and efficiency to steer conversations away from drama easily attracted one of the supervisors to moderate the exchange and shut her down.

As admins, we had the ability to move freely around the chat client to different rooms, as well as move temps and in-house agents alike from room to room by their request.

We could also invite some qualified first level agents to help out in chat at times.

Carrie's latest trick was to move other admins into the chat room where *she* was struggling, then demote their admin status so that they'd be unable to leave.

Matthew failed to address this behavior effectively, and Carrie's battle cry was, "I'm putting these people where they need to be!"

She'd also be seen berating the temps in chat with sarcasm and disparaging comments.

I mentioned to supervisors that this was unacceptable, and as a co-worker [not a manager], Carrie had no right to assume authority over anybody in the department.

Until the issue was addressed, I was left having to frequently send a message to *other* level III co-workers to restore my admin status so that I could move back to my primary room.

This came to an end only when the temps had started reporting that I'd been disappearing from my assigned chat room in the middle of them asking me questions, leaving them wondering where I'd gone off to.

I was happy to direct management to the chat client logs indicating exactly how Carrie had been operating.

Their method of resolving the issue was requiring all admins to enter "split view" in which *all 4* chat rooms were tiled on the screen simultaneously.

This fractional view only caused the speed of temps' chat messages to scroll by even *faster*, as the windows were now so much smaller.

Communication had become more convoluted, and both Carrie and management were responsible for it.

By winter, nearly 80% of the temps had already been let go and swapped out twice over again with those of the same caliber; they'd not the slightest experience with professional telephone etiquette, or the discipline to actually add any notes to their cases.

We'd seen a sharp increase that year in repeat callbacks from irate customers whose issues hadn't been properly resolved on their first attempt.

They only grew *more* angry when providing us with a case number that contained no troubleshooting notes, having to begin from scratch.

Flashbacks of my legendary battle of the motherboard sickened me as I'd realized... that was *my* employer's behavior right now.

I pitied our customers, the poor bastards.

They knew it, too. Many asked us straight up if we'd outsourced our team, because, "Your tech support was always so great over the years, and all of a sudden most of you people don't know what the hell's going *on* when I call!"

We'd already been given a strict briefing not to acknowledge any staffing changes on any calls, and it's not as if The Empire sent our customer base an email notice of scumbag outsourcing tactics — but it really wasn't difficult to catch on. They all knew. They most certainly knew.

The Dangling Of A Carrot

I'm fairly confident most working people gauge their success by recognition.

Job recognition in the form of money is usually preferred.

Work harder, produce more results, get paid more.

There are retreats and seminars aplenty that exist to teach the importance of praise and the value of positive attitudes.

Yes, those traits *are* of inarguable value, but let's cut to the chase, shall we?

If you were to go several weeks at your job without congratulatory praise, or if somebody a couple of cubicles down was in a sour mood, I'll play the odds that you likely wouldn't up and quit your job that day because of it.

Spend several weeks at a job without a paycheck however, and I'm fairly certain you'd stop showing up.

Compensation is primarily why the vast majority of us work, and we expect to be paid *fairly*.

All of us level III agents had our responsibilities increased substantially without making an extra dime.

The Empire had grown a tumorous idea that they should recognize the highest performing third level agents by weakly rewarding them with nothing but an unofficial new title to show their gratitude.

They started to toss around the militaristic acronym of "PIC", meaning "Person In Charge."

We didn't actually have any authority, and no monetary compensation was involved.

No matter — The Empire had a game plan to squeeze more performance out of their agents.

They teased that they were *considering* making the PIC title an official position in the near future. Though they were still ironing out the details of what PIC duties would entail, any extra efforts in helping bring the temps up to snuff in the meantime were promised not to go unnoticed... *maybe*.

No monetary raise was guaranteed.

Good Coffee, A Good Book, &
A Nicer Friendlier Chat

There's nothing like a bold cup of coffee and a good book to raise one's spirits.

Thanks to another tip from Chris Pirillo in early 2015, I'd been enjoying the finest cups of coffee I'd ever brewed at home.

I'd long ago graduated from a standard drip coffee maker back in high school, to a french press when moving out on my own. I never imagined I'd make coffee any other way.

Pirillo's video demonstrating the sparging method with the Aeropress convinced me otherwise.

I understand that coffee is a belovéd drink that's held sacred, but many drink it for different reasons.

Some truly love the aroma and flavor of coffee, partaking in a classic black brew, sipping a delectable espresso, or enjoying a traditional cappuccino.

Others — dare I say most people I know — consume coffee for the sugary syrups, flavored goops, and excessive creams they order to be dumped into it.

There's also that caffeine kick they can't go a day without lest they suffer a withdrawal headache, but if that makes them happy, then more power to'm!

Many of them write me off as a coffee snob due to the fact that I... actually enjoy the taste of coffee.

It's usually when they head off to a certain massive coffee chain that's so incapable of brewing a decent cup of coffee, that they need transform them into cloying dessert drinks for nearly six dollars a pop.

The *looks* I get when I tell people I don't want to join them!

"Wha-? Don't you like *coffee*?"

With a modest grin, I always clarify:

"Me? I **love** coffee; that's exactly why I don't go there."

Apparently all one needs to do to be filed away as a pretentious coffee snob is to prefer your cup of coffee *not* taste like cotton candy from 10 servings of sugar, or like a radial tire from being burnt and stored in a hot vessel for 8 hours too long.

In truth, I don't insist on single-source beans, I couldn't tell you the name of any famous latte artists, and I don't frequent any coffee houses that price a single espresso for more than the cost of the ceramic cup from which it is drank.

Though I don't frequent any of the aforementioned sugar-obsessed coffee burning chains, I honestly have no problem occasionally purchasing a bag of their unflavored beans, grinding them fresh daily and making a cup myself at home; it'll taste a lot better to me than how **they** make it...

Especially when I use the Aeropress.

It's worth seeking out Chris's video, and absolutely worth the purchase. When you do, enjoy your arrival to flavor country.

Whether you take that trip or not, the coffee and book pairing never ceases to be a sure thing. I find it difficult to not relax and be sucked into a great book regardless of genre when there's a nice cup o' java nearby.

A favorite that year when spirits really needed lifting was, *You're Never Weird On The Internet (Almost)*, a memoir by Felicia Day.

Being a gamer, a band geek, and growing up in the same generation as Day, it pushed all the right buttons for me.

I couldn't put it down, as many of her tales were rather relatable, and the book was hilariously uplifting. I recommend it for anyone seeking sincerity and charm.

It also served as a fantastic confidence booster when I'd been losing my belief that I could get through the latest developments at The Empire.

I'd long been suspicious that I'd be laid off anytime or the company would completely sell out, so thoughts of looking for another job and leaving them *had* been swimming around in my head for a spell.

By the time one year had passed since "The Wreckin'ing", I'd been with The Empire for over 12 years. I was making $26.50/hour, was among the top performers in my department, and I had the luxury of working remotely without a commute.

Did I really want to walk away from this gig?

The Santa Ynez Valley didn't offer tech jobs in the same realm; I'd have to work in downtown Santa Barbara to make this kind of money.

At 35 miles one-way, that was an annual transportation expense of over $8,000, not to mention losing 80 minutes of my personal time every day to the commute.

Quite the demotion, that.

Fortunately, in summer of 2016, the department finally made a change that improved agents' quality of life once more.

They ditched the temp agency's web-based chat client for a much better product.

It allowed for tagging posts as official questions, and our opted *direct* replies would show indented below in an organized manner. Questions could also be tagged by the temps as "answered" when needing no further assistance.

Admins could filter the view to reflect how many open questions were still active, easily revealing those who were awaiting answers.

Finally there was hope for no more exhaustively redundant inquiries:

"Did you still need help?"

"Were you responding to me or someone else?"

"Can you re-post your reply? The chat was scrolling too fast, and I missed part of the last message."

We still had our assigned rooms to monitor, but could once again view them full-screen which was a breath of fresh air.

Tensions were lower. Demeanors were pleasant. Negativity subsided from the chat rooms!

Management was able to utilize the new system well, and was able to much easier give credit to those who were the most active in resolving the questions posted.

Our performance stats soared.

There's nothing like a bold cup of coffee and a good book to raise one's spirits...

Not using a rubbish chat client also seems to help.

I Don't Carrie Anymore

So, there's this fella who inherited his initial wealth, filed multiple business bankruptcies throughout his career, and had been exposed boasting about his unsolicited groping of women.

When being called out, his response was proclaiming that other politicians were even worse.

Political party blinders knowing no shame, apparently many Americans found a way to justify these acts, and thought he'd make a good President.

Other than that embarrassment, 2017 didn't start off too shabbily.

The Empire had actually made good, promoting all five level III agents to another newly established department position: Senior Support Technician.

My own promotion came with a 9% raise, and our names in the chat client were now shown with the prefix of, "PIC -", which was the title that temps would now refer to us by.

The Empire also contracted a new health insurance carrier offering a basic group plan at $380/month to cover Kelly and me.

...less than half the price of the ACA plans!

We took it. Though still over 3 times the cost of our prior individual coverage, it was the first time we'd been able to *somewhat* afford health insurance in seven years.

With the acceptance of our new position, it was explicitly promised that we would not be required to answer any more front line calls, **ever**.

We were to focus on our primary duty of assisting the outsourced temps in the chat rooms.

Access to software that allowed us to record and/or listen in on their live calls for training purposes was also granted.

Any spare time we'd have between their questions was to be put to use closing out their backline cases.

If we had any time beyond *that*, we were encouraged to publish or revise any articles that were needed, as the new Knowledge Base was still lacking.

Many level I and II agents were promoted to the next respective tier.

Jordan had given notice, as did another supervisor upon learning of his planned exit.

In addition to her lead duties, Moira was asked to step in and directly fill one of the lost supervisor roles, and The Empire brought on another direct hire, Jaina, to replace the other.

Along with Matthew, that made only three in-house supervisors.

Teams were once again adjusted accordingly: along with Carrie (unfortunately) and a few others, I'd now be answering to Jaina, who was an absolute pleasure.

She'd not only had experience supervising and providing training in the past, but was formerly a tech support agent herself.

She knew the ropes, had intricate knowledge of computers, and was able to relate to and empathize with us more closely than any other supervisor I'd been assigned to since Jerry.

Life as a PIC had started off swimmingly.

Soon The Empire would announce their latest upcoming product, ReportsPro Cloud. It was a web-based application, and had all information from ReportHUB conveniently integrated into it.

By slowly transitioning users over from ReportsPro, it would render that most difficult and time-consuming issue of database corruption a thing of the past.

Our department had yet to have any training on ReportsPro Cloud, and our customer base was strangely told of its official release date before *we* were.

When it went live, the software was highly limited in function compared to ReportsPro, which was still by far the flagship product.

Several issues were reported daily to Rowena in TSE, who as usual, relayed those details to the outsourced Development team.

Of all the TSEs that we reported bugs and errors to, Rowena had always been my favorite to work with. She always appreciated the level of detail I observed, and she'd always backed me up involving my escalations.

For the first couple months of its initial release, ReportsPro Cloud was quick to gain notoriety among customers and tech support agents alike — as a steaming pile of trash.

Many had chosen to go back to using classic ReportsPro until the kinks were worked out.

When once reporting a batch of issues for the day to Rowena, I voiced how perplexed I was that The Empire would dare release ReportsPro Cloud in such an unpolished state, for fear of losing a large number of customers.

Her response revealed strategy most *scandalous.*

"Mike, in a development meeting years ago, it was explained by upper management that The Empire's long-term strategy by releasing ReportHUB was as follows: they wanted our customers to become so entrenched and invested in the software... to have it worked into *so* many aspects of their business, that it would be an excessive cost and inconvenience for them to decide dropping us for a competitor. That was their plan."

I can't imagine having spearheaded such a movement in a big business meeting, but somebody did... and enough of those listening thought it was a great idea to go forward with.

Rowena continued:

"Our long-time customers don't have much of a choice; the Empire's got'm by the throat."

It was clear my time with them wasn't going to last much longer. The only mystery was whether I'd be laid off, or if their corporate scumbag tactics would finally drive me to quit.

That holiday season was the next little test.

I'd worked on the skeleton crew for both Thanksgiving and Christmas holidays the last five years straight. *That* particular year, family members were visiting from out of state to gather for Thanksgiving, and I was eager to celebrate with them.

Others in the department had already scheduled extra vacation time around the company holidays, so I was simply planning on spending Thursday alone to visit with family. We'd planned wine tasting, restaurants, going to the park, and visiting at family friends' houses as well.

Lo and behold, an email popped into our mailboxes in early November. There hadn't been enough volunteers to cover for Thanksgiving's skeleton crew, so names would be drawn by management to fill the need.

It didn't matter that I'd volunteered for and worked both winter holidays the last several years; I wasn't exempt.

My name was drawn. I was required to work it.

Jaina saw this, and agreed it was bogus when I told her about my plans and the situation. Though she didn't have the power to override management's decision, she *was* able to approve and ship a loaner laptop to me for the holiday. I could retain my plans to accompany family and friends, while keeping an eye on the chat rooms through VPN with the company machine.

It wasn't the best situation, toting around an open laptop everywhere we went, but at least I got to spend some time with family instead being stuck at home or in front of my desk.

Soon after the holidays, we'd learn that there would be no raises in the new year as budgeted funds had been depleted, this time from the expense of the new software release.

Call queues were again on the steady rise, with backline cases piling up at an increasing rate.

Special "PIC meetings" were soon established, in which all PICs met with Jaina, Matthew and Moira every two weeks to discuss concerns.

These meetings quickly grew stagnant and melancholic, with many frustrations being voiced from PICs.

Most were regarding the low level of talent from temps still being the number one difficulty — one of which we had no control.

Plentiful examples were given of how extremely lacking in technical aptitude they still were, and how nominal their Operating System knowledge was.

We pointed out the inefficient cycle of having in-house agents providing technical support to unfit temps that were outsourced to in turn provide technical support to customers.

It was unfathomably absurd.

Our once-proud department's previously efficient operation had become a dual-layered handholding service.

Some supervisors were empathetic, yet made it clear that the temp agency's management had sternly told The Empire that they'd tired of hearing negativity about the skill level of the temps, and didn't want to hear any more.

That's right: they were banning any future negative feedback regarding those placed in tech support positions who were uncertain of how to reboot a computer.

Not unlike painting over fresh mold, that.

This was no fault of the temps. It was the fault of an upper management team that decided to place them in a business where they had no business being placed.

Seeing an opportunity to insert a fresh dagger during that meeting, Carrie responded to the supervisors' statement about negativity with a real zinger.

"Yah I was — *hesitant* to bring this up, but I'm hearing a lot from some of the temps that Mike White has been behaving very negatively and is hard to work with. I'm not saying it *myself*, I'm just saying that's what I've heard..."

Oh, I wasn't letting *that* one go.

Carrie's verbal flint had scraped off a spark inside me, and I would use to ignite a firecracker loud enough to leave a ringing in the ears of every co-worker for the rest of their days at The Empire:

"I have brought up these concerns here in this meeting with proactive intent because I was under the impression that's what these meetings were for, but the last thought I'd like on everybody's mind as we leave is that Mike White is difficult to work with. If you like, I'm willing to compare PICs' stats indicating the quantity of resolved chat room questions and backline cases anytime."

With an excessively sarcastic Jimmy Stewart-like inflection of pseudo-cheer, I continued:

"I'd also be *more* than happy to get some live collective feedback directly from my fellow PICs *and* the temps in regards to who's been treating them in a negative manner, and who hasn't. How about you, Carrie?"

Heavy silence set in, being broken a few seconds later only by a slightly audible nervous laugh let out by Matthew.

You see, months prior, Victor had privately informed me that Carrie had been given a terrible annual performance review back in January. She'd been called out for unprofessional conduct, and was taking it out no longer on her own, but on several of the temps in *Sheryl's* assigned chat room.

Victor had witnessed a few of these said acts, and had already testified with Sheryl to the entire supervisor team. Thus, after Carrie's sad attempt to misdirect the threat of aggro onto me, I knew I could afford to put her in her place.

Though, in reality, she'd merely put herself in it.

Matthew picked up after a moment with, "Okay well let's not get into a rivalry among our own, let's get back on track here..."

I dialed Jaina after the meeting to follow up on my statement, and in so many words she said that although it was unexpected, it was understandable. She declared she'd observed both me and Sheryl tolerating Carrie's behavior well.

Feeling confident, I made the decision to gently request of her that I not be required to abide Carrie anymore.

Ever.

I would behave in a professional manner, but I no longer wished to answer any of her direct calls, work on any backline cases that she was involved with, answer direct messages, and during our team meetings if she ever dared address me personally I would be offering nominal, curt responses.

She was generous enough to abide my shun request.

Rancid Cultures

It had been well over a year since I'd had any time to even touch our KB, and though it was a difficult crowd to work with, I never personally berated any of the temps in the chat rooms.

I discreetly brought up concerns to Jaina and Matthew of some temps who'd shown no improvement after several years, but they went unaddressed.

It was obvious the supervisors were intimidated by upper management.

The fact was that the temps were affordable labor, and that's all that mattered to The Empire.

How affordable? Well, we'd all know *exactly* how affordable after one of them decided it was of professional demeanor to blurt out their rate of pay in one of the chat rooms.

They had resolved a case after working on it for nearly an hour, and one of the other PICs had congratulated them on finally resolving it. Their cliché response was seen by all:

"Hey, that's why I get paid the big bucks! Gotta work for my $9.50 an hour!"

The temp happened to be on my team, so I sent them a direct message to let them know some may be uncomfortable publicly discussing wages in the workplace.

They replied that they were so very proud of what they made at this job, they were having a hard time keeping it bottled up.

My attempt at dropping a hint by not responding proved ineffective, as they went on... still in public chat.

They noted this was $2.00/hour *more* than their last assignment with the temp agency, and since their mortgage payment for their house on a half-acre was only $400/month, they were living very comfortably.

They were indeed. You can't do *that* in California!

As TSE sometimes monitored the chat rooms to assist when PICs were inundated, Rowena had seen the discussion and called the temp on the phone to finally silence them.

She'd restated to the temp that wages were not to be discussed in the chat rooms... but the damage had been done. Everybody saw it, and it was the subject of scandal.

All in-house agents learned that The Empire was paying less than California minimum wage for the co-workers that replaced those who were laid off en masse, and *we* were being held responsible to carry them.

It felt like no matter how much coaching was provided, they didn't have any interest in retaining the knowledge.

Case notes were still void, troubleshooting skills still null, and — like clockwork — par times for case resolutions were exponentially surpassed before the issues were dumped backline.

In addition to showing no long-term improvement, there were other behaviors that had developed among those who had been around since 2015.

When temps posted questions in chat, PICs would usually answer within two minutes after analyzing the provided case number. In return, it became typical for some temps to take 10 minutes or more to write *back.*

We PICs would be left wondering if they saw our reply, whether they were disconnected, if our advice had worked, if it hadn't, et cetera.

After being met with this silence, we'd struggle to do what we could in the meantime — checking for updated case notes, and viewing the queues and phone statuses to see if the agent was even still on the phone with their customer.

Soon we were on to them: they'd been placing customers on hold in order to take additional breaks.

Reporting this behavior merely resulted in them being re-briefed of their break time policy.

It wasn't long before they learned new tricks.

No matter — after listening to a couple recorded calls, we caught them again.

The customers were being told by temps that they'd be put on hold while researching the next steps, but no hold music commenced for near 10 minutes of silence.

The temps discovered they could avert attention from their active calls showing on "Hold" status by instead engaging the mute button.

When one temp was confronted, they played the "emergency restroom break" card.

They weren't *all* so crafty, nor did many of them seem to care about consequences.

Another who'd been confronted about their excessive idle times explained they were feeding their livestock.

"I've got two acres of land, and I had to feed my cows and the goats…"

Many would also run the clock, staying in "Wrap" status for over 10 minutes. Explanations ranged from one temp taking their dogs for a quick walk, while another brazenly admitted they'd craved an extra cigarette.

The recorded call revealed they'd literally told their customer that they'd call them back in a few minutes because they "needed to go out for a quick smoke."

Time and time again, PICs reported that many of the temps were doing as they pleased until it was time to leave, and nearly always dumping their last call of the day into the backline queue so they could clock out.

Jaina was still doing what she could to support us. She'd informed me that substantial evidence and high quantity of these occurrences were confirmed, and all infractions had been reported to the outsourced agency.

However, per their contract agreement, no details involving any disciplinary measures that may or may not have been taken would be reported back to The Empire.

It was moot; all the temps I'd reported clearly hadn't been disciplined very strongly, as they remained employed, and PICs were left frustrated with their continued lack of improvement.

It was as if they could get away with anything.

Even upper management could tell the temps weren't taking well to coaching, so they in their infinite wisdom had the perfect solution:

Cultural Management.

To be taken only by the PICs and supervisors, we were registered for a Cultural Management Course consisting of recorded seminars to view at our own pace.

It was roughly 3 hours of content.

The supervisors were then to involve themselves in every agent's daily tasks at a pedantic level — PICs included.

Jaina behaved the most pragmatically, maintaining her distance and cordiality while Matthew and Moira obeyed this new charge with militaristic zeal.

In an attempt to separate me from Carrie, I had been moved to Matthew's team. I would have much rather preferred to stay with Jaina, as I felt more appreciated.

She respected my ability to handle my duties more independently, as well as realized that the high volume of backline calls, and futility of educating the temps were problems that *wouldn't* be solved by breathing harder down our necks.

Matthew would privately message us asking if we'd seen the latest question in the chat rooms, even if we were already busy answering another.

Call Queue details had always been largely displayed in the corner of every agent's monitor; one couldn't miss it.

Yet, we'd be reminded of the current queue count and hold time even if a single call was waiting. This was the case even if we were already on the phone ourselves resolving a backline case.

Supervisors could *see* everybody's phone status, chat room activity, and active cases to know we were already extremely busy — yet — continued micromanaging us per these seminars.

Every one of the Big Six became required of the agents, and to be sure that PICs kept up their game as well, a major promise about our new role was retracted:

We now had to take front line calls, and a minimum number of them every month at that.

New scripts were established, and were to be followed verbatim.

The seminars had also introduced a new method of giving feedback that would be enforced going forward:

Mandatory praise.

A charming little scripted introductory ritual had been inserted into every proceeding PIC meeting:

We were each required to seek feedback from a random fellow PIC. It was to be answered with a reply containing an element of praise, along with a suggestion of how to *further* increase performance.

We'd then acknowledge in a scripted gracious manner that demonstrated not only that the feedback was understood, but with a short example of how we'd try to implement the provided suggestion in the future.

It was beyond pretentious; it was disgusting.

We'd also be required every meeting to creatively conjure up a minimum number of praises for the temps on our team for demonstrating any of the five Empire Values, which were to now be officially referred to as "Cultural Beliefs."

These praises were then documented on a spreadsheet stored on the intranet for management to see.

Even more than ever, we knew these beliefs well: Talent, Teamwork, Reliability, Communication, and Praise.

Lengthier, more hackneyed descriptions had now accompanied each, which we had to again learn verbatim and take an updated test to receive a graduation certificate from this Cultural Management Course.

We all wanted to vomit.

Naturally, these seminars did absolutely nothing to address the crisis of The Empire having hired temps who lacked Talent, didn't practice Teamwork, were devoid of Reliability, incapable of Communication, and... were now to be given Praise for it.

This was The Empire Way.

Coach Doubt

The latest development was a shining example of psychological abuse in the workplace, but hey, it wasn't a total loss.

The Empire was able to boast their "Cultural Management Awareness" and "Distinguished Corporation" statuses by brandishing said logos on their website for all to see.

Weird Al's parody "Mission Statement" from his latest album *Mandatory Fun* hit the spot, and it was circulated amongst my co-workers with appreciation.

It nailed the pretentiousness of the corporate world, to a tee.

Though there were still close to 20 temps on staff, less than five of the original hires had remained after the first two years.

It's rather difficult to instill long-term knowledge into short-term employees.

As the Cultural Management movement reached its peak, so did our supervisors' micromanaging practices.

This *broke* the temps, and before long they'd embraced defeatism.

Matthew and Moira had grown more stiff, but Jaina still retained sincerity in private messages and over the phone. She called me often to thank me for handling difficult cases, diffusing drama in chat rooms, and taking escalations that nobody else would.

If it weren't for her still being with the department, I could have seen myself quitting.

This rotten recipe that had been embraced by The Empire put us in a nasty position. PICs had begun to combat the micromanagement, exhibiting passive-aggression in our direct message replies, *and* during meetings.

The whole department's level of quality, and our customer satisfaction rating had both long plummeted, and PICs had grown tired of carrying rookies' workloads.

Enveloped by such a large fog of failure, supervisors finally gave in as well, and had begun to let up a bit; the mandatory praise segments during our PIC meetings had begun to slowly wane without mention, and much like the expensive Problem Analysis Seminars over a decade prior, these Cultural Management policies had slowly proven to be a farcical waste of company time and money.

Management had made the decision to try a different approach to improve temps' performance, and ordered them to start being held to performance stats and receive QA Reviews.

Gosh, were they sorry they did — but it was for the best.

The QA Reviews ended up being the smelling salts upper management needed to realize on paper just how sorely underqualified the chosen temps were; they'd had their faces so buried in dollar signs and corporate politics, that they'd not once set foot on the department floor, glanced at the hilarity of chat rooms, or attempted to read any atrocities of case notes.

Not a single temp scored a suitable review after two months, and the vast majority scored under 50% when held to the same standards of in-house agents.

They were worse than embarrassing.

The cases they sent backline were still often devoid of *useful* case notes, others some of any at all.

Alas, there are worse things than emptiness to be found in case notes, such as aggression and unprofessionalism.

It started showing up in droves from the temps who had been there the longest, with ramblings resembling lite streams of consciousness peppered with the berating of customers and co-workers alike.

"Dont know what error is cant find in ANY ARTICLES in the knowlege base that work!......... Asked for help but nobody is helpng me in the chat room... i guess they don't care!"

"This customer has no clue and is hard to work with. They keep clicking around on things and not listening to me."

"Rebooting the 'puter didn't work. Giving up on this one for now... need to go to lunch and will try calling them back after I eat."

"This is clearly a PICNIC issue."

These were a small handful of the entries I'd spotted in their case notes.

For those not in the know, PICNIC is one of those lovely tech support acronyms to imply that the problem isn't with software, but rather an inexperienced user. It stands for: "Problem In Chair Not In Computer."

PEBKAC is another variant, "Problem Exists Between Keyboard And Chair."

I can't neglect the classic "ID-10-T issue.", which when spoken verbally, is a subtle way of calling a customer an IDIOT.

Of course I've laughed at all these terms, but fitting as they may be at times, they're certainly not a tactful acronym to include in the troubleshooting notes of a customer's case — especially since those notes may be sent to the customer anytime by request.

That temp was the real ID-10-T.

Their outbreaks of such audacity went unappreciated by management.

Still, not a single one of the offending temps were *effectively* disciplined, as they kept their jobs, and the behavior continued.

Verily, it appeared as if poor performance was not only accepted and approved of, but enabled.

Their QA Review scores had been so consistently scathing, that the temp agency's management soon told The Empire of the temps' displeasure. They weren't appreciative of the negative light that the numerical scoring system of reviews was shining on them, and requested that it be redesigned.

Our minds were **blown** when The Empire folded without a fight, and agreed to revamp the QA system.

Did the temp agency have some dirt on somebody in upper management at The Empire? Was there a sex scandal or drug dealing ring that was being covered up? Why would they *agree* to such a thing so effortlessly?

Whether it was blackmail or the worst contract agreement in The Empire's history, it was all so highly suspect.

We only knew that The Empire didn't want to lose their dime-a-dozen labor force, so they prioritized a restructure of QA Reviews.

The result was a review process infused with cloying levels of rainbows, roses, and chirping birds sufficient enough to nauseate a unicorn prancing atop a fluffy cotton candy cloud.

QA Reviews no longer revealed a numerical score, because anything less than a passing grade could offend the temps.

Pointing out any negative behavior, irresponsibility, lack of professionalism, or even gross negligence was likewise preferred — nay — *required* to be padded with equal amounts of carefully formulated praise.

Otherwise, it could offend the temps!

The QA Review still analyzed the same criteria, but no matter how many elements left unchecked on the review card, a saccharin-laced line of encouragement, following by tips to improve were to be entered at the bottom line of the form before presenting it to the agent.

No negative verbiage could be included in the summary, as that might just offend the temps.

To give an example of a common result, say a temp had been reviewed on a case in which they'd taken an hour to resolve a call with a 10 minute par time. Case notes would be incomplete, yet also contain comments insulting the customer's intelligence.

Their supervisor would be obligated to praise them for actually resolving the issue. They could then *mildly* suggest the temp reach out for timely assistance next time, and gently request they exercise more empathy with the customer by *trying* to omit any degrading comments in order to reflect improvement in their next review.

PICs were treated to this review method as well, which we found offensive and condescending.

As an additional illusion of hope for improvement, a new training system had also been established.

PICs were encouraged to report to management any items of concern that would suggest an employee was under-trained or behaving unprofessionally in any manner.

The special email group that was created to send these requests to was called, "Training Opportunities."

We sent them in *droves*.

Despicable acts and embarrassingly poor behaviors were reported frequently. Things for which a respectable company would instantly terminate an employee were revealed.

For every training opportunity sent to the team, the temp agency's management would hold a three way conference with the offending temp and their supervisor to provide them with supplemental coaching.

Rowena had seen how bad the situation was and how hard I'd taken it, so she called me to provide a taste of insider information... discreetly.

It seemed the contractual agreement with this powerful temp agency had begun to prove a more poisonous affliction than it first let on.

It had been made clear earlier that year by the agency that in order for The Empire to continue letting temps go at the developed turnaround rate, substantial documentation displaying clear equal treatment, methodical efforts to provide proper training, and ample time allowed for said education to be practiced and retained would have to be established to avoid unpleasantness... such as law suits.

Their fate had been sealed. They were screwed.

After that little heart-to-heart with Rowena, I realized I'd have to play the game.

I reminded myself that the PICs weren't the only ones suffering this whole time; the customers had been taking it up the tailpipe as I had with the shady dealership, poor public transportation, and Mr. Smarmypants those many years ago.

I still had to sleep at night, so I very discreetly *shared* Rowena's tip-off with Victor, Sheryl, and Danny about the reason for training opportunities.

We soon sent them in even *larger* droves!

Temps continued to feed their livestock and go on smoke breaks while on calls. They kept berating co-workers and customers alike in case notes when they weren't leaving them blank.

Management took notice.

By the time early 2019 rolled around, PICs were discouraged from submitting training opportunities unless the temps' actions had *directly affected* the customer's live support experience.

Supervisors hadn't the bandwidth anymore to follow up on the mounds of manure we'd been sending.

On paper, the PICs were merely indulging management's new system, and our zest doing so was clearly documented. A 1% raise was granted across the board that year.

As we'd received nothing in 2018, we gladly took it.

Fixing Myself

My weight loss continued. I'd dropped further to 230 and was still standing up most of the day at my computer desk, but history had taken its toll.

Car accident, depression, life, work stress...

It added up, and I'd previously lacked ample fortitude to keep myself in the best possible shape.

Chiropractic adjustments alone had stopped being so effective.

I still wasn't exercising, as it was painful on my joints.

Seeking a low impact activity, I'd started to explore local hiking trails and discovered that I found them pretty darn thrilling.

My spine did not.

Before long, jolts of pain shot through sensitive nerves, absurdly tight muscles spasmed, and swollen tendons fought back. I found myself struggling to stand up straight, hunched over like a suffering creature in a bell tower.

I tried over-the-counter painkillers, but they'd never worked for me. I really didn't want to rely on any long-term prescription drugs as to avoid risk of damage to my organs, as well as that of forming an addiction to powerful painkillers.

After my years of suffering chronic back pain, my latest major attack had convinced me to *maybe* consider the latest trend: CBD.

Decriminalization of cannabis was nothing new to many states, and California had finally embraced it as well.

The negative stigma and taboo around the plant had started to give way to education and realization of its medicinal — and particularly to my interest — anti-inflammatory and pain-relieving properties.

As we all surely did, I'd known of several burnouts back in high school and didn't ever want to end up that way.

Paired with the D.A.R.E. program that we were all put through in elementary school, I'd been brainwashed into thinking this CBD racket was surely another exploit for stoners wanting to get high.

Finally the time came when my back pain was so excruciating, a good night's sleep wasn't a reality for several months. I could hardly hobble from the bedroom to the office without being doubled over while wincing and clutching my lower back in pain.

I officially decided CBD *may* be worth looking into more, and researching if it would be truly effective for my back pain without buzzing me up for work.

Completely skeptical, yet unable to bear the suffering anymore, I caved out of desperation.

Consulting with a local medical doctor, it turned out that my car accident history, having extra weight on my body, and working a desk job in a chair for a couple decades made me quite the candidate.

I was very specific that I was interested in products that would not get me high in any manner, as I wished to be able to drive, focus at work, and even operate heavy machinery if needed, without sacrificing any mental ability or motor skills.

I was assured that several products and forms of CBD could be extremely effective for my type of back and body pain, and if they contained none or only nominal traces of THC, then it was a certainty I'd not be getting high from them.

I had been approved, and was soon mailed a legitimate certificate and medical marijuana card valid for purchasing licensed products from certified dispensaries in California.

I located several products in edible form for convenience, trying out a few brands. Gummies and taffy were most commonly available.

I was at my worst, hunched over about 30 degrees, hardly able to sit or get up from a chair without debilitating pain stabbing my lungs with the fury of a cactrot's thousand needles.

Each whole taffy contained 50mg of CBD, with less than 1% THC. The dispensary pointed out each taffy was five servings, but not to worry. Even consuming several of these whole taffies wouldn't get me high.

I sliced off the recommended dose and ate the tiny sliver.

It had a sugary caramel flavor upfront, but it definitely had an odd, earthy aftertaste. It was like the rind of a brie cheese mixed with musty old concrete basement floor, and stale hops.

No, I've never licked a basement floor, but that aroma was unmistakable.

The taffy wrapper indicated to wait up to 60 minutes for full effect, so I sat on the couch and tried to relax.

By 30 minutes, I was still in just as extreme pain as I had been. I grew frustrated, felt swindled and began cursing for wasting my money and holding hopes that this stuff would work at all...

But the wrapper said *60* minutes.

After 35 minutes, I noticed my breathing had relaxed a bit; I wasn't intoxicated or buzzed, but was able to take fuller breaths without a pinching ache in the back of my torso.

Trying again, now daring to inhale much deeper, I could **really breathe!**

I huffed, puffed and sucked in a massive breath of air into my lungs as if preparing to belt out some low B-Flat whole notes on the tuba.

Holding it for several seconds, I fully and steadily exhaled without difficulty. Shoulders rolled and flexed, with my chest expanding and contracting comfortably.

Dare I try standing up?

I didn't need to try. I leaned forward from the couch with nary a single painful ping down my spine, and stood fully upright for the first time in weeks.

Standing there breathing was all I could do for a few moments, as I was in awe at what had happened.

A single dose of CBD was able to do what over-the-counter painkillers, heating pads, and the occasional chiropractic adjustments weren't able to do for me anymore on their own.

I must have been walking slowly around the apartment for a good 10 minutes with a grin on my face, enjoying full painless breaths for the first time in too long when Kelly came home from work for her lunch break.

Realizing that I wasn't hunched over and that I was smiling, she froze mildly in surprise.

"So, um... I'm guessing it... worked?"

I laughed so excitedly, she suspected at first I'd been day drinking. I assured her I wasn't.

I was overjoyed to be standing upright again without pain, and immediately called family and friends to share my exciting new discovery.

The next week brought some different discoveries when the taffy ran out, and I had only the package of gummies to try.

With great disappointment, the gummies turned out to be garbage.

They did nothing for me, and my back pain had slowly begun to return about two days after my last morsel of taffy had been depleted.

By the end of the week, all the gummies had been consumed, proving nearly useless as my back pain had come back in full force, as bad as it was before.

I went right back to the dispensary and bought several more of the taffy candies. In fact, they only had five of them at $15 each, so I bought them out.

They again proved effective, and lasted me nearly a month.

By that time, their inventory was restored at the dispensary, but the prices had *sharply* risen. They were suddenly $22 each.

Supply and demand.

I bought two, realizing I couldn't afford these prices long-term and would have to find other less expensive forms of CBD.

Edibles, drinks, tinctures, topicals, actually smoking it... there were so many options.

I'd never smoked any marijuana strains myself, and wasn't interested in trying. A far cry from my preference for pipe tobacco and cigars, burning marijuana has always smelled to me like a jar of mildewed sage leaves found in a public dumpster after being sprayed by a skunk.

It's not for me.

I ended up trying several products throughout the year trying to find one that was reputable, affordable and most importantly, one that worked.

The industry and market was so bloated that there didn't seem to be a better method other than trial-and-error to find a product that was consistently effective.

Many brands wouldn't list strains or ingredients, and regulation of every single product wasn't feasible with such a growing market.

Some edibles were so ineffective, I suspected they may very well have been regular candy.

I found a couple tinctures that worked as well as that taffy, but they were either exorbitantly priced, out of stock, or eventually replaced by another product that didn't work as well or even at all.

Perseverance in my search would soon pay off.

Following freestyle motocross pioneer Carey Hart on social media, I noticed him mentioning on one of his posts how helpful CBD had been for him to manage pain, and that's saying something.

On that very same post, somebody had asked what brand of CBD he used.

Carey has healed through a serious number of broken bones; if he had a preferred brand of CBD that effectively provided **him** with relief, I really wanted to find out what it was.

I combed through every comment, finding his answer.

He'd replied by saying he was hoping to officially announce his own brand in the near future, and to be on the lookout.

I was indeed.

Trying numerous brands after looking at hundreds of reviews and ratings, my efforts seemed moot; they were all so hit-and-miss.

Needless to say, come summer of 2019 when Carey announced his HartLuck CBD brand, I ordered some as soon as it became available.

No medical card was required, as it was THC-Free.

Having gone through so many upsets, I went in with no expectations so that I wouldn't be disappointed.

I'd made the mistake of being overexcited before just to be let down, or find another product that worked only to soon see it go off the market, so I tried to remain neutral.

A few days later the order arrived, and — well...

Since then, I've enjoyed the full line of Hartluck CBD products, with great success.

I use the tincture as a flagship go-to in the morning, gel-caps for strong long-term relief, a warming salve and a cooling lotion when needed, and an inhaler which is extremely convenient during outdoor exercise such as hiking.

Which, by the way, I'm able to now enjoy without pain.

It works great for me, and meets that balance of being effective, affordable, and available.

I hope the brand is around a while, as I've since been able to adopt a regular exercise regimen, no longer suffering from stabbing, lung-stifling pain.

It's helped me sleep through the night, increase my quality of life, decrease stress, continue to stay active, and get in better shape.

To be clear, this isn't to proclaim that any CBD product is a cure-all. It's not a sleeping pill, a multivitamin, an energy drink, a weight loss drug, or a fat burner.

CBD won't do a lot of things many companies proclaim, but what it's done for me is provide incredibly effective anti-inflammatory and pain-relieving effects to give me that edge — that breath of fresh air after years of ineffective over-the-counter medications that left me with nothing but an upset stomach and a body still in pain.

It served as a great start, and that gave me the motivation to formulate a game plan and do the rest.

The Hartluck CBD tagline is, "Fix Yourself."

I think it's pretty apt.

Fashion Over Function

As the PICs had been inundated the last several years, the Knowledge Base had suffered well.

Sure, many legacy solutions for basic issues were all there and mostly still valid, yet a high number of articles still needed to be updated.

The last few years had spawned a hefty laundry list of those that needed to be written, but nobody had the time.

To save the day, some disconnected clown in upper management spawned yet another brainchild, and had fed it steroids.

In efforts to uphold their facade to investors and continue defending their proud decision of outsourcing to save a buck, they were bent on proving the temp hires weren't useless.

They would do so with a bright idea to formulate an in-house course to designate any and all employees who completed it as certified article authors.

That's right, those who struggled themselves using a browser would soon be authoring articles for others to follow.

Mental, that.

The certification course was a sham. It focused only lightly on technical grammar, lexicon, and the troubleshooting process. It was *largely* about the formatting and structure of how the article appeared.

Not a thing was mentioned during training or the test about the actual *quality* or *efficacy* of article steps being of any concern. As long as the right words were capitalized, and the article steps were stylized nicely with numbering and bullet points when applicable, that was all that mattered.

I was the first volunteer to take the course, failing it due to several test questions having **incorrectly assigned answers...**

I tell you, I wouldn't have believed it either.

Management was getting tired of hearing from me, but they'd brought it upon themselves.

Like before, a department-wide email was sent explaining that the test was temporarily taken down for maintenance and would be re-released the following week.

It was, I passed, as did others.

To have an unchecked free-for-all of invalid articles being submitted by the droves from unqualified temps would be silly. Luckily, the PICs were directed to constantly monitor the submitted article sludge being flung into the once-respected KB... that KB that I'd spent so many years creating and now *recreating*.

As was inevitable, newly approved authors who were desperate for recognition started submitting the most heinous article drafts faster than we could burn them.

Hundreds were submitted in the first few months, rife with invalid troubleshooting steps.

Formatting flubs, not to mention typos and grammatical errors were predominant enough to invoke an eye-roll and facepalm upon every fresh article glance.

If the submitted article contained *mostly* valid troubleshooting steps, we were to notate any corrections and reassign the draft to its author for revisions.

If the steps were for the majority *invalid,* or if an article already existed for the issue in question, we could quickly mark the draft rejected, queuing it for deletion and informing the author of the result.

At first, all PICs had jumped in with gusto, as our precious KB was the last element of true quality that fueled the remaining pride in our department.

Several temps were creating articles for nearly every case they'd resolved, without even checking if a solution already existed. Thus, the vast majority of the article submissions were superfluous.

Fewer things in that era were more gratifying than tallying up the article draft's errors, sending off the results to the author and management to see, and queuing it for deletion.

Tenth-rate filth!

A great deal of them literally gave steps to simply restart Windows to fix a variety of issues.

Don't get me wrong, the legendary British sitcom, *The IT Crowd* is well-known by many a tech support agent in America, as is their running gag of rebooting a computer to solve the majority of customer issues, but...

It's a joke. It's not reality.

When dealing with many software issues, rebooting *can absolutely* serve as a workaround, but as a drawback, postpones and avoids discovery of the long-term resolution, while teaching a customer poor habits.

As articles containing more errors than they had *words* were being submitted for approval constantly, this incredulous reality was enough to send most PICs over the line, and into the land of don't-care-anymore.

That made things difficult on Danny and myself, as the others seemed to accept defeat and slowly stopped reviewing the submissions.

I couldn't blame them. In a way, they were wiser than I for doing so.

They knew when to pick their battles, and had long seen there was no convincing management to embrace any shred of proactive behavior, authenticity, or quality.

I do understand that unwillingness to admit defeat could be subjectively considered a weakness.

I also enjoy having a clear conscience — and when I'm being paid money to resolve technical issues to the best of my ability including any and all tasks set forth, I do exactly that.

It seems there is no other way.

On The Spot

One of The Empire's many bookkeepers had happened upon a damaging little scrap of info.

It would seem that the luxurious chat client we'd been using in order to handhold our temps so they could handhold our customers... was an unnecessary expense.

There was yet another chat client already being paid for as part of our email service. Our department management had not realized this.

Naturally, it was brought up at the very next quarterly meeting.

Though this newfound chat client was paid for, our supervisors guaranteed us that before it would be considered for use by our department, management would be fully reviewing its functions to ensure it was an acceptable fit.

It would need three features:

To offer the ability to flag posts as questions, the option to reply directly to them, as well as mark the questions as answered. These were the much-loved and necessary features we'd enjoyed that allowed us to avoid the blurred wall of chaotic scrolling which we'd suffered with the prior chat client.

Management completed their assessment of the software, and despite lacking two of the features, it replaced our existing chat client by year's end.

One out o' three ain't bad...

Outrage from the PICs filled the very next team meeting, and our lead supervisor Moira gushed promises of a remedy.

We'd once more been sent years back in time to an archaic process, butchering chat room efficiency.

No more tagging posts as questions, or marking them complete. One could only reply directly to a comment, displaying them indented below it as expected.

As an added bonus when typing a direct response, the chat room had a bug that would sometimes allow the reply field to jump around on the screen, causing you to easily to lose your place. It was hard on the eyes.

Its performance was lacking and quirky, as sometimes the direct reply feature wouldn't function correctly, instead placing one's response at the bottom of the chat room as a new post. Thus they were not easily seen by those looking for the next indented direct reply.

Disaster.

At the following team meeting, new chat room practices had been formulated to help alleviate our woes:

The PICs had been added to a "group" within the chat client, which could be tagged for easy visibility.

When a temp asked a question in a chat room, the "PIC group" was to be tagged by them, much like tagging a friend in a social media app. This would send PICs a popup notification as to easily reply to that post directly.

When a question was answered and the case closed, the temp was to *edit* their originally posted question, marking it with a heart emoji to indicate that they *loved* the help they'd received by the PIC, and needed no further assistance.

As to receive credit for the assist, the PIC was then to add a note in the temp's case with a hashtag #PICassist which could be easily tracked and tallied by supervisors for our performance stats.

This tedious exploit of nominal chat client functions proved excruciatingly difficult for the temps to abide by.

They'd often forget to tag the PIC team, which caused an influx of complaints that they weren't being helped.

Likewise, their inability to mark posts with the heart emoji left PICs constantly unsure if cases were successfully resolved.

By nature, once a temp got an answer they needed, they'd naturally stop looking at the chat client and leave PICs hanging; as soon as they got what they were after, they were gone.

Trying to smooth over the mess that ensued by skimping on chat client costs, an incentive was quickly established by management that very same week.

A monthly poll was to take place in which all temps and in-house teams were to cast their vote for MVP - (Most Valuable PIC) - one they thought had been both the easiest to work with, and most helpful.

Additionally, supervisors had the ability to grant a $50 "On The Spot Bonus" to any PIC showing performance above and beyond, such as often taking difficult escalations, not passing responsibility off to others, or receiving personal customer praise by name to a supervisor or manager.

Though the temps continued to cause us endless grief in-house, I always tried to perform my job with a positive *outward* attitude, never treating them rudely or in a disparaging manner.

Were they under-qualified for the position? Absolutely. Did they get thrown into the job without requesting a technical role? Sure they did.

That didn't warrant berating them; they didn't know any better, and were only trying to get through the day to make a buck.

Their inability to learn from the more than 400 training opportunities I'd submitted over three years was anything but acceptable, but *that* was management's decision to keep them on staff.

Or rather, contractual obligation...

I had a job to do, and I'd continue to do my best at it.

By the time I was given my review in January 2020, the MVP incentive had been in place for over six months.

I'd won the title three times, and scored two On The Spot Bonus awards.

In that last year, I'd also reviewed over 500 submitted article drafts, marking over 400 for deletion. I was told during my review that this was an overwhelmingly impressive number, as some of my co-workers had been reviewing only a couple per month.

I also had the highest number of #PICassist tags by a long shot.

Matthew, who had shown signs of one being beaten up by management over the recent years was quite ecstatic, and expressed how glad he was to see such energy still in the department.

Though my performance stats showed 70% higher than the next for #PICassist tags, far more backline cases closed, chat questions answered, and article drafts reviewed, 1% compensation was all the department could muster.

I was running out of reasons to continue working so hard.

I'd finally breached $30, though; that was a fun landmark. $30.01 was my new hourly wage. Respectable for a paltry high school education, but I knew I was worth more for the caliber of work I was providing.

I had still been holding on simply due to the convenience of working at home.

No matter — all the PICs were about to fall into a great deal of extra time in the upcoming months.

Everyone's usually grateful for spare time, but a pandemic is **not** the preferred driver of such a break.

I trust I don't need to elaborate on the details of COVID-19.

At the start of the new year, our Tech Support department had still been receiving nearly 800 incoming calls daily.

By mid-March, we saw that number drop to under 400 a day.

California's governor instituted full lockdown policies the day before my 40th birthday.

No big celebration for me. Kelly had to cancel all her secret plans which she still hasn't divulged, as she's hoping to throw a belated landmark birthday party when it's feasible in the future.

Bummer, but we did what we could. Kelly and I scandalously violated the lockdown policies by having a small celebration with immediate family and a few friends at our apartment.

Being robbed of a landmark birthday was lame, but my heart goes out to those who had to cancel wedding plans, or worse: suffered from the virus. I'm quite aware the world doesn't revolve around me.

When the month of May arrived, the call count dipped below 200 a day.

In-house agents feared another layoff as countless businesses throughout the country had already started to downsize or even permanently close.

I wouldn't have to wonder for very long; on the morning of May 12th, I would speak to my supervisor Matthew for the last time.

I'd had an issue for the first hour that day with my emails not being received by anybody, and had sent Matthew a couple direct messages to which he replied he'd "look into it."

He never did, though; he didn't have to.

The poor bastard knew exactly why it wasn't working.

At 10 a.m., he called me with a robotic, miserable inflection.

"Hi, Mike? This is Matthew, how are you doing this morning? ... with us on the line is a representative from HR..."

That's never a good thing.

As soon as I heard those words, I *grinned* slightly.

Partly in shock — well, **mostly** in shock of course, because I'd just heard the toll of the bell.

I was amused that it had taken so long, and that it finally happened.

With many trite and obviously scripted phrases, Matthew stated that many industries throughout the country had felt the economic effects of the COVID-19 pandemic. It was professed with clarity that the company was forced to make a decision based purely on financial elements, and I quote:

"Unfortunately, due to the financial impact of the lockdown policies on the industry and our company, we have been forced to eliminate one of the PIC positions.

"...this is not a decision based on performance, but purely a financial decision that is best for the department."

My superior performance stats didn't make a difference.

My winnings of several MVP awards and On The Spot Bonuses weren't enough.

By being among the most decorated and highest paid employees in the department, I'd only made myself the next target for upper management to snipe.

... like those of the last layoffs.

I was thanked sincerely for my 17 years of service, and was told that a generous 19 week severance package including health insurance had been prepared.

Matthew and the HR rep offered to stay on the line to answer any immediate questions I had. Following the end of the conversation, I would have 10 minutes to tactfully and privately bid my farewells to co-workers before my access to email, chat, direct messaging and company phone would be blocked.

I had unknowingly worked my final shift. I was to log out as soon as possible, and would be paid for the remainder of the day.

Whenever somebody was laid off, they were done so without notice, on the spot.

That was The Empire Way.

Immediately following the end of the phone call, I privately messaged my fellow PICs Victor, Sheryl and Danny, as well as Rowena and a couple other TSEs — all of whom were taken aback and asked if I was joking.

I gave them my personal contact information so we could stay in touch, and told them I was as shocked as they were.

It was as cookie-cutter as cliché moments come.

I didn't wait to be disconnected; I powered down as fast as I could, accepting the fact that my ties to The Empire had been cut.

After my work PC completed its shutdown and I unplugged all hardware from every power outlet, I remember stopping and taking several deep breaths.

I never hyperventilated, never entered a state of panic, never got choked up or cursed The Empire for their ways...

I only took another deep breath and uttered out loud to myself in the room:

"Wow. What a *ride.*"

I didn't realize until later that month, but those deep breaths had in fact been of relief.

I was no longer working for The Empire.

FOURTEEN

'Tis All Fun & Games

...

When I first started working in The Dungeon back in September 2003 for $13/hour, The Empire was made up of thousands of employees. Upon getting laid off on May 12, 2020, their total in-house population had been reduced to mere hundreds.

I try not to let myself dwell on how things were handled at The Empire, as I remained in their employ by my own volition.

I still have family living up in Oregon, and it doesn't really matter that living there didn't work out for Kelly and me; we still enjoy visiting, and I miss the craft beer, the food, the people, and one of the best arcades in the country.

I'm talkin' about you, QuarterWorld.

I'm still good friends with several of my former co-workers, and it was heartwarming to hear them reporting many in-house agents and other PICs pleading to management to reach out for me to come back.

They haven't, of course. If they did, their offer would need to be *much* more generous than $30.01/hour, as I'd decided shortly after my final shift that The Empire can no longer afford my services as a Senior Support Technician.

In fact, I don't believe many can.

I've made some decent honest money telling folks how to operate a keyboard and mouse, but I no longer wish to do so.

Having for years told Kelly that I didn't know how much longer my job at The Empire would last, I'd often say, "If nothing else, I suffer through this job long enough to get us debt-free, then I'll have no regrets."

I'm proud to say that I indeed have none.

It's an incredibly odd, new feeling being able to keep your hard-earned money once you're debt-free. Your checking account balance actually keeps increasing.

You don't ever want to go back, either.

We keep a disciplined entertainment budget, and try to limit our restaurants to a few outings a month.

It feels special every time.

We've continued to improve our health, increasing activity slowly and steadily.

My outlook on life has changed drastically, feeling liberated and self-assured.

In late 2020, Kelly and I had stopped into a very large and well known electronics store chain, out of town. Upon checking out, we heard a foul-mannered, miserable human several check-out counters away, barking at the poor cashier:

"YOU need to be more accommodating to SENIOR CITIZENS, ya know that?! ...and ya need to get me something to *sit* on, I can't stand up for very long, I'm disabled!"

We continued to check out as the employee scrambled to appease them.

When we were handed our receipt and purchased goods (in a plastic bag!) we headed toward the exit, but not before passing the miserable old crab, catching the end of their rant to the cashier *and* their supervisor who had now made an appearance.

"...or is that above your pay grade?!"

The supervisor pushed back.

"Excuse me. You're going to have to behave in a respectful manner or you *will* leave the store."

Great supervisor! We couldn't help but to laugh as we exited, hearing that customer get shut down.

I really don't miss dealing with that.

I'll be turning 41 in a couple months, and I'm optimistic that our county lockdown *might* be lifted. We'd love to support local restaurants by celebrating a birthday with the taboo act of enjoying a meal on-premises.

After all, of our plan of 15 days to slow the spread, today marks day 356.

The economy in is still in the toilet, and small businesses everywhere have been financially eviscerated.

Our country has just finished enduring the latest less-than-stellar Presidential experience, so I'm trying to maintain hope the next one does a better job.

I won't hold my breath. My political party loyalty lies with none, and I've yet to be impressed with any since I've been alive.

All I know is that there are a lot of people in our country that are hurting, and we could all use better leadership.

Like many, I'm still without a replacement job. It feels awfully strange never having been unemployed.

During my job hunt, I've recently entertained the idea of applying for a certain non-profit organization that requires a qualifying IQ score from an approved supervised test. The Stanford-Binet score from my youth more than qualified me, and I was hoping to immerse myself in the social networks of their touted special interest groups to discuss and expand upon my musical, culinary, and technical hobbies; I might acquire more contacts and increase chances for success during my job search.

As it turns out, I encountered multiple issues on their rather poorly designed website, including authentication bugs, and numerous dead links & orphan links alike. For an organization that boasted itself as the largest and oldest high IQ society in the world, I had the expectation for their website to be more functional than that of the average food blogger.

I also experienced a nasty vibe of both pretentiousness and used car lot smarm during their application process — that of which was very quick to incite the perception of nickel-and-dime ploys.

Non-profit? *Pff...*

Hard pass.

Kelly has been fortunate enough to have selected a vocation that remains essential in these times.

Due to our proactive and self-disciplined behavioral changes the last couple of years, we're in a position that has allowed me to be a tad choosy in my pursuit for the next place of employment.

I'm no longer at the mercy of taking the next temp job that comes around to afford my next meal.

It's taken getting laid off to realize how used to being miserable I'd become at The Empire, and I've never been so energetically busy at home since then.

When I'm not spending my time job hunting, I'm expanding my cooking skills, and thoroughly enjoying the local blends and seasonings from Solvang Spice Merchant.

I've dabbled in candle making, with many people having purchased them for gifts.

I've upped my homebrewing skills, with now seven years of experience crafting ales and ciders, and have recently begun brewing several styles of mead.

I've designed a few custom wooden board games, selling most of them and donating one to a silent-auction fundraiser. It went for $100, which was a great feeling.

My healthy obsession with music is also stronger than ever.

A fantastical musical group out of San Diego by the name of "Steam Powered Giraffe" has made their way onto my radar, and I couldn't resist binging their entire discography upon discovering their absurdly addictive, eccentrically charming style. I hope to catch a live show as soon as possible.

I've been more frequently playing and recording tuba, trombone, euphonium, melodica, accordion, and a cajon that I've recently crafted from beechwood.

I was able to outfit an inside corner of our living room with modular acoustic treatment for under $200, creating a budget home studio. With it, I've begun producing my first album with a couple songs near completion.

I'm still using ProTools LE on an old iMac running OS X 10.5, along with that DigiRack 002 signed by The Flecktones years back because it still works perfectly. I'll surely upgrade when necessary.

Taking time to relive all these old memories, and heal from the recent ones while accurately documenting them in segments has taken nearly half a year.

It's been incredibly cathartic.

Kelly and I are again without health insurance coverage as of my final severance check last year. Even with Kelly's sole income, the government still deems us "rich" here in the top cusp of the lower class; the cheapest Covered California plan quoted to us this year was $798/month.

Well, at least it's below $800 now...

This week, I was overjoyed to have completed the process of rolling over my 401(k) to an IRA. The Empire had chosen a bottom-of-the-barrel investment company which resulted in another painful customer service experience.

I spent too many hours on the line with an outsourced staff that was unable to understand many of the words coming out of my mouth and vice versa. A great majority of that was hold time, which wasn't all that less productive than the time spent actually *speaking* with them.

In the end, they had my 17 year old retirement fund pulled out of the market for 148 days. It took them *that long* to mail a check to my newly selected investment company despite the seven to ten day expectation they gave me.

My 401(k) went without gaining interest for the duration.

I spent several weeks looking for an attorney, but it appears my losses were above what I could get from small claims court, yet far too *paltry* for any of the 30+ law offices I'd contacted across the country to be willing to accept the case.

That's a raw deal.

I decided to let it go, and keep living my life rather than stew in the company of anger: that unconquerable enemy.

This despicable company in question, along with many other large corporations seem to have taken to blaming the COVID-19 pandemic for recent plunges in quality customer service.

On the contrary, I've personally observed a steady decline long before the pandemic.

The convenience of online shopping has for years seen great customer service slowly dwindle, making its way into history books as a lost art as more brick and mortar stores lose the battle against internet retailers.

This has been a free choice made by consumers, as they wish. Whether they even realize it, or have any regrets of these ramifications will be told in time.

It feels we're all at the mercy of a suppressed economy, but I'm still pushing forward with full steam.

Though the downfall of The Empire was my latest experience in the technical support industry, it's not come close to detracting from my love of working with computers.

Integration, Programming, Game Development, Composing, Audio Engineering, Music Production...

There's a multitude of directions I can choose to go from here to allow my creativity to thrive, and there's a pile of up-and-coming smaller companies devoid of micromanagement, corruption, or cubicle drama.

I aim to seek them out.

Having gone through what I did, if my next chosen workplace gravitates in any of those directions, I'll be swiftly giving notice after finding another that deserves my personal time.

They'll be acquiring a powerhouse that they didn't see coming.

Though my career might be slightly changing, I'm still me... still following Chris Pirillo's work, and still using Hartluck CBD to fix myself.

I'm occasionally doing my part for The Alliance in *World of Warcraft*, and *Minecraft* continues to please with limitless possibilities.

My Nintendo fandom has never dwindled. I keep a couple of small CRT TVs around so I can play zapper games like *Duck Hunt*, *Gumshoe*, and *Hogan's Alley*.

I also recently held one **stellar** *Zelda* Anniversary party to celebrate the original title's release, complete with themed food and drink.

GRUMBLE, GRUMBLE...

I still love watching '80s movies, episodes of *Firefly*, *The Twilight Zone*, *The IT Crowd*, and enjoy both the *Star Trek* and *Star Wars* media franchises alike.

No need to discriminate.

I'm still cranking up The Flecktones, Billy Joel, and P!nk, as well as thoroughly enjoying her wine releases from Two Wolves; the 2015 Petit Verdot paired beautifully with an Alec Bradley Prensado cigar.

Intel's twelfth generation of processors is releasing soon, and I'm planning on building a new gaming rig once their eleventh generation gets a price drop.

I'll absolutely be sticking with an MSI motherboard again.

I'll always hold myself to high standards regardless of the task I'm performing, and will always do the best, most honest job that I can whether I end up self-employed, or working for someone else.

As it turns out, I learned as much about *myself* as I did of the industry while at The Empire.

Pride in one's hard work should never be confused with blind loyalty to one's employer.

Loyalty can be misplaced, and making that mistake can be potentially self-destructive.

I've learned that one should never tolerate being taken advantage of, not being paid their worth, or drudging through a job they no longer love.

It seems there *is* another way.

My name is Michael Anthony White. I'm a Trekkie, a Padawan, Band Geek, Computer Geek, and '80s Geek.

I'm a Gamer, a Homebrewer, Browncoat, Ravenclaw, and Musician.

You can find me in the land of digital sand.

ACKNOWLEDGMENTS

My Wife, Kelly: For always being there for me with love and support throughout life, this entire project of passion, and beyond.

My Parents & Sisters (Michael & Nanette, Genevieve & Vanessa): For love and support, always.

Jeffrey & Melissa McConnell, & Matthew Truman: For providing massive inspiration and encouragement, great friendship and laughs, and of course, initiation into the zany realm of band geekery!

"Jay", "Liam" (Judoyak!), "Raymond" (pwned!), "Victor" (isn't it *true...*), "Sheryl", "Dylan", "Jerry", "Ben", "Danny", "Rowena" & "Jaina": For great friendship & camaraderie throughout this adventure.

Janis Ian, Billy Joel, & Alecia Moore (P!nk): For your songs and heartfelt lyrics that — to me — continue to be the benchmark of sincerity, insight, honesty, & affection. For this I hold you all with great respect.

Matthew Broderick, Neil Patrick Harris, Cree Summer, & Wil Wheaton: For jump-starting, and always sticking up for the geek in all of us. Thanks for your works during my childhood, and your continued performances today.

Chris Pirillo: For incredible educational entertainment, always geeking out, looking beyond hardware specs, being honest, infectiously humorous, encouraging the thought process, and being you. MTFBWY.

Béla Fleck & The Flecktones (Jeff Coffin, Howard Levy, RoyEl "Future Man" Wooten, Victor Wooten, & Richard Battaglia): For blowing my mind with incredible audio that took my musical studies and practice to the next level, for making me lose count to deliciously complex time signatures, and always teaching.

Blood Sweat & Tears, Chicago, Danny Elfman, Detektivbyrån, Freezepop, Squirrel Nut Zippers, Steam Powered Giraffe, Savant, Sahaj Ticotin & Ra, Wintergatan, & "Weird" Al Yankovic: For getting me through all times, both rough and wonderful, and fueling my creativity. Your music is always on my playlist, and I wouldn't have it any other way... Oh, and uh — an extra shout out to Al for the sophisticated culinary masterpiece that is the Twinkie Wiener Sandwich.

Ernest Cline & Patrick Rothfuss: For restoring my love of reading with heavy hitting powerhouses of fantasy, charm, and geek bragging rights.

The Good Life, & Valley Brewers: My favorite Solvang haunts to *enjoy* a fine drink, and *brew* a fine drink, respectively! Thanks for these years, and to more, Cheers!

Carey Hart & Hartluck CBD: For helping me fix myself. Your products have helped me change my life.

Atari, Blizzard Entertainment, Harmonix, Koji Kondo, Markus Persson (Notch), Manami Matsumae, Nintendo, Sega, Sony Interactive Entertainment, Square / Square Enix, & Nobuo Uematsu: For creating my favorite video games and the incredible music that will always have me using my brain and imagination with a massive grin on my face.

Acer, Atari (again!), EVGA, IBM, Intel, Microsoft, MSI, & Texas Instruments: For hardware and software that has made me love being a computer geek.

LeVar Burton: For your captivating enthusiasm and zeal for the magical possibilities of books. This has always been a powerful sentiment that is positively infectious...
BYDHTTMWFI!

Felicia Day (Last yet absolutely *not* least...!): For supporting the band geek, computer geek, & reader in me through your many works — serving as a major driving force that convinced me to write this first book.

~ many thanks, everyone ~

Michael is a computer geek/band geek hybrid from Generation X, raised in the quaint Danish village of Solvang, California. Venturing to San Diego, and later to the Pacific Northwest before returning to his hometown, he has enjoyed a fruitful career in the computer and tech support industries for nearly 25 years.

Outside the cubicle, he can be found recording music in his home studio, brewing ale & mead, hosting board game parties, as well as playing plenty of video games with powerfully moving soundtracks.

Always one to enjoy spinning a witless yarn, he's at last fulfilled his desires to tell of the exploits of madness and tomfoolery he's observed over the years.

He still misses Saturday morning cartoons and music videos, dearly.

CPSIA information can be obtained
at www.ICGtesting.com
Printed in the USA
FSHW020331080921
84565FS